FACES IN
MY TIME

BOOKS BY
ANTHONY POWELL

NOVELS
Afternoon Men
Venusberg
From a View to a Death
Agents and Patients
What's Become of Waring

A DANCE TO THE MUSIC OF TIME
A Question of Upbringing
A Buyer's Market
The Acceptance World
At Lady Molly's
Casanova's Chinese Restaurant
The Kindly Ones
The Valley of Bones
The Soldier's Art
The Military Philosophers
Books Do Furnish a Room
Temporary Kings
Hearing Secret Harmonies

BIOGRAPHIES
John Aubrey and his Friends

PLAYS
The Garden God and *The Rest I'll Whistle*

MEMOIRS:
To Keep the Ball Rolling
Vol. I. Infants of the Spring
Vol. II. Messengers of Day
Vol. III. Faces in My Time

The Memoirs of
Anthony Powell

Volume III

FACES IN MY TIME

HOLT, RINEHART AND WINSTON
New York

Library of Congress Cataloging in Publication Data
Powell, Anthony, 1905–
Faces in my time.
(His To keep the ball rolling ; v. 3)
Includes index.
1. Powell, Anthony, 1905–   —Biography.
2. Novelists, English—20th century—Biography.
I. Title.   II. Series.
PR6031.074Z514   1980   823'.912 (B)   80-14843
ISBN 0-03-021001-1

Faces in My Time is the third volume of an autobiographical
series by Anthony Powell entitled To Keep the Ball Rolling.

CONTENTS

LIST OF ILLUSTRATIONS

Between pages 38 and 39

Between pages 102 and 103

List of Illustrations

Between pages 166 and 167

Between pages 190 and 191

FACES IN
MY TIME

I

O saisons, ô châteaux!

In the spring of 1934, the world heading for trouble, my own existence, personal and professional, showed no immediate prospect of organic change. I should be thirty the following year, more than eighteen months to go, but that ominous milestone looming into view. A current love affair still possessed charm, though—as ever—a charm tinged with anxiety.

> . . . it's half past six she said—if
> you don't like my gate why did you
> swing on it, why *didja*
> swing on it
> anyhow——

Even if Hart Crane's lines, so often applicable, did not altogether meet the case yet, there was a shared awareness that things could not go on like this indefinitely.

Writing books was still underpinned by a half-time job in the publishing house of Duckworth; three novels (even if none, including cheap editions, had sold much above three thousand copies) now possible to regard as a modest *œuvre*. The new literary fashion then in the ascendant dominated by what Jocelyn Brooke (himself homosexual, but detached from 'committed' writing) used to call The Homintern, was unsympathetic to me; at the same time the fourth novel on which I was now at work—to have the title *Agents and Patients*—did not entirely satisfy my own standards in breaking fresh ground. Its theme attempted that only in tentative exploration of a central idea, the difference between those who do, those who have things done to them. The narrative, treated lightly enough and set contemporaneously in the Thirties, showed little or no departure from the mood of the Twenties.

Forty or more years later I find *Agents and Patients* an odd book to re-read. Full of private jokes, deviating a little from the bare naturalism that had once seemed the only proper literary goal, the technique is somewhat filmlike, the dialogue reasonably taut. Characters and situations bring back the period more vividly than I had expected, some of the less plausible happenings nearer to life than might now be supposed. Tragedy is not attempted, but there is a persistent sense of nervous tension; it might be conceded even menace in the Berlin sequences.

Probably I am surveying my own work too complacently. After publication *Agents and Patients* (like its predecessors) was censured for lack of seriousness, an objection always posing complex questions; notably Nietzsche's conjecture that the individual when closely examined is always comic, the reason why the Greeks kept the individual out of their tragedies. This last concept certainly helps to explain occasional disharmonies in contemporary novels, where an obsession with the explicit can attempt to accommodate, with a romantic aim, essentially unromantic physically sexual detail.

In any case, whatever the mode, the novelist can write only the novel which emerges from within, ideally bringing to each new book those consuming hopes and fears characteristic of embarking on a first novel; the same concentration, sense of surprise at what is taking shape, constant apprehension that something has gone wrong, above all banishment of anything in the least like self-satisfaction. To combine these constructive elements after publication of several novels is a hard discipline. Valéry's words in those stimulating essays *Degas Dance Dessins* are always to be borne in mind: '*Tous les arts regardés longtemps s'approfondissent en problèmes insolubles*', and, elsewhere in the same collection on the same subject, '*les problèmes sont toujours indéterminés, les résultats toujours contestables, la sanction toujours incertaine*'.

All this professional talk is becoming tedious. Technicalities of writing are inflicted merely to denote my prevailing mood, working on my novel— much more likely lying at full length on the long rickety blue sofa—in my top-floor flat at 26 Brunswick Square (part of the Foundling Hospital

Bloomsbury Estate, landlords, Constant Lambert remarked, who always made one feel like a foundling), when one April evening in 1934 the telephone bell rang.

The voice, a woman's, gave in tone the impression of being a slightly disgruntled parlourmaid, not best pleased at being made use of as secretary by her employer. Whoever it was announced herself as 'speaking for Lady Pansy Lamb', pausing slightly after that statement, as if requiring assurance from the receiving end. On the reaction proving positive, the intermediary asked if I would come in for a drink a day or two later at 12 Rutland Gate. By no means overwhelmed at that moment with invitations, I unhesitatingly accepted, requesting that thanks be conveyed to the hostess, whom I had not seen for some little time. Such were the first words exchanged between my future wife and myself.

2

In *Messengers of Day*, second volume of these memoirs, I said something of Pansy Lamb, eldest of the four Pakenham sisters (at this time the only married one), and her painter husband, Henry Lamb. When we first met, about six years before this, she had been sharing a flat with Evelyn Gardner, both girls still unmarried. Since then we had come across each other only once or twice; for instance during a not very recent weekend at a country cottage taken by John Heygate and Evelyn Gardner after marriage. The Knightsbridge address to which I was invited was unfamiliar; the formality of a third-person telephone transmission of the invitation most uncharacteristic of the Lambs, though I did not give much thought to that at the time.

An oblique approach had in fact been decided upon with the object of ascertaining whether my Bloomsbury address in the telephone-book housed the right man. Violet Pakenham, the third sister (just twenty-two), had volunteered to implement the enquiry in the rôle of secretary or maid; assuming that character-part with all the verve of old-fashioned music-hall.

The house in Rutland Gate, so it appeared in due course, had been rented as tail-end of a lease by the Pakenhams' mother, the widowed Countess of Longford, who had died five or six months before. The eldest son, Edward Longford, by now married for eight or nine years, rarely emerged from Ireland; his younger brother, Frank Pakenham, also married, was a don at Oxford; the Lambs lived in Wiltshire, not far from Salisbury. During the few months before the lease of Rutland Gate fell in, the three unmarried Pakenham sisters—Mary, Violet, Julia—were getting a good deal of fun out of continuing there on their own, while other members of the family found Rutland Gate a useful base for such a round-up of friends as the present one.

At the Lambs' party, not knowing her to have been the heroine of the innominate telephone-call, it fell out I scarcely spoke to Violet Pakenham herself after being introduced. She was, in fact, undergoing the disembodied state of one about to collapse with the pneumonia which overtook her a day or two later. I did, however, have a long conversation with Frank Pakenham's wife (also met for the first time), who, as Elizabeth Harman, had been a celebrated belle of the undergraduate generation following my own at Oxford. Our talk must have taken a literary turn, because I remember her expressing doubts as to the lasting value of Proust's novel, owing to the worthless nature of the society there depicted.

Some mutually acceptable compromise must have been arrived at on the subject of Proust, since, when we met again by chance at another party a few weeks later, Elizabeth Pakenham suggested that in the summer I should come for a week to the Longfords' house, Pakenham Hall (now Tullynally) in Co Westmeath. Although attracted by this invitation, I was contemplating a usual routine of crossing the Channel for a holiday in August. If the Continent were included, a week in Ireland might be awkward (and expensive) to arrange.

Elizabeth Pakenham swept such pretexts aside. The answer was an easy one: make it an Irish holiday; stay at Pakenham for a fortnight; in fact, stay as long as I liked; although a week in Dublin was worth considering, if that city had never been visited. She herself returned to England at the end of August, she said, but the Lambs would not arrive until the first week in September—and of course I should want to be there for the Lambs.

'You'll be getting a formal invitation from Christine,' were her final words.

I am now a little appalled at the ease with which Elizabeth Pakenham overcame any doubts that may have arisen in my mind as to the seasonableness of imposing myself for a fortnight on her brother-in-law and sister-in-law, two persons I had never met. Indeed, I am reminded of the social manoeuvring of such equivocal Surtees heroes as Mr Sponge on his sporting tour (though this would infallibly be an unsporting one), or Fine Billy Pringle's adventures and misadventures in *Ask Mama*. For that recklessness—as my wife has often observed—I have been paying all my life.

3

I had some slight preconception of the household to be expected, though not at all a clear one. I assumed, for instance, that to have written a book or two would not be considered abnormal (my hostess having written several), and that probably an agreeable element of eccentricity might be looked forward to in my host. At some stage of negotiating the journey Christine Longford sent a picture postcard of the house (grey stone with neo-gothic castellations), some preparation for its outward appearance, a quiet and dignified one. I had been given no clue to the terms the Longfords were on with the rest of the family, but saw no reason for that to be a cause of concern.

At Eton I had known Edward Longford and Frank Pakenham by sight, but, apart from the Rutland Gate party, only once, at a dance, exchanged a few formal words with the younger brother. Both, like myself, had been born in December, one three years older, the other the same age. All I knew of Frank Pakenham was that he moved in political as well as academic circles. I could, however, recall an occasion at school when Edward Longford had stood out as more than just another boy passing up and down the road outside my window. Very fair, not bad-looking, with a rather petulant air, he was even as a schoolboy getting decidedly plump, though not yet unduly troubled with a glandular disturbance, which caused him in quite early manhood to grow fat beyond even the tendency to that condition for some reason oddly prevalent among Irish landowners. He had come into his inheritance at the age of thirteen on his father's death in action in the first war.

One evening in the Studio (scene of much of my own realized life and adventitious education at Eton), Mr Evans, the drawing-master, was laughing in his good-natured way, while offering advice regarding a large composition in charcoal on blue-grey paper at which Longford was at work. The picture on the easel, plainly symbolic, showed a female figure loaded with chains. Ambitious in conception, the emphasis on subject rather than medium, the lady—possibly basis for a poster—evidently personified Hibernia, Dark Rosaleen, the Spirit of Ireland. Why that was at once obvious, I don't remember; a caption may have stated the fact above, below, or on a shield that was part of the design.

This remembered vignette (which must have taken shape before the Irish Free State came into being) could not have been more apposite. Irish Nationalism was then Edward Longford's most passionate enthusiasm. This fervour, at variance with family tradition, possibly owed something to personal rebellion, sense of frustration, above all uneasy relations (felt by all her children) with his widowed mother; in his own case aggravated by Lady Longford's unrestrained regard for him in his family position as eldest son.

At Oxford, a speech made by Edward Longford at the Union (condoning the murder by Irish terrorists in London of Field-Marshal Sir Henry Wilson) had proved unacceptable to contemporaries at Christchurch, leading to immersion in Mercury, the fountain dedicated to such expressions of undergraduate disapproval. This ducking was the great event of Longford's career, ever afterwards a gratifying memory, his favourite set-piece. I don't think I have ever been in his company for more than a couple of hours without his making reference to the occasion. According to himself the ceremony had been mildly—even courteously—performed, leaving him on a warm summer night lying in his pyjamas slightly submerged in a few inches of water.

The Mercury incident had taken place the year before I came up to Oxford, where my sole recollection of Longford—again characteristic owing to his devotion to the Theatre—was seeing him arrive, accompanied by a girl, in the front row of the stalls at some performance of the Oxford Players, a much frequented repertory company established my first term. I thought the girl might be from one of the women's colleges, then remembered being told that Edward Longford was unofficially engaged to Christine Trew; in those days even an unofficial engagement between two members of the University being sufficiently exceptional to be generally known.

O saisons, ô châteaux!

Christine Trew, whose widowed mother lived at Oxford, had been up at Somerville. She had also figured as one of the protegées of Lady Ottoline Morrell, and it was at Garsington that she and Edward Longford had first met. Henry Lamb, who painted all his in-laws, described her looks, not altogether inappropriately, as Aztec. I saw her again that term or next (though not to speak with) at a party given by Robert Byron in Merton, as she was one of the two or three 'undergraduettes' who had penetrated the more respectable outskirts of the Hypocrites Club world; a milieu not at all Longford's (who lived a fairly reclusive Oxford existence), though he knew several Hypocrites members in their more staid moments.

Her eldest son's early marriage was welcomed by his mother as a lucky escape from the scheming débutantes of Mayfair and Belgravia. Hitherto the family had lived most of the year in Oxfordshire, but the young Longfords naturally decided to settle for good in Ireland, where, disengaging themselves so far as possible from all English ties, they turned their attention to the arts and crafts of the country under a new régime.

Dublin's two theatres of intellectual flavour—known locally as Sodom and Begorrah—were The Gate and The Abbey; the former casting a net wider than merely Irish drama; the latter traditionally dedicated to plays of essentially ethnic complexion. The Gate had fallen into financial difficulties soon after Edward Longford's marriage, and, at short notice, he came to the theatre's rescue. Henceforward (subsequently in the Company's derivative as Longford Productions) he was not only The Gate's patron, but also impresario, playwright, actor (Hymen in *As You Like It*), scene-painter, prop-man (supplying Pakenham family portraits etc. for stage-sets).

These theatrical activities naturally demanded fairly prolonged residence in Dublin, *villeggiatura* in Westmeath becoming increasingly reduced to a month or so in the summer, even such interludes punctuated by occasional flying visits to the capital to keep an eye on plays and players. At an earlier period, a few former Oxford cronies of the Longfords might from time to time turn up for a short stay in Westmeath. Latterly house-parties had on the whole tended to be made up from the families and friends of the younger Pakenhams.

In short, the Longfords had begun to make little or no secret of the fact that they themselves were becoming heartily sick of these exiles in the

7

country, with the deprivations entailed of all The Gate meant to them. Guests from other worlds provided no sort of compensation. These were almost certainly unversed in Dublin theatrical gossip and intrigue; at worst, might even lack interest in the Theatre at all. The Longfords' sentiments were entirely understandable, but I had been given no hint in preparation for such an eventuality.

4

My only previous visit to Ireland had been to stay in Ulster with an Eton friend of unintellectual habit of mind, a house dedicated to fox-hunting and drinking. This household would have fitted to perfection into the Surtees novels, and, although in the North, tolerably well into the Somerville and Ross stories, *Some Experiences of an Irish R.M.* (1899). I had been recommended to this last book in early life, and found the collection wholly unreadable. It took over thirty years of marriage for my wife to persuade me again to try the works of Edith Œnone Somerville and Violet Martin Ross, advising the masterpiece of that talented couple, *The Real Charlotte* (1894); a novel I would now propose as not unworthy of comparison with, say, *Middlemarch*.

In supposing the atmosphere at Pakenham would have little in common with the horsy hard-drinking Anglo-Irish goings-on in general accepted, not without all justice, as representative of that very distinctive social order, I had made a correct assumption. Nevertheless I have since wondered whether Somerville & Ross, in their more subtle inspiration, might not have found useful material in Pakenham at the moment of my own fortuitous arrival; although, so far as horsiness was in question, they would have had to make do with Edward Longford—an MFH who did not ride to hounds—being titular Joint-Master of the Westmeath Hunt. In other respects there was rich material.

Christine Longford's first book had been a short but accomplished study of the Emperor Vespasian, an academic work followed by several novels, individual and sardonic in style. She also wrote occasional plays, which were performed at The Gate. I had taken particular interest in the first of these novels, *Making Conversation* (1931, republished 1970), since it appeared in the same year as my own first novel, *Afternoon Men*. Both books were docketed by reviewers (often apt to confuse satire with comedy) as satirical, but must have been issued at different seasons, as I have no recollection of their having been noticed together. In the fashion of the moment, neither had much plot in the popular interpretation of that term.

Making Conversation observes the Oxford scene of an undergraduate generation just preceding my own, through the eyes of Martha Freke, a girl of dutiful behaviour, if somewhat haphazard background. Martha Freke comes up to one of the women's colleges determined to work hard, also to find out what life is about, unassured, but far from uncritical. The usual disillusionments—mild enough by present day standards—take place. She finds herself sometimes bored, sometimes thwarted, sometimes melancholy, though always remaining an anti-heroine on the look out for a chance to become a heroine. Allowing for differences between the women's colleges and the men's, I found, broadly speaking, nothing from which to dissent in Martha Freke's picture of Oxford.

This sense of having more or less shared a common experience of Oxford, combined with both of us later receiving similar treatment at the hands of reviewers throughout the production of several novels, made me feel I had almost met Christine Longford already. She has, indeed, over the years in her capacity as critic, written of my own work with a generosity that seems to confirm that my surmise in supposing us to possess a parallel viewpoint as writers was not altogether misplaced. Nevertheless I had not been in the house long before I began to suspect that, so far from being accepted as a colleague of much the same approach, who *mutatis mutandis* had experienced many ups and downs comparable with those depicted in *Making Conversation*, I was in fact not far from being regarded as personifying something little short of those specimens of unwarrantable sophistication and intellectual worldliness so neatly burlesqued in the pages of that novel.

London literary patter would be playfully dismissed as much too grand to be valid currency in these wilds. Edward Longford, whose temperament was not easily geared to interests other than his own, did from time to time display bursts of curiosity about sides of London life, social or intellectual, of which he seemed by then to have felt a trifle starved, though making such enquiries with a kind of implied guilt, as if a betrayal of his principles. The two Longfords were perfectly friendly, perfectly

9

hospitable, but deprecatory laughter often suggested that I was rambling on about a society which, even in its more bohemian expression, was painfully overcivilized for those with simpler cultural tastes. What seemed the commonplaces of English life (in this respect Oxford given a special dispensation) were accounted no less remote than conditions on Mars; and decidedly more pretentious than those on Mars were likely to turn out.

There is much to be said for limiting certain aspects of the arts, perhaps especially those of the Theatre, within a deliberately restricted field of vision, but the extreme inwardness of the viewpoint with which I felt myself suddenly confronted was, at first onset, a little disconcerting. In those days even in England I was almost abnormally unstage-struck, and in most other respects too I felt myself to have strayed into regions where I lacked equipment to be anything approaching an ideal guest.

One's impressions can be misleading to oneself. My hostess saw things from quite another angle, later presenting her own view in one of her plays performed at The Gate, by good fortune included in the Company's repertoire on a London tour. The picture given there, at variance with what remains in my own mind, is also a far more bracing one.

This allegory of my visit is built round the embarrassments of a noted London theatrical-director, who turns up in an Irish country-house, the owners of which are for some reason unknown to him. Emphasis is laid on his appearance being 'very English'. Among those already assembled there are various ladies, married and unmarried, who see this as a situation of which to take advantage. One girl is drawn in the Irish fictional tradition of extreme harum-scarumness. For example, she becomes involved in a brawl which includes chasing another member of the cast with a broken umbrella. In choosing from this rich assortment of rivals, the theatrical-director opts for the rampageous tomboy.

Before the real-life dénouement could be even anticipated, I had (unlike the theatrical-director, so far as to be judged) developed those inner uneasinesses mentioned earlier, doubts to some extent counterbalanced by the energy and gaiety Elizabeth Pakenham brought to the household. Notwithstanding, as the second week of my stay approached, prospect of a change-over in the party imminent, I began to wonder whether her boundless optimism had not for once overstepped itself in arranging for my installation in her brother-in-law's house over quite so long a period. All was buoyant enough while she was there. How would things be after she and her family returned to England?

In short, I was conscious of a growing sense of insecurity, increased apprehension of a coming week that might mean making conversation indeed, with all the uncomfortable implications latent in that phrase as title of Christine Longford's book. On the other hand, the invitation having been issued (anyway so far as Elizabeth Pakenham was concerned) for two weeks, to announce premature departure might seem odd; perhaps even give the impression of having taken offence at something. Besides, I wanted to see the Lambs, and had no particular plans for spending more than a week in Dublin.

5

The writing of today, in winning an absolute freedom of expression within certain hitherto prohibited areas, has proportionately lost ground where much could formerly be said with effortless grace. John Aubrey, for example, makes the autobiographical note: '1651: about 16 or 18 of April I saw that incomparable good conditioned gentlewoman, Mris M. Wiseman, with whom at first sight I was in love—*haeret lateri*.' Again, James Boswell, in his Journal (14 December, 1762), a century later unaffectedly records: 'I got up in raptures and kissed her with great warmth. She received this very genteely.'

Neither Aubrey nor Boswell, it is true, was speaking of his future wife. Even so it is plain enough that the disenchantments of our own day, in discarding a formality of language which had its uses, have replaced that by informalities, not only by their nature more self-conscious, but presuming on all sorts of over-simplification of another sort, contemporary debauchment of words having sabotaged phrases previously regarded as universally admissible for definition of emotional life in almost all its aspects.

Accordingly, I shall not attempt to describe how my personal problem was (to borrow a favoured Jamesian idiom) beautifully solved, when Violet Pakenham arrived at the house in the company of the Lambs. She herself has in any case touched on that in her own autobiographical volume, *Within the Family Circle* (1976). It was at once clear that the situation had been saved; or—if the imagery of my future sister-in-law's play is to be retained—the curtain had gone up on the final Act, with its (apparently) unexpected climax.

I did not then know the Lambs at all well, nor had the least notion of the interior patterns obtaining among the Pakenham family; for instance, that the two pairs of sisters fell into separate couples: Pansy and Mary, the elder; Violet and Julia, the younger. Indeed, of Mary and Julia I knew next to nothing. Violet Pakenham, so far as categorized in my hearing at all, was spoken of as rather different from her sisters (she liked polo, night-clubs), but, having no reliable guide to the Pakenham norm, these labels did not convey much. They were, in fact, if not always untrue, like certain trade descriptions, largely misleading.

The whole atmosphere of the house was now transformed. Lamb, so it turned out, regarded himself equally suspect as purveyor of an alien culture. As he enjoyed a touch of conflict in life, this rôle was perhaps not wholly misprized by him. Clandestine visits to neighbouring pubs became one of the changed patterns of behaviour, and Lamb immediately established a studio in one of the bedrooms, into which he moved a large 18th century screen for the background he preferred.

In connexion with this last matter, Lamb had a story of his sole meeting with Henry James, which had taken place at Lady Ottoline Morrell's house in Bedford Square. That, as he put it, had been in the days when he was 'the sort of person who didn't own an overcoat'. Lady Ottoline, who had been one of Lamb's patrons, had accompanied some departing guest down the stairs from the drawing-room to the front door. Lamb and James were left alone together. There was a dreadful silence. Lamb did not feel he should speak first; James, visibly agitated, agonizingly gestant with an ideal sentence. The words came out at last: 'I hear you are the *fortunate* possessor of a studio?'

There is much to be said for James's opinion. Studios have their own particular intimacy. To keep his hand in at work Lamb suggested painting a portrait of me. We used to have sittings every morning. After an hour or two in the chair, models, becoming stiff in their joints, develop a life-lessness inimical to the painter's vision. Accordingly, Violet Pakenham used to attend these morning sessions, enliven them with conversation to keep the model alert.

My scheduled stay at Pakenham ended, I left to spend a week exploring

Dublin before returning to work. Violet was committed to a short round of other visits. We were not able to meet again until she came back to Rutland Gate in the latter half of September. That gave time for adjustments in certain spheres, which—something by no means to be dismissed as negligible—were brought about *sans rancune*.

On the last day of September, 1934, I invited myself to tea at Rutland Gate. The condition of being engaged was in those days allowed more attention than today. It was one in which we now found ourselves. If time apart from each other is subtracted from the span of days dating from our meeting at Pakenham (the Lambs' Rutland Gate party scarcely counting, still less the earlier telephone conversation), we had known each other about three weeks.

The decision could hardly be regarded as less than rash on both sides. Undoubtedly it was rash. On the other hand, there is absolutely no knowing what being married to someone is going to be like, short of marriage to that person. Nothing else will do. The state is quite different from any other relationship. People can be close friends for years; cohabit, sometimes under the same roof, for decades; meet and marry on sight. All are equally chancy once the knot is tied.

Even in marriage at least twenty or thirty years are required to test the implications of a given partner; both parties, in the nature of human beings, changing in the Hegelian manner all the time. On this delicate question it might be added that, by the age of close on twenty-nine, I had never asked another woman to marry me—nor indeed thought much about marriage—and, after nearer fifty than forty years, to speak unequivocally, have never wished to be married to another woman. In consequence, taking a risk in the matter seems something not always to be condemned.

6

This drastic step transformed me, from someone with rather remarkably few relations, to becoming an element in a large family with extensive ramifications, a condition totally different from that in which I had previously lived. The metamorphosis at once poses a question, tedious to myself, but congenial to readers of novels: the extent, if any, to which the Pakenhams (Earls of Longford) are to be identified with the Tollands

(Earls of Warminster), the family to which the Narrator's wife (née Isobel Tolland) belongs in *A Dance to the Music of Time*.

Excluding for the moment husbands and wives, combined Pakenham, brothers-in-law and sisters-in-law were six in number. In the novel, the Tollands are ten. This increase was designed for two reasons: first, with deliberate object of bypassing crude comparisons made by chronological enumeration of the respective families, real and imaginary, as a means of supposed identification; secondly—more important—to give wider scope for *dramatis personae* known to the Narrator through close family connexion; thereby increasing sources for animating the story, only to be looked on as easily available to a brother-in-law, though not necessarily to other people; a novelist's useful card of re-entry.

It has been suggested (by a member of the Pakenham family belonging to a younger generation than my own, who at the same time agreed not even approximate individual portraits existed) that the general tone of the Tollands in facing life is not unlike that of the Pakenhams. Such a possibility is something of which I cannot be sure (novelists possessing less conscious control of what they write than is supposed), and the comment may well be true. Indeed, it would be surprising were no similarity at all observable. In one particular case I would go further, conceding that in Isobel Tolland faint nuances (of which I am myself probably unaware) may to some extent mark her out as my wife; part of that autonomous side of writing which can carry more conviction than careful thought on the part of an author.

On the other hand, if no Pakenham model is used for an individual, a general family orientation is to some extent reproduced in equating the separateness from his brothers and sisters of Erridge, Lord Warminster, with that of Edward, Lord Longford; though the vaguely Orwellian lineaments of the former do not in the least match those of the latter; nor are the two earls in the remotest degree alike in outward appearance, political views, matrimonial life, general demeanour.

Including husbands and wives, out of ten brothers-in-law and sisters-in-law, only two—a professional painter and professional soldier—did not at some time appear in print. Frank Pakenham (only a couple of days in the house when I stayed in Westmeath) has more than once written autobiographically. He had already been created a baron (not a life-peer), when he succeeded his elder brother in 1961, and—antithesis of those

individuals who lack 'image'—is in other respects a public figure of whom
few cannot have heard. A different manner of looking at the world has
never in the least impaired our mutual relationship.

Mary Pakenham, too, has written autobiographically. Dealt an excellent
hand in the way of looks and talent, she had published several books,
made a career in journalism, before marrying Meysey Clive in 1940, a
Grenadier and Herefordshire landowner. At the time of her wedding I
was with the army in Northern Ireland, so that I never knew Clive
(only eighteen months younger, but never run across at Eton), met solely
for a few seconds, when he and Mary Pakenham were walking out
together. He was killed serving with his regiment in North Africa in
May, 1943.

The youngest of the Pakenham sisters, Julia—as a child almost twin
with Violet owing to closeness of age—a plump blonde beauty of sharp
wit, also occupied herself in occasional journalism. In 1938 she married
Robin Mount (another Etonian eighteen months younger than myself,
remembered by sight), the most elegant amateur rider I have ever seen
going over the jumps at a steeplechase. He, too, practised intermittently
as a journalist (sporting-columns, light verse), but was not well adapted
to earning a living.

Mount exchanged from the Wiltshire Territorials, joined shortly before
outbreak of war, into the Commandos, and saw service in the Middle
East. Tubercular, he was finally invalided, never really recovering his
health. Devoted to racing, inclined to drink rather more than was wise, he
too would have fitted easily into the world of Surtees. He is memorialized
not unmovingly in a novel, *The Man Who Rode Ampersand*, written by
his son, Ferdinand Mount. Julia Mount died in 1956; Robin Mount in
1969. They had a small house at Chitterne in Wiltshire, one of those
forgotten villages 'under the Plain', where, both before and after the
war, we used to have some very good times.

II

Great Ormond Street

During the next two months, a short if gruelling interlude of meeting relations, collating friends, making preparations for a new life (to be lived on about eight or nine hundred between us), we began to look for a flat, something slightly larger than Brunswick Square though in the same neighbourhood. One we inspected, not quite big enough, belonged to the librettist of that pre-1914 War classic:

> I'm Gilbert, the Filbert,
> The Knut with a K,
> The Pride of Piccadilly,
> The blasé roué.

An upper-part was advertised in Great Ormond Street, where several Oxford contemporaries were still to be found in the fine sub-divided 17th century houses (at least one formerly an embassy) at the east end. This house, 47 Great Ormond Street, much smaller, probably a shade later in date, was at the west, Queen's Square, end. Facing the Children's Hospital, a red brick building of unmatched hideousness, it was divided into three flats.

The tenants of the upper-part were not at home the afternoon we called, but the name under the bell was that of a couple—the B's—whom I had come across when guest at the sittings of the Society for Psychical Research (*Messengers of Day*). I knew neither of the B's at all well, the husband better than the wife. She, somewhat older, gave the impression of keeping a strict eye on him, particularly when the assembled psychical researchers held hands and sang, while the medium 'went under'. It was agreed that Violet should try to gain access again the following morning (I should be at the office), reporting later on the flat's possibilities.

When Violet rang the bell in Great Ormond Street the next day, the door was opened by Mrs B in person. Violet said her piece, rehearsing the fact of my acquaintance with the B's, together with the news that we were getting married, and looking for somewhere to live. Mrs B's reaction was disconcerting.

'Well, I hope your married life will be happer than mine,' she said. 'I've been married for nine years, and my husband's just left me with a woman he's known for five weeks.'

Notwithstanding this unpromising reception, Violet spoke favourably of the flat itself. We decided to make a further inspection, this time together. Mrs B showed us round, divided between despondency regarding the prospects of all marriage, and hope to get the flat off her hands. The panelled sitting-room looked out over the street. There was a much smaller room at the back, beyond it a minuscule kitchen. Bedroom and bathroom were on the top floor of the house; above the bedroom, in a loft, the water-tank; a fact of ill omen.

In the bathroom, Mrs B drew attention to the rowing-machine she and her husband had installed for daily exercise. This contraption was now for disposal, she said, speaking nostalgically of the rhythmic creak made by its sliding seat, to be heard in the bedroom while husband or wife was next door, rowing an imaginary course from Putney to Mortlake. Mrs B did not effect a sale of the rowing-machine, but we arranged to move into the flat early in the New Year.

2

We were married at All Saints', Ennismore Gardens, parish church of Rutland Gate, on 1 December, 1934. There was no formal reception after the service, but a party had been given in the house the night before, which, beginning at 5:30 and extending to past 10 o'clock that night, had included every form of friend and relation. On the following morning Wyndham Lloyd, my best man (an old friend, reliable for such an occasion), arrived at Brunswick Square with half a bottle of champagne to ease the journey to the church. Constant Lambert had arranged the music (Handel's *Water Music*, and, he insisted, the *Lohengrin* Wedding March rather than Mendelssohn's), but was himself too incapacitated by the party to attend the church.

The honeymoon was to be in Greece, a country neither of us had then visited. The first night was spent at The Orleans Arms, Newhaven (booked by John Heygate, then living nearby), the room King Louis-Philippe had occupied on arrival in England as a refugee. December seas were rough the following morning, a stiff gale blowing, great green waves, clouds of white spray, bursting over the jetty of even the inner harbour.

The four or five travellers on board included a mother and grown-up son, the latter immediately overcome with the direst form of seasickness the instant the ship cast off. Ladies were forthwith ordered below. It was not long before I followed them. Neither of us is a bad sailor, but that was the most malign crossing I have ever experienced. The old Orient Express, a different *cuisine* at every frontier, gave three nights to recover. When a new restaurant-car was put on at Nish the diners all looked like exiled kings.

In those days Athens, archaeological glories apart, was a small Balkan capital, dispraised on the whole by tourists, though by no means without charm. Greece, out of season in winter, was absurdly cheap, except for the Grande-Bretagne, where we stayed only a short time, moving to a lesser hotel in a street almost opposite. Food was not good on the whole (one tolerable restaurant run by White Russians), wine drinkable, if at times recklessly labelled. Only men frequented cafés, but no objection was raised to the presence of foreign ladies.

Between Athens and the port of The Piraeus, now a continuous suburb, then stretched open country. The view from Sunium's marbled steep had scarcely changed since Byron's day. At Delphi, no more than a village, we were the only guests at the small inn, the slopes of the eagle-haunted mountain as deserted as the ruined shrines.

The climate of Athens can be unsympathetic. Friends, on our return, hastened to explain that everyone feels ill on their honeymoon, but subsequent visits to Athens during the next forty years have convinced me that the capital is the one place in Greece where one is apt to suffer malaise. Those who agree attribute that discomfort to dust, and certainly spirits rose on trips made out of the city, declining again as the suburbs were entered again on the way back.

We had been given one or two introductions, including a young Englishman working in 'The Power' (the Electricity Company), and a Greek MP, school friend of an uncle of Violet's. This Greek Old Etonian, Alexander Pallis, distinguished classical scholar as well as politician, had also been contemporary with Tom Balston (*Messengers of Day*), who said that, when both of them were not far short of Sixth Form, they had fought, rolling over and over on the ground; an incident, had we known it, that would have added flavour to meeting Pallis.

Before we had time to deliver the letter of introduction, Mr Pallis himself arrived at the Grande-Bretagne to pay a call at ten o'clock in the morning on his way to the Chamber of Deputies. Violet, feeling a trifle off colour that day, was still in bed; in fact holding a levée in our fairly spacious bedroom, the young man from The Power having also come to see us. When Pallis was announced we invited him up too.

Afterwards we wondered whether, in terms of Greek etiquette of that date, this was carrying informality too far. Pallis, wearing the subfusc suit customary for Greeks in the capital, mentioned that he was on his way to the Parliament House. Conversation was a little stilted, something uncharacteristic of Greeks, especially anglicized ones, usually equipped with an easy flow of cosmopolitan talk.

After a while Pallis, issuing an invitation to his house, where a day or two later he was to deliver a lecture on Alexander the Great, rose from a small bedroom chair by the dressing-table, and took formal leave. Only as he disappeared through the door, gone beyond recall, did it become clear to those who remained in the room that the whole of the back of his dark suit was flecked with white powder; in fact Violet's bath-powder. He had been leaning against her dressing-gown. Pallis was decidedly an unmarried man. One could only hope that too many jokes were not made when he arrived at the Chamber of Deputies.

3

Ghiolman Brothers, an efficient and obliging travel agency, arranged tours in Athens and further afield, but when we wanted to make a trip to Crete (the mythology of which had always particularly interested me) objections were immediately put in the way. The island was difficult of access; accommodation there could not be recommended; there was really nothing much to see when you got there. Firmness had to be exercised before a booking was allowed.

In the event we crossed to Heracleion (then Candia) by night, a boat called the *Lesbos*, the name in Greek characters on the sailors' jumpers, garments which would have reaped a brisk sale in London boutiques. On arrival we put up at the King Minos Hotel (now demolished), friendly, but unluxurious, indeed little developed since the days of the Minotaur. On the following morning Violet counted forty-nine mosquito bites on her face, then gave up the numeration.

If the Greek mainland was cheap, the islands were even cheaper, a glass of *ouzo* in Crete costing the equivalent of the then British halfpenny (admittedly two rounds required for a lift), while a pleasant wine labelled Malvoisie recalled false fleeting Clarence's butt of Malmsey. By the harbour, the Middle Ages were again summoned up, where two men displayed a performing bear—always a sad sight—but the little quite elderly cripple, with Pan-like beard and satyr's shrivelled legs, yelling with laughter while he darted about pretending to assault the longshore-men sexually from behind, belonged essentially to cheerful classical myth.

In Crete, often revisited, we saw for the first time the Minoan palaces—Knossos, Phaeistos, Ayia Triardha, the last the most finely situated, all now much further excavated—driving across the island in that incredible Cretan light, which, especially towards sunset, turns the mountains into every colour of the spectrum, the sky all but black in one direction, dull gold in another. We were to see this phenomenon repeated on a smaller scale years later, when Violet lived at Shoreham in Kent during the war. Our Greek trip, most of all the time in Crete, opened my eyes to the Ancient World in a manner I had never known before.

4

On return to London there was a short interim at my old flat before moving to Great Ormond Street. On the first morning at Brunswick Square, when Violet went out to do the shopping, the front-door of the

flat below (something quite unusual) had been left open. The tenant
was E. M. Forster, a writer not personally known to me. The novelist
was standing in a room beyond the small hall, thoughtfully arranging his
ties. He gave a quick glance over his shoulder as Violet passed down the
stairs, curiosity having apparently overcome an avowed distaste for the
opposite sex.

We took over the two top floors of 47 Great Ormond Street in about
February, remaining there for two years. Below, on the first floor, lived
a bachelor in the Treasury; a German refugee on the ground floor. The
Treasury official, small, consequential, preoccupied with his own affairs,
was not much in evidence, except for one unhappy occasion, when the
photographer come to take a picture of Violet for an illustrated paper,
managed to fuse all the civil servant's lights.

The German refugee, quiet and sententious, also rarely appeared. In
the basement lived a caretaker, whose duties included stoking the furnace
for the boiler, the landlord providing hot water for the whole house.
Various families or single individuals presided over the caretaking at
different times; one couple, a middle-aged chef and his much younger
wife, doing a midnight flit with all their belongings on a barrow, which
we watched from our window. They were never seen again. These last
black sheep were replaced by an elderly window-cleaner, a widower.

Soon after the window-cleaner's installation in the basement we were
woken in the small hours by the sound of dripping water. It was soon
revealed that a steady stream was pouring through the ceiling and down
the walls of the bedroom. Clearly all was not well with the storage tank
at the top of the house. I quickly descended to the lower regions, where
the caretaker slept. Blundering about there in the dark, I at last found a
door and an electric-light switch. When the light was turned on, a bed
was to be seen with two heads on the pillow: one that of the old man;
the other, a boy of eleven or twelve years old. The boy woke, uttered a
piercing cry, disappearing at once under the bedclothes. This disturbance
aroused the other occupant of the bed.

I explained what was happening about the water, but felt I must hurry
back upstairs to Violet as soon as possible to give an account of the
grotesque scene below. The bed-sharing was, in fact, as likely to have
been a consequence of hospitality (possibly even temporary accommodation of a grandchild) as an occasion of pederasty, which was my

immediate assumption, and certainly the boy seemed deeply embarrassed at being discovered in these particular circumstances.

Meanwhile boiling water had begun to course down the walls of the main staircase and flats below our own. When I returned to the hall, after telling Violet my story, the other tenants were assembled in a state of some disquiet. The Treasury, in the best tradition, could offer no easy solution nor practical wisdom, but the German refugee—perhaps a scientist or engineer—pedantically explained in his slow precise English that the answer to our problem was to turn on all the hot-water taps in the house. This was done. The deluge slowly abated. Everyone went back to sleep.

The elderly window-cleaner vacated the post of caretaker after this débâcle, whether or not on account of it, I am uncertain. He remained, however, in our own lives, continuing to clean the windows when we moved later to Regent's Park. During the course of our association (ended only by the war) Violet paid for him to be fitted out with a new set of false teeth.

5

At one time or another we had various cooks at Great Ormond Street (none of whom lived on the premises), far the most remarkable and accomplished of these being Clara Warville. Mrs Warville never spoke of her husband, who seemed to belong to an infinitely distant past, though I think 'Mrs' was probably not, as the case with some cooks, a courtesy title. She had been cook-housekeeper to George Moore during the writer's Ebury Street period. In theory now retired, living in Chelsea on a pension, she preferred to have some not too demanding job, rather than doing nothing, but it was essential that she should be the sole member of the staff.

We were indeed lucky to find such a cook, not only an admirable exponent of the art at its simple English best—a *cuisine* by no means to be despised—but also a person of quite unusual gentleness and niceness of character. She used to wear a cap reminiscent of Falstaff's Mistress Quickly, though her temperament was far other.

Clara Warville had contributed a chapter to Joseph Hone's biography (1936) of George Moore, in which she gives a most convincing account of the writer and his quirks. She inscribed this book for us. While she was at Ebury Street cooking for Moore he paid a visit to Paris, on his return bringing a present for the parlourmaid, but either forgetting Clara Warville or unable to find one for her. In consequence he asked Lady Cunard to get something suitable the next time she was in Paris. Lady Cunard bought an exceeding pretty oval broach, ivory with a motif of flying birds, which the Empress Eugénie might well have envied, the piece belonging very much to what was worn at that day. Moore also gave his cook a photograph of himself, a picture that had once included Edmund Gosse, whose hand was resting on Moore's shoulder.

'I had Mr Gosse's arm painted out,' said Clara Warville.

6

At an early stage while living in Great Ormond Street we became possessed of a Siamese cat, Bosola, named after that devious character in Webster's *The Duchess of Malfi*, a play then recently performed. Bosola was a strong feline personality, intelligent, serious, noting such things as Violet tying an unaccustomed ribbon in her hair, but also a trifle neurotic.

We thought a companion of his own breed might steady Bosola's nerves, give him a friend to confide in, so a year or two later, after we had moved from Bloomsbury to Regent's Park, acquired another Siamese neuter. This was not a success. Paris (his pedigree name), younger than Bosola, was hearty, carefree, bouncing, not unfriendly, but Bosola could never get used to his extrovert ways, was indeed a little afraid of him. Nevertheless, although not developing truly fraternal feelings towards each other, Bosola and Paris would occasionally enter into a temporary alliance to exclude from what they regarded as their own territory any cat they both looked on as a social inferior.

I do not record the names of these two Siamese cats from mere sentiment. They were to play a decisive rôle in my own life.

7

I continued to work at Duckworth's, and Violet (together with occasional articles on horses and equitation) wrote the 'Mary Grant' column for the *Evening Standard*. This was a feature dealing with shops and their current stock, one inherited from her sister, Mary Pakenham, who had originated it. Sorting out some kind of pattern from this period, the few years that remained before war came, is not at all easy. Engagement-books, entries often illegible, are like the dial of a compass that is out of order, the needle circling first in one direction, then in another. Names recorded in memoirs have to possess some tag making them comprehensible to the reader; therefore the picture given here is often arbitrary, coherence, if any, emerging only decades later.

Among weekends out of London some were still spent at Woodgate, Gerald Reitlinger, 'The Squire's', house in Sussex (*Messengers of Day*), where fairly consistent discomfort blended with a good deal of random fun. Violet was infinitely tolerant in accepting conditions against which many of The Squire's female guests had rebelled, and, though perhaps less engrossed by his own eccentricities than myself, appreciated entertainment resting on minimal accomplishments in the host as such.

David Talbot Rice—Reitlinger's archaeological colleague in the Near East—used to insist that The Squire's alimentary system was equipped with a crop like a fowl, enabling the ingestion of only gritty substances. This was borne out to a large extent by the cooking at Woodgate where, in spite of the pressure of friends, tolerable food and drink were hard to come by. All sorts of stories centred on subterfuges to increase the flow of alcohol. On a certain Monday morning, driving back to London, Basil Hambrough quite simply made off with a bottle of champagne (used as prop in a posed photograph the night before), which the three of us drank at luncheon. Constant Lambert, lying on the lawn, accidentally upset a glass of sherry, at which the Squire had rapped out: 'Wasteful beast.'

One of these Woodgate visits was devoted to making a photographic sequence of the Tranby Croft case, the Yorkshire country-house, where, as Prince of Wales, Edward VII was staying when another of the guests, Sir William Gordon Cumming, was accused of cheating at cards. Other Woodgate guests enacting these Tranby Croft scenes were the Widow Lloyd (spoken of in earlier volumes of these memoirs), and Francis Watson, another connoisseur of Woodgate, and later head of the Wallace Collection.

Some now think the stigma on Sir William Gordon Cumming unjust, none the less he boasted to Lady Jersey (who repeated his words to Violet, her grand-daughter) that he had 'broken all the Ten Commandments except Murder'. Cheating at cards is not specifically mentioned in the Decalogue, but, if intent on covering everything but a capital charge, the baronet might not have made an exception of tampering with baccarat stakes.

Some forty years after this photographic diversion at Woodgate, a Television Company, contemplating a programme on the Tranby Croft scandal, approached me with the request that I might be prepared to consider releasing for that purpose contemporary photographs I was believed to own, showing the Tranby Croft house-party, perhaps the actual scene at the gaming-table.

Reitlinger, even if some of his statements were to be accepted with caution, possessed an extraordinary fund of information on all sorts of unlikely subjects. His collection of pictures and artefacts was equally varied, including a large assortment of Oriental pots kept in glass cases. Some of these pieces had been varnished—deemed undesirable by experts—and he would wander abstractedly about the house, scraping away with a sharp instrument at one or other of them; a process Violet named de-sharding.

No one guessed for a moment that Reitlinger's ceramics (bequeathed on his death to The Ashmolean) would turn out to be one of the finest collections of its kind ever brought together, worth today nearer two than one million. When fire destroyed Woodgate in 1978 fortunately all the best pieces survived.

This disaster, bringing about The Squire's own end, at not far from eighty, from shock at his loss, had come about in a characteristic manner. One winter afternoon the chimney of the room in which he was sitting caught fire, the flue, in the tradition of the house, probably unswept for immemorial ages. With typical stubbornness Gerald Reitlinger, having managed to extinguish the blaze, lighted the same fire again in the evening, the calamitous consequences of which took place that night. It was a suitably tragic climax for a figure whose strange nature, macabre humour, disconsolate appearance, might fittingly have found a place in the pages of Dostoevski.

8

Great Ormond Street's comparative nearness to Sadler's Wells increased contacts with the Ballet. The flat contained a small upright piano (part of Violet's dowry, later sold), which Lambert begged might always be kept locked, in case some guest tried to play it. The only occasion when the piano was, in fact, put to any use, so far as I remember, occurred on a warmish day before a party, when Lambert himself removed his waistcoat, concealing the garment under the lid of the keyboard. Another—mulled claret—party attended by the Lamberts, Freddy Ashton, Billy Chappell, Bobbie Helpmann, no doubt some of the *corps de ballet*, was followed the next day, during a matinée of *Apparitions* (Liszt, selected by Lambert, choreography by Ashton), by some heavy thuds on the boards of the Sadler's Wells stage.

9

Cyril Connolly was then married to his first wife, Jean Bakewell, one of two sisters from Philadelphia, though for some reason Connolly preferred to emphasize their upbringing in Baltimore. The other sister, Annie Bakewell, and her American husband, Bill Davis, lived much of the time in Spain. We did not know the Davises at this period, but after the war used to stay with them at La Consula, an attractive Italianate house, a touch of English Regency about its exterior, near Malaga.

A perpetual flow of variegated guests passed through La Consula, scene of continuous hospitality. Ernest Hemingway (whom I never met) was a friend of Bill Davis dating from the war, and stories stemmed from his visits there. Connolly, for example, described how, after Hemingway had been egregiously rude to a fellow guest, their host had explained to the latter later: 'He doesn't like you.' On another occasion Hemingway had been at La Consula at the same time as Lord Christopher Thynne, then an almost painfully emaciated-looking young man, who had just completed his National Service with the Household Cavalry. Hemingway used to swim a regulation number of lengths in the swimming pool every day, marking each length by removing a pebble from a pile kept at one end for the purpose. Thynne entered the pool while this rite was in progress. Hemingway at once challenged him to a race of two lengths.

There was absolutely no means of guessing from Thynne's outward appearance that he had represented the British army's swimming team a short time before. Hemingway's defeat was so unexpected, so overwhelming, that the writer confined himself to his bedroom for the next twenty-four hours.

Connolly's keenness on food, much propagated by himself, was usually beneficial for his guests, the wine always, but at the King's Road flat the succession of cooks went up and down in quality, sometimes sharply. Whether or not the proprietor of a mobile coffee-stall got wind of this, one of these was certainly parked every night in a strategic position just opposite the house. There Connolly dinner-guests would sometimes end the evening with a sausage-roll or two.

I had first met Elizabeth Bowen with Connolly (who greatly admired her writing), and once, after one of these somewhat unfulfilled dinners with him, we left in her company. The coffee-stall had perhaps been suggested, but Elizabeth Bowen, with that slight hesitation in her speech, said: 'Come back with me to Regent's Park. I've got a h-ham.'

As Mrs Alan Cameron she lived with her husband in Clarence Terrace, as it happened, next door to my parents. When we arrived at the house she led the way to the kitchen in the basement, and began to look about for the ham. Elizabeth Bowen rarely wore spectacles, and perhaps did not see very clearly without them, the possible explanation of her next remark. 'Some people complain of cockroaches in the basements of these Regent Park houses,' she said. 'Your parents do, but they say their cook doesn't mind a bit. She just stamps on them. I never seem to see any here.'

In one of the Dr Fu Manchu stories (I quote from memory) the sinister Chinese doctor, by the use of hypnotism, causes the wallpaper of a room to appear to be writhing with huge beetles. That was just how Elizabeth Bowen's kitchen floor looked at that moment.

10

Connolly (who always remained an encourager of young writers) spoke of a Welsh poet recently come to London, whom he judged to have talent.

His name was Dylan Thomas, and he was, so it seemed, an agreeable young man. New blood always welcome, we suggested that, when the Connollys next played a return at dinner, they should bring this young Welshman with them. In due course a party of the five of us took place at Great Ormond Street.

Much that is disobliging has been written of Dylan Thomas, the chip on his shoulder, his boorish behaviour, his drunkenness. No doubt all these could be trying enough at a later date. The evening he came to dinner should be recorded as one of perfectly normal drinking and talking, even if a good deal of both took place. Odd as the judgment may now sound, Thomas gave the impression of being quiet, amusing, good-natured.

As an example of the last, Thomas spoke appreciatively of Richard Church, a middle-aged man of letters of somewhat prim exterior, easy to make fun of, if only for a rather schoolmasterish championship of then unfashionable writers like Arnold Bennett. Church was, in fact, a capable critic, and, as literary adviser to a publisher, had (rather in the manner of Edward Garnett) helped Thomas to publication, an act which had not been received at all ungratefully.

Thomas talked for the most part about such things as his recent brief employment as reporter on some newspaper. He had been sent to interview Charles Laughton, an actor who excelled in explosive parts like Captain Bligh of the *Bounty*. Perhaps not very tactfully, Thomas had asked: 'How do you act, Mr Laughton?'

Laughton's reaction had been violent.

'How do I act? How do flowers grow? How do birds sing?'

Thomas had attended a party in Paris a week or so before, where, feeling very drunk and seeking respite, he had gone upstairs and crawled under a bed. Soon after withdrawing to this retreat he heard two lesbians, unaware of his presence in the bedroom, come and recline on the bed above him. Sounds took place of unsuccessful efforts to achieve a physical relationship. For a while he listened, then sleep overcame him. He passed out utterly. Hours later, so it seemed, he came to. He felt awful and could not remember where he was. Then, as consciousness slowly returned, stirrings took place somewhere above his head, the sound of voices. The lesbians were still there, still unable to realize their mutual passion, conveying an awful sense of unremitting yet fruitless human exertion.

Thomas inscribed a copy of *18 Poems* (1934) at this dinner, and we met again quite soon after at the Connollys', a biggish dinner-party round which a certain amount of legend, largely spurious, seems to have grown up; for instance, that the party was given specifically for Dylan Thomas, and that he caused offence there by telling bawdy stories. I have no recollection, when invited, of even being told that Thomas would be present. I was not at his elbow all the time, and, when drink has flowed, few can claim never to have attempted a lurid anecdote that missed fire. Apart from that local possibility, certainly no atmosphere of failed jokes on Thomas's part at any stage dominated the evening.

One of the guests was Desmond MacCarthy, in his late fifties, more than twenty years older than anyone else. The rest of the party included Evelyn Waugh, Robert Byron, and—so far as I remember—ladies representing on the whole fashion rather than literature. Waugh, who seemed depressed, left early. Jeanie Connolly thought he had been made melancholy by some remark, possibly Byron's, to the effect that Thomas's looks resembled Waugh's own when younger. In *A Little Learning* Waugh speaks of a Welsh great-grandfather claiming descent from the Glamorganshire chieftain, Cadwgan Fawr. There was certainly an outward impression shared with Thomas of reddish hair, small stature, steeply banked fires within.

I had met MacCarthy, a link with a much older world of writers, but we knew him much less well than his daughter, Rachel, married to David Cecil. That night, the women having left the dining-room, conversation turned to Swinburne and the poet's exuberant correspondence, some of which MacCarthy had seen, on the subject of flagellation, and kindred erotic topics, with his friend George Powell of Nanteos (Gorge of the Nightingales), an ancient house in Cardigan, alleged repository of the Holy Grail.

Speaking of these letters, MacCarthy asked if I were any relation (George Powell's was a different family) to Swinburne's correspondent, all of whose letters (by then in the National Library of Wales at Aberystwyth, not far from Nanteos) are believed not to have come to light to this day. Thomas questioned MacCarthy about them.

'What are they like? Oh, bloody bottoms, all that.'

Thomas pondered.

'I wonder whether one could pretend to be writing a book about

Swinburne. Take a look at those letters some day when in the neighbour-hood.'

I ran across Dylan Thomas again only a few times, once at one of Edith Sitwell's parties at the Sesame Club; then after the wedding reception given at the Savoy on John Heygate's second marriage. Violet and I walked up Kingsway on our way back to Great Ormond Street. Two young men strolling just ahead of us were revealed to be Thomas and a companion. Rather full of champagne, I caught Thomas from behind with the rolled umbrella I was carrying. As he was dead sober this seems a mild instance of *Man Bites Dog*, or rather bites artist as young dog. The other young man was David Gascoyne, poet, and his-torian of the Surrealist Movement. I had not met Gascoyne before, though he had sent some poems to Duckworth's I had thought well of. The firm showed no enthusiasm.

The Surrealist Exhibition of 1936 at the New Burlington Galleries was the last occasion I saw Thomas. Surrealism had long ceased to be a novelty even in London, but, the Press giving a good deal of publicity to the show, quite a lot of people turned up at the Private View in hope of an incident.

We were talking to Thomas at the Exhibition when a young woman wearing over her head what appeared to be a fencing-mask covered with red roses, accompanied by a *quadrilla* of associates, entered the gallery holding the model of a female leg high in the air. The object must have been one of those furnishments for displaying women's stockings in shop-windows. This 'happening'—to use a modish term of later date—fell uncommonly flat to all appearances on the assembled company. Thomas explained that the Surrealist significance of the gesture was vested in the surname of the bearer (whom he designated by a rather rude phrase) being Legge. Although Thomas was friendly, I had the impression that some degree of success had not improved him. There was a sense of his having coarsened as a person. We never came across each other during the succeeding years when his name became increas-ingly well-known, and his behaviour proportionately declined.

Nowadays people almost literally start back with the words: 'Ah did you once see Dylan plain, and did he stop and speak with you?', a reverence spreading almost immediately after Thomas's death into areas far beyond those where people take an interest in what poetry is being written. This was brought home in the late 1960s, when, passing through the town of Carmarthen, we took the opportunity of seeking out the museum there housing the Voteporix Stone, an historic pillar of which I had often read but never seen.

This 6th century memorial to King Vortipor, earliest surviving monument to a monarch in the British Isles, has on it an inscription written both in dog-Latin and slanting Ogham (Vortipor's dynasty having intruded from Ireland into South Wales), which calls this petty king of the Demetae by the title of Protector (spelt wrongly), that is to say Officer of the Roman Imperial Bodyguard. It is much as if an Asian or African ruler had been accorded honorary rank in the Life Guards (or at least heard of such being granted), and his descendants continued to use the honorific long after; for by Vortipor's death Rome's rule in Britain had lapsed for a century and a half.

Nevertheless, the style had been remembered from other days. In some countries a relic so venerable might be displayed with all the pomp of a national treasure. In Great Britain—perhaps on the whole preferably —things are otherwise. In any case, historically speaking, nothing much is noticed here, except by those specially interested, between Stonehenge and Hastings.

From the outside the Carmarthen Museum looked like a small private house, of which the front-door happened to be unfastened. We entered. The Voteporix Stone was within, just by the door. A moment later the curator appeared from a room at the back. He seemed surprised by being confronted by visitors at all, positively astonished by a couple who had heard of Vortipor, a king exciting little interest since excoriation as a tyrant in the chronicle of the monk Gildas, his contemporary.

No doubt feeling the occasion both a good one for revealing the extent of the treasure he guarded, at the same time opportunity for exercising that South Wales irony with which the army had made me by then familiar—a tone particularly pleasurable to the ironist, when applied to a fellow countryman become a shade too eminent outside the locality—the custodian observed: *'And we've got Dylan Thomas's cuff-links too!'*

12

In the autumn of 1935, after a trip to Portugal, there was a disaster. Violet suffered a miscarriage. I have spoken earlier of the unfamiliarity with the condition of marriage owing to the break in the succession of domestic life caused by the first war—something common to all my generation. Such mishaps were thought of as belonging to the uninstructed Victorian past. That was not so, as we were sadly to learn.

The following year we brought off a project much discussed, a trip to Russia to see the architecture and galleries; also the home-ground of the great Russian writers. No one was then aware how sinister a juncture that moment was for the world, the Stalinist immolations just about to gather momentum. The year, 1936, was indeed the last of the routine InTourist visits then in operation.

The *Smolny* (her name suggesting aristocratic cadets and budding Maids of Honour) sailed from the London docks direct to Leningrad. The small ship's company included a commissar and his wife. Our table-mate was the wife of an Embassy official known to have been arrested in Russia. She would jump up at the end of every meal, cross to the table of the commissar and his wife, talk frenziedly to them.

The crew, evidently chosen for their good-looks and aggressively cheerful bearing, sang to the balalaika in the evening, but an elderly man, rather shaky on his legs, did all the waiting single-handed. One night the captain made a speech, translated by the commissar. The captain said that he believed there were English people and French people on board. He was well disposed to English people, because they had cut off the head of Charles I; to French people, because they had guillotined Louis XVI. His words now strike rather an old-fashioned note in Soviet propaganda.

Peter the Great's city on the islands startles by its magical beauty, some of the prospects up to even Venetian standards. The dreary and squalid quarters far exceed in extent these gorgeous backdrops (no addict of the

Russian novel would expect or wish otherwise), but the pellucid northern light gives an amazing radiance to the pastel shades of stucco and sparkling onion domes.

No doubt all races have their favourite colour combinations (a comparative study might be interesting), the Hermitage and other Russian galleries indicating the Russian collectors' taste for deep crimsons and dark greens; a coalescence noticeable from, say, Rembrandt to the 19th century genre canvases of the Tretiakov. In the United States one is struck by what seem typically 'American' subjects, rather than colours, chosen from the Great Masters, but probably close investigation would reveal every nation's preferred subjects and colours too.

The Torgsin stores were still in operation during this trip, vast marts of miscellaneous objects confiscated from private owners, not of museum level, therefore put on sale to bring in much needed foreign currency. Most of what was on display was in poor condition, often mere rubbish, but a few items of Empire furniture (not of high quality) might have been tempting had not prices been higher than Bond Street's, to which expense and hazards of transport would be added.

We went by train to Kiev, a city less attractive than expected, but of interest on account of the striking racial difference between Ukrainians and Russians. The street crowd in Leningrad had not greatly differed from that in a Finnish town, something not at all true of Kiev. One reads of this contrast in Gogol and elsewhere, but I was unprepared for stepping off the train into a different country. They were having an anti-gas exercise at the station—precautions a little unusual at that date—several female porters wearing gas-masks.

On the journey back to Leningrad we were lucky enough to have a wagon-lit compartment to ourselves. Violet was knitting a jumper, copying the design from the cover of a knitting-magazine, which showed the garment worn by a girl with slightly Slav features. At regular intervals through the day the conductress, one of those weather-beaten elderly women who play such a prominent part at the lower levels of Soviet officialdom (and could be a great nuisance by their bossiness in museums), would look in to punch the tickets. This one was gnarled and toothless.

Returning for yet another check, the conductress carefully slid the door behind her, and pulled down the blinds. Then she took from the buttoned pocket of her uniform what appeared to be an identity-card. She

33

pointed to the embossed hammer-and-sickle crest at the head of the document, emphasising the emblem several times with her finger. She followed up this action by producing a wad of rouble notes from another pocket, thumbing them over, once more indicating the hammer-and-sickle, then taking hold of the half-finished jumper. In short, she wanted to buy the jumper on the Black Market.

Violet conveyed as kindly as possible that the jumper was not for sale simply because she wanted to wear it herself. The conductress accepted that fairly philosophically, and withdrew. Naturally enough the tickets had to be examined again an hour or two later. By that time Violet had rummaged about in her luggage to see if a present could be found. A jumper, old but originating from Fortnum & Mason, was dredged up.

At first the conductress could not understand what was happening. Then, when she grasped that the jumper was being given to her, she flung her arms round Violet's neck, kissing her ecstatically. I was laughing at this scene when, without the least warning, I too was included in a fervent toothless embrace.

13

At that period the ambition of most young novelists, many elder ones too, was to find employment scriptwriting for a film-company. In the autumn of 1936 my agent arranged some weeks of probation with one of these, with any luck to be followed by a six-months contract. Accordingly, I resigned my job at Duckworth's (the firm having published *Agents and Patients* earlier in the year, last of my novels to appear under that imprint), bringing to an end an association of close on ten years.

I was not sorry to leave, feeling by then that my days in Henrietta Street had lasted long enough. Nevertheless, such early experiences of life are never quite rivalled in sharpness of outline by most of what follows, and, after fifty years of authorship, I find difficulty in not looking on even my own books from a publisher's point of view. Gerald Duckworth himself accepted my departure with composure, indeed a more than oriental impassivity.

The work to which I now transferred myself, one of the humblest categories of 'The Industry', was known colloquially as 'quota quickies'. At that era (in this respect soon to improve) anything like a good British film was rare to the point of being almost unknown, most movies originating from the US, with an occasional highbrow treat from Russia,Germany, France. In order to assist British films a protective tariff had been imposed, laying down that for every foot of foreign film, a proportion of film made in the UK must be shown in British cinemas. This was called The Quota.

Some of the larger Hollywood studios conformed with this measure by establishing their own subsidiary companies in England, where the pictures produced would be technically British, written on the whole by British screenwriters, while so to speak officered by American executives and scenario-editors. Naturally such American companies did not want to compete with their own parent company in Hollywood, so that this was not a milieu in which to find the art of the film at its most dextrous and imaginative.

The American company in question was Warner Bros, then renting a studio in Teddington. The pay offered was the dazzling sum of fifteen—rising to twenty—pounds a week, but the six-months contract laid down that the writer worked from ten to six every day, including Saturday. In practice, Saturday afternoons were not usually exacted (though there were exceptions), but this oppressive threat was always a possibility, and a reprimand was issued to any writer who arrived more than five minutes late, or departed more than five minutes early.

The Teddington studio was not at all easy to reach from Bloomsbury, the alternatives being a series of trains and trolley-buses, followed by a brisk walk, or taking a car through the centre of London twice a day during the worst of the traffic. On the way to Teddington the first morning I mused on what might befall, deciding that something like 'Write a story about postmen' would come near the least welcome assignment.

Telepathic influences must have been at work, because, when the half-dozen or so probationer-scriptwriters, of whom I was one, were divided into syndicates by the American scenario-editor, my own group was instructed to devise a film about messenger-boys, a now departed race, who wore a para-military black uniform, pill-box cap on the side of the head, a shiny bandolier slung across the shoulder; even in those days having about their duties and turnout something of an Edwardian past.

The two other aspirant scriptwriters with whom I was teamed up on this unstimulating theme were in marked contrast to each other: a middle-aged Irish journalist (in fact my agent's husband, though that was not revealed at the time), and a *beau jeune homme* in his very early twenties, whose charm and goodlooks seemed the chief assets. The Irishman, shabby, good-natured, inarticulate, not very quick off the mark, did not survive the probationary period, but the younger colleague turned out to be one of the few bright spots in this purgatorial underworld of film-life.

In the course of about a month the three of us produced certainly not less than nine stories about messenger-boys—a fat boy, a thin boy, a bespectacled boy; a brave boy, a cowardly boy, a studious boy; an English boy, a Scotch boy, an Irish boy; in brief, exploring almost every aspect of messenger-boyhood. The homosexual angle, which time out of mind has played so prominent a part in sportive anecdotes connected with the vocation, was not then available, though messenger-boys were the pivot (if that is the right word) of a Victorian scandal in Cleveland Street, which might nowadays provide a dramatic messenger-boy background.

At the close of these wrestlings of the imagination with the essences of messenger-boy life and character, the subject by then as threadbare as the creative faculties of the scriptwriters concerned, the scenario-editor agreed that perhaps messenger-boys were not a good notion as material for a film. Instead, he handed out typescripts of an unsuccessful stage play dating from ten or fifteen years before, with the command to adapt it for the screen. The play, too, one of unguessable silliness, was in due course scrapped; on which the whole process would start up again in a different form—suggestion, application, abandonment.

I found these labours profoundly unsympathetic; indeed, during later uncomfortable moments in the army, I used to buoy myself up by thinking that at least I was not trying to compose quota-quickies. Teddington seemed to combine some of the dreariest aspects of office-life with making demands on the machinery of creative invention in a manner that was at once superlatively exhausting, yet wholly unsatisfying.

The regimentation was as futile as it was irksome. Few writers would be able to sit six or seven hours on end, working six days a week, incarcerated in a small strip-lighted whitewashed cell, producing the desired product of their own imagination. It could be argued that the banalities prescribed for that sort of film make, in one sense, less demands than truly imaginative work. Even so, the writer must possess the appropriate instinct—which certainly quite a few good writers have shown—for turning out what is required.

Left to do the job at home, one would in general have accomplished much more, but that location would not have allowed for the syndicate system, a necessary part of the process, one certainly more applicable to plays and films than to a novel. In practice, the scriptwriters, cooped up from ten to six in this barrack, would spend most of the time chatting among themselves.

The higher echelons of the Teddington set-up, not a particularly prepossessing crew, were accustomed to eat together at a kind of roadhouse in the neighbourhood, where a heavy luncheon, formidable in its number of courses, was provided. Scriptwriters anxious to make a good impression (a harsher image comes to mind) on the senior executives of the Studio would habitually eat there too. A fair number of drinks would be consumed before sitting down at a long table in a private room, where, throughout the meal, a spelling game was played. I can't remember the precise rules, but everyone present put down a pound, the object of the game being to avoid the word's last letter terminating at oneself; upon which one's money became forfeit.

I dislike all parlour games (except as otherwise specified in these memoirs), but, above all, I hate parlour games which involve spelling. This is not so much from inability to spell, as on account of their tedium and profanation of language, but even spelling games, detestable as they can be, are not normally played at meals. A more barbarous form of disturbing the pleasures of eating and drinking, such as they were in that place, while at the same time debasing the dignity of words, would be hard to conceive; not to mention adding a further hazard to an indigestible menu and overplus of midday aperitifs.

I attended this macabre feast not more than a couple of times. There appeared to be no snack-providing pubs of the right sort in the vicinity, but I nosed out a Cranfordian tea-shop, where refined spinsters laid on some form of light refreshment at the luncheon hour, a repast infinitely preferable.

I learnt later that the chief executive—who was in the habit of circulating fiats couched in some of the strangest prose I have ever read on such weighty matters as writers not allowing wet umbrellas to drip on the floor of their rooms—suffered from chronic dyspepsia, and had been advised by his doctor to rest every afternoon for ten minutes after the midday meal before beginning to work anew. His daily indigestion caused me neither surprise, nor, to tell the truth, great regret.

14

The youngest member of our syndicate, Thomas Wilton Phipps, an Etonian, had recently eloped with a pretty American girl even younger than himself. He was three-quarters American too, his mother (separated from his father and living in the US) sister of Lady Astor, the MP. Tommy Phipps's own sister, Joyce Grenfell, was already becoming known as a *diseuse* in very much her own manner. These connexions made Phipps a rich source of gossip, not only from Cliveden's proud alcove, but cutting a wide swathe through both sides of the Atlantic, anecdotes brightening an otherwise sombre scene.

Phipps owned a secondhand (nearer twentieth-hand) car of daunting ramshackleness, which seemed operated by will-power, since neither gears, brakes, nor engine reacted with the smallest conviction of reliability. Notwithstanding this vehicle's crumbling body, the alarming sounds that issued intermittently from under the bonnet, it conveyed him daily from Chelsea to the Studio, sometimes accommodating me too.

One night Phipps was giving me a lift back to London, when (at a point on or near the Great West Road) the highway narrowed sharply, probably owing to repairs on the surface taking up most of the width. Suddenly three high-powered cars of considerable size, travelling at a great rate almost abreast of each other, bore down from the opposite direction. Seizing the hand-brake as we sped towards what seemed imminent collision, Phipps muttered to himself: 'This is just going to be a question of upbringing.'

Even at the time I thought that a suitable title for a book, but fifteen years passed before I found an opportunity to use it.

15

Moving at a more elevated level in the Studio than people like Phipps and myself, since he had written a play which had been performed, albeit

1. AP—oil painting by Henry Lamb, 1934

2. Edward and Christine Longford,
Violet Pakenham, 1933

3. Elizabeth Pakenham, 1935

4. Violet Pakenham at Pakenham, 1934

5. Pakenham Hall, Co Westmeath

6. Violet at Sunium, 1934

7. AP at Sunium, 1934

one in collaboration, was Terence Rattigan, who now had another work soon to be put on in the West End. This new play, staged a month or so after I came to work at Teddington, was *French Without Tears*, which turned out a resounding hit at the Criterion.

In consequence of the immediate success of *French Without Tears*, Rattigan naturally wanted to escape from film hack-work as soon as possible, settle down to the profession of dramatist, but his contract with Warner Bros ran on for at least six months, possibly an option existing for an even longer period.

One of the most oppressive of Hollywood's methods imported into the UK (like working on a Saturday afternoon) was that an actor or writer, under contract to one studio, might be hired out to another. In the case of stars large sums could be involved, but even a scriptwriter making twenty or thirty pounds a week, might be loaned at, say, sixty, the company pocketing the difference. I believe Rattigan, as a promising new-comer, had already suffered one of these exchanges. His present good fortune made a repetition of such borrowing probable. At first Warner Bros refused to release him on any terms, but compromise must finally have been reached, because he disappeared from Teddington to write further plays.

Although he had sidestepped his father's efforts to put him into the Diplomatic Service, Rattigan was outwardly very much like the popular notion (as opposed to the usual reality) of a young diplomat: tall, good-looking, elegant in turnout, somewhat chilly in manner. He had been a cricketer of some eminence at Harrow. His homosexuality, of which he made no particular secret, probably unswerving, was not at all obvious on the surface.

In the final act of *French Without Tears* the predatory girl, man-eater of the French cramming establishment, whose bitchy behaviour has caused two rivals for her love to become friends and abandon her, plans to sink her talons into a young lord due to arrive there. As played at the Criterion, the new *pensionnaire* turns out to be a boy of twelve years old, but, as originally written (and produced on the Continent), the curtain goes down on the entrance of a middle-aged homosexual, his tastes unmistakable, leading on a leash two large Afghan hounds.

Over a period of about three weeks Terry Rattigan and I were immured together with the purpose of producing a story between us. This brief collaboration added no classic to movie history, indeed professionally speaking, was totally barren, but we laughed a lot over preposterous subjects discussed as possibilities.

One was always aware in Rattigan of a deep inner bitterness, no doubt accentuated by the irksome position in which he found himself at that moment. In the Theatre good publicity such as he was enjoying is something to be taken advantage of without delay. He had a touch of cruelty, I think, and liked to torment one of the male executives of the Studio, who showed signs of falling victim to Rattigan's attractions.

When I asked Rattigan if the French crammer's in his play bore any resemblance to that he had himself attended at Wimereux (one specializing in Foreign Office candidates), he replied: 'Not in the least.' This did not bother him at all. He was a thrusting young man whose primary concern was to make himself financially independent, not interested in 'art' so much as immediate effect.

Rattigan would talk entertainingly about the mechanics of how plays are written, always consciously from a 'non-artist' angle, though in a manner never to bring in doubt his own grasp and intelligence. One of his favourite formulas was: 'Take a hackneyed situation and reverse it.' His own natural abilities always seemed to me to conflict with this disregard for more than popular success, even if a popular success that designed to be a cut above run-of-the-mill banalities.

It might well be argued that certain popular successes (Shakespeare's, for instance) have become classics, while many 'artists'—indeed most— are forced to work from time to time at something less than their highest potential in order to live. Nevertheless, Rattigan's freely accepted approach in this respect poses the question to what extent any writer can control what emerges, or, put in another form, whether escape from too much 'popular' writing, once indulged, is ever possible.

16

The last task undertaken for Warner Bros—like the final labour imposed by an enchanter into whose power one has fallen through imprudent search for hidden treasure—was to produce a 'treatment' for a film about the life of the Victorian philanthropist Dr Barnardo, creator of the

Barnardo Homes. A 'treatment' is the technical term for the narrative of a film story before being dramatized into dialogue.

Dr Thomas Barnardo (1845-1905), a medical man first intending to become a missionary, was so appalled by the condition in his day of destitute children in the East End of London, that he began rescue work on his own in a small way. This finally grew into the extensive organization to which Barnardo's name is now attached. Like most persons of his kind Barnardo had a fiercely polemical side, the ups and downs of his career offering a promising basis for the semi-fictional semi-documentary type of film about meritorious achievement, which was then having some vogue.

No other scriptwriter being associated with this project in the first instance, I was allowed to work at home, where naturally something more serviceable was produced at greater speed than could have been hammered out in the cells at Teddington. When submitted to those who made such decisions, this 'treatment' of the Barnardo story was considered sufficiently satisfactory for the scheme to be followed up.

The question now arose of how to make sure that surviving representatives of the Barnardo family would raise no difficulties about an exceedingly free and easy version of the philanthropist's biography. On enquiry it turned out that Barnardo had left only one child, a daughter, Syrie Barnardo, who, after marriage to a pharmaceutical tycoon, had abandoned her first husband for the writer, W. Somerset Maugham. The marriage with Maugham had also broken up about ten years before this, and, under her second married name, Syrie Maugham now ran a fashionable interior-decorating business, often mentioned in the gossip-columns.

How best to tackle the problem of obtaining Mrs Syrie Maugham's clearance for the intended Barnardo picture much exercised the Studio executives concerned. As London based, they were perhaps less at ease than in Hollywood, and—so it seemed to me—they now showed an artless lack of aplomb in handling the matter. My own view was that, even if the precise sum was not specifically stated at this stage, a hypothetical subvention should at once be adumbrated as preliminary for permission to go ahead. That might well save much beating about the bush. Those in authority, however, possibly from mere parsimony, showed an extraordinary coyness about mentioning money to someone they regarded as a lady of quality.

After various comings and goings, it was finally agreed that Mrs Maugham should be invited to luncheon, and, during the course of the meal, I should read aloud to her my (preponderantly fictional) account of her father's rise to fame, trimmed up in such a way as to make a saleable motion-picture. The scenario-editor thought a *partie-carrée* preferable to a trio. This would obviate his having nothing better to do at the luncheon-table than follow Mrs Maugham's changes of expression as I unfolded my largely imaginary narrative of her father's life and good works. Violet, though she had not otherwise met her, had once attended one of Mrs Maugham's parties, so she too was invited to make a fourth.

The scenario-editor rented a flat in Whitehall Court, a large block in Westminster, housing not only individuals but also the premises of many small clubs, including The Authors, of which more later. The scenario-editor, who had written a play produced in New York some years before, but failed to follow up, was a bachelor, a decidedly gloomy one, the antithesis of traditional American high spirits. His flat, where the party met, monastically austere, was in key with its owner's temperament.

When Mrs Maugham arrived she remarked rather grimly that, having lived in Whitehall Court with her first husband, she knew the journey from where we sat to the dining-room took twenty minutes. Her estimate proved no less than accurate; the restaurant itself, catering for the convenience of residents rather than professional gourmets or those who liked a chic atmosphere, not warming up our party by a sense of riotous conviviality. The tables had, however, the supreme merit of being set far apart, particularly merciful for an audition likely to require a good deal of carrying off.

Mrs Maugham herself maintained a demeanour of inscrutable severity throughout my embarrassed recitation, entoned between gulps of the Whitehall Court table d'hôte. There was, indeed, no earthly reason why she should dissipate her energies, on which there were no doubt many demands, in conventional courtesies or an engaging manner. She wisely attempted neither. In fact the proposal to make a film about her father did not appear to interest her in the least. It may well be that she preferred that aspect of her background to remain unemphasized. Violet and the scenario-editor chatted of this and that. I felt considerable relief when the macabre performance was at an end.

Back at the Studio, the whole question of the Barnardo picture was allowed to remain in the air. No one seemed to know what to do next. Further action in the matter never took place, and not long after this my own contract with Warner Bros ran out. No suggestion was made that it should be renewed. I cannot remember whether or not I had any hopes that such would happen. As means of earning a living I should have been quite happy to continue with the Barnardo project, but the moment coincided with one of those periodic recessions in the British film industry, studios closing down right and left. Perhaps my 'treatment' of Dr Barnardo, deep in the vaults of Warner Bros, still lies waiting for the Last Trump, when all shelved 'treatments' come up for judgment before the Great Executive.

17

This passing encounter with Mrs Syrie Maugham (whom her husband in his old age handled, at least on paper, rather roughly) gives excuse for saying a word about Somerset Maugham himself, when we talked together at a much later date. In earlier, more puritanical, days I had looked on Maugham as a mere story-teller for tired businessmen (and why not?), but in the end one learns how hard is all writing, growing grateful for what holds the attention at all, even if only at certain points. Maugham's style can be uninspiring, but, as remarked earlier, some of his short stories seem to me in a high class, while *Cakes and Ale* contains comedy that rises well above the commonplace.

I had met Maugham perhaps three or four times over a quarter of a century before exchanging anything but a conventional sentence on reintroduction. We sat next to each other in the mid-1950s at a luncheon party given more or less in his honour at the *Punch* 'table'. He was then far less publicly revealed than later as an undoubtedly tragic, if sometimes not very attractive figure, whose immense popular success in one area of his life contrasted with ghastly interior misery at the other.

The stutter—referred to so often by Maugham himself, as well as those who have written about him—was in ordinary conversation far less in evidence than I had expected. No doubt the impediment was a recurrent personal annoyance in disturbing the climaxes of his own anecdotes, the delivery probably deteriorating when he was angry (apparently no uncommon condition), but otherwise the slight hesitation had charm rather than the reverse. He took charge of the conversation at once, detonating a few near epigrams in the Nineties manner, which seemed to indicate a desire to keep matters at a formal rather than easygoing level. Then he began to discuss young writers, saying that he admired, for instance, John Lodwick.

It happened that, while employed on the *Times Literary Supplement*, I had reviewed John Lodwick's two last novels. Perhaps not now much remembered, Lodwick was then making some name, but, in consequence of a car accident in Spain, died soon after this in his early forties. One of these novels, *The Cradle of Neptune*, was clearly an autobiographical account of being a naval cadet at Dartmouth. I had thought Lodwick's writing competent, in places a trifle undisciplined, and gave Maugham a guarded answer, saying I liked what I had read, but thought there was not yet sufficient work to judge Lodwick's staying power. Maugham replied rather huffily: 'He writes a book a year. I don't know how many more you expect.'

Years later, I found that my friend and publisher, Roland Gant, had been also Lodwick's friend and publisher. I mentioned this conversation with Maugham. Gant was able to add a footnote. He described Lodwick as an adventurous type with a lively war record, a man always involved in love affairs and travel. Maugham, on account of his approval of Lodwick's books, had extended a rather vague invitation to come and see him as Lodwick then lived in the south of France. Some time later, Lodwick, fairly dishevelled and somewhat drunk, turned up at the Villa Mauresque allegedly leaving outside the gates a gipsy girl he had picked up on his wanderings. The visit, so Gant understood from Lodwick, who was unnerved by Maugham's icy politeness, had not gone with a swing.

The snobbish overtones of the next stage of my conversation with Maugham need no apology, since one of the best of his short stories, *The Outstation*, turns on that very theme; while in *Cakes and Ale*, Alroy Kear (prototype of Hugh Walpole) is specifically described as a novelist in whose works 'You will never find any of those solecisms that disfigure the productions of those who have studied the upper classes only in the pages of the illustrated papers'.

Having found me wanting in my attitude towards John Lodwick's writing, Maugham now moved back to Victorian times. He remarked:

'It's amusing in Trollope's novels how the Duke will address his son by his courtesy title.'

One should always reflect, however briefly, before answering. I spoke thoughtlessly. I was influenced by the knowledge that, when their father was killed, the younger Pakenhams had been sent for by their mother, and told that in future Silchester would be called Edward. Indeed I could remember at least half-a-dozen boys at school to whom that convention (probably now fallen into disuse in a more down-to-earth world) equally applied. Without the need of anything like Alroy Kear's expertise, the practice could, in fact, probably have been gleaned from the illustrated papers themselves.

Incautiously, I said: 'But surely that quite often happens in these days too?'. The moment the words were out on my mouth I saw I had blundered. Maugham did not reply. He simply turned to his other neighbour and conversed with him throughout the rest of lunch.

III

North Palm Drive

In the course of my scriptwriting interlude, temporary increase in earnings seemed to make this a good moment, if we were to have children, for moving into somewhere rather less restricted in space than Great Ormond Street. The man from the Treasury had expressed a wish to take the top-floor flat if vacated, so there would be no trouble in finding a new tenant. The property market was at that moment in a fairly stagnant condition. We acquired the lease of a small house in Regent's Park, which we were to own, though not live in continuously, for seventeen years. This was 1 Chester Gate, probably planned with several others nearby as bachelor residences of the period, situated in a short turning leading into the east side of the Park from Albany Street, a long road, stretches of which were of village-like character; including a jobbing tailor with a notice in his window announcing: 'Soonest with the Latest'.

For a time Clara Warville came to cook for us, but bus routes from Chelsea to Regent's Park were less convenient than to Bloomsbury. Moreover, in a slightly larger establishment, she could not always rely on being alone in the kitchen, a state she preferred. To our great regret she left us, but wrote Violet a letter saying that the previous year had been the happiest in her life. However well she had adapted herself to looking after George Moore—there was no doubt she felt an affection for him—Ebury Street must have known many nerve-racking crises.

46

2

I had not much enjoyed being a scriptwriter, but the experience was not without its uses. A shortcoming of which I became very conscious at Teddington was lack of histrionic ability in putting forward my own ideas, such as they were for films, to American executives, who could grasp a dramatic situation if acted out in front of them, but were unable to take in a proposal made only by word of mouth. The work, partly for that reason, did teach me a little about narrative construction, chiefly the necessity of 'establishing' early on in the story circumstances to be used at a later stage. This is a technique to be observed in the books of, say, Proust or Joyce, as much as in any competent detective story. The lesson is particularly important for any writer embarking on a long novel, akin to that principle inscribed in James's *Notebooks*: 'Dramatize, dramatize'.

Meanwhile some other employment had to be sought. Plans were known to be on foot in Hollywood (the term I shall use generically for the cluster of merging townships associated with the South Californian movie world) for making a picture to be called *A Yank at Oxford*. There seemed hope of getting a job in this production, since I could now be deemed to have scriptwriting experience (though in fact no syllable written by me had even been spoken from the screen), and had spent three years at the university which was to be the background of the story.

Negotiations were opened up between my agent in London and the firm's collaborator in Hollywood. Some hope of a deal was held out if I were on the spot. The next thing to do was to get to 'the Coast'. It was said that a year's sojourn there could allow some earnings to be retained. A longer period, entailing an ever expanding standard of living, was better avoided for those who did not wish to settle down to those expensive habits, which could result in a life-sentence to the weariest of treadmills.

Deciding to approach California by sea, we set out in May, 1937, on a voyage due to take four weeks. The *Canada* (a Danish vessel sunk a few years later by a German mine) put into harbour only three or four times. We reached St Thomas in the Virgins (islands formerly Danish, by then sold to the US) on the morning after the coronation of King George VI had taken place in London. There had been celebrations on board too, and, seen through the porthole of our cabin, the green downs of St

47

Thomas shimmered and heaved no less than the waves of the Atlantic. It was one of the worst hangovers I have ever experienced. Tom Collinses in the shadow of Morgan's Castle did something to restore the equilibrium.

At Jamaica we visited the Mona House (in Jamaican terms, we were told, not unlike Rosa Lewis's Cavendish Hotel*) in the company of an American married couple, part of that flow begun some years before of American expatriates no longer able to afford life in Paris. The wife was much the dominant partner, vitalizing so far as possible a husband whose claims to be a writer seemed fairly nebulous. They were very characteristic of those more obscure American dwellers on the Left Bank, sometimes satirized by Hemingway and Fitzgerald.

These two, so it appeared, had been lucky enough to find an inestimable *bonne* for their Montparnasse household. When they planned to return to the US they put an advertisement into the local paper of the *arrondissement*, stating that this maid's services were available, and that she could be interviewed in their flat any afternoon.

The following day two ladies arrived on the doorstep. They turned out to be no less than Gertrude Stein and Alice B. Toklas. The famous couple were in search of a maid. The employers, overawed by such eminence under their roof, summoned the unparagoned *bonne*—among whose other qualities was a total self-possession—and themselves retired from the sitting-room to the kitchen.

The murmur of interrogation could be heard through the wall. Suddenly the door between burst open. White and trembling, almost in tears, the maid burst in.

'No, madame, no! I cannot go to those two sorceresses!'

3

The *Canada* sailed on, and entered the mouth of the Panama Canal. At one point a break in the luxuriant marine vegetation of the banks showed

*Speaking of Rosa Lewis in *Messengers of Day*, I mentioned that, when the American painter, J. O. Mahoney, stayed at The Cavendish during and after the second war, she often addressed him as 'Ambrose Clark'. I had not then identified Ambrose Clark (of Cooperstown, NY), renowned in hunting and racing circles on both sides of the Atlantic in the years between the wars. I must thank my correspondents, American and British, for rectifying this ignorance.

the remnant of the canal de Lesseps had attempted, a forlorn and mysterious Lost World. We emerged into the Pacific, going ashore only once at some Panamanian port, where bananas were taken on board, visiting a bar housed on stilts, where a man was playing with a large crab on a lead, sometimes secreting it under his sombrero. Then we arrived at Los Angeles.

There is nothing specially welcoming about Hollywood, rather the reverse, especially as I was greeted by the news that my agent had died while we were on the high seas. The replacement, as an individual, was wholly antipathetic. This was getting off to a bad start. After a day or two at the Beverly Hills Hotel, money—of which there was not an inexhaustible supply—seemed to be disappearing at an alarming rate.

In fact, so one fairly soon discovered, Hollywood, if you kept your head, was not necessarily expensive for those who designed to enter The Industry, provided they had not yet found a job. Indeed, certainly in relation to availability of passable accommodation, Hollywood was cheaper than London; at least for those prepared to live as Untouchables 'on the wrong side of the track'. In that far-from-chic area we found a self-contained furnished flat in a two-storeyed house, 357 (not 347, as elsewhere stated) North Palm Drive, Beverly Hills. There were two quite sizable rooms, another much smaller one, kitchen, bath, for sixty dollars (about the then equivalent of twelve pounds) a month, including one day's cleaning. The next necessity was a car. A secondhand one was acquired for two hundred and fifty dollars.

Such a 'life-style' would scarcely have been tolerated had one found the kind of employment sought. It is interesting to speculate what nemesis would have been visited on a comparatively highly paid scriptwriter, who firmly insisted on saving the bulk of a substantial salary by existing as we did.

A male songster in one of the Hollywood night-spots (another of his lyrics 'Bring me a lei from Hawaii') used to sing:

> I'd like a little shack
> On the other side of the track,
> And a man who doesn't limp
> To be my p . . .

The final word was lost in the wail of the saxophones. Apart from the energetic entrepreneur specified in the song, our Beverly Hills flat was pretty well what was described.

The car, an Oakland, deserves a word. The model had been only briefly produced (two years, I think), then withdrawn from the market, perhaps (a purely British phrase I was recently told by an American) because too 'good value for the money'. It came from a used-automobile lot, personal property of the salesman, a sympathetically inscrutable Missourian, and served us well.

At first, after this car became my property, when asked by parking-attendants: 'What make?', I would reply: 'An Oakland'. Later, even when row upon row of shining new automobiles stretched far away to the horizon and beyond, I changed the answer, not without pride, to: '*The* Oakland.' That was enough. By this time it must have been the sole example still on the road. I returned the Oakland to the Missourian, who, on its resale quite a long time later, forwarded to England a very respect-able proportion of the car's cost in the first instance.

Now began the depressing round of being interviewed by executives for a job. The executives themselves were often friendly enough, even more so their secretaries. One of these said: 'You're English, aren't you? And I *think* you come from London'—a diagnosis for some reason lacking that complimentary ring of being immediately marked down as a Parisian or New Yorker.

I soon became increasingly tired of retailing my life-story in pursuit of what was revealing itself as a mirage, so far as any clarity could be dis-tinguished through that utter stagnation of movement, total inanition where action is concerned, characteristic of almost all theatrical negoti-ation, perhaps most of all apparent in the film-world's dealings. No one would say; 'We haven't got a job for you', while at the same time no summons came from those visited, who were supposedly looking into the matter.

4

While trying out the Oakland for the first time in some secluded neighbourhood of Beverly Hills, I all but collided with an infinitely larger and grander vehicle containing two celebrated stars of that period,

Ronald Colman and his wife, Benita Hume, but in general film stars were not greatly in evidence, except at certain restaurants or night-clubs currently fashionable, where naturally prices were high. At that moment the favoured bar was The Cock n' Bull. On our sole visit there, film-stars stretched as far as the eye could reach, among them Marlene Dietrich, perhaps the only one I had any wish to see in the flesh, who did not at all disappoint.

This recognized concentration of celebrities of one sort or another in a given public place is—even apart from Hollywood—a phenomenon more Continental and American than English. Americans have often asked me: 'What is an amusing place to visit in London?', but (in days when one was comparatively in touch with such things) the question, anyway in the terms implied, was unanswerable. There might be restaurants, bars, night-clubs, pubs, where there could be a good display of lions on a lucky night, but, at all levels, the English take their pleasures in an indefinably intimate and complex manner, which inhibits the snap answer to be provided (anyway formerly) in Paris or New York.

The Eiffel might have qualified in London of the Twenties, but the restaurant was not large, the company often humdrum enough, strangers far from welcome, meals consumed in almost total darkness. At the Café de Paris, then and much later, Douglas Byng, with an ineffable sparkle, sang his own songs for the piano, to what was usually a conventionally smart world. Nearer the mark as an 'amusing' place demanded by foreign visitors was the Café Anglais in Leicester Square, where, for a very brief period in 1928, Rex Evans put on a similar, though individual, entertainment, to a large audience, lions in reasonably high proportion, evening dress optional, prices not high. Rex Evans was to be one of our supports in Hollywood.

Our only Hollywood contact of a non-professional sort was an American-born great-aunt of Violet's, Mabel Leigh, who with her husband, Rowland Leigh (seventy-eight and fairly shaky), had come to visit their son, also called Rowland, who was making a successful career as a scriptwriter and librettist. Mrs Leigh, an altogether delightful person (whose father, a professional soldier, had fought for the Confederacy with unhappy results for their fortunes in Savannah), had married a younger son without prospects. Fortunately old Rowley Leigh combined the usually conflicting traits of devotion to racing with total abstinence from betting, a peculiarity that perfectly qualified him as handicapper for the Jockey Club, an appointment which brought in a modest livelihood.

Young Rowley Leigh, much more ambitious, had been prominent as actor and producer in the OUDS during the Oxford generation immediately before my own, but it was through his mother that we met such few stars as came our way. It was possible to possess no great wish to frequent the star-world—for which in any case our station in Hollywood life far from equipped us—while at the same time to feel a term there had been rather flat, on return to England, without some minimal contact with the element that made the place famous; notwithstanding the fact that those biblical emblems of plenty, wine and oil, were looked on locally as of at least equal account.

Mabel Leigh had travelled to America on the same boat as the sister of the current Mrs Douglas Fairbanks Sr (formerly Lady Ashley), in consequence of which we were taken to see Douglas Fairbanks, even then regarded as a giant (in fact, almost dwarf) from Hollywood's Heroic Age, at his Santa Monica beach-house, a residence bolted and barred like a fortress.

There was a heavy sea-mist that day, and the atmosphere of the Fairbanks household was not easy. Violet recalls that Sylvia Fairbanks remarked that Douglas Fairbanks (like most Americans) was a great luggage snob, while she (like most English people) travelled with suitcases which looked as if they had been rescued from the rubbish dump. This, she said, greatly shamed her husband. On other occasions we met one or two more stars, the exuberant comedienne Sophie Tucker, who at once started up a flirtation with old Rowley Leigh, and the Mexican vamp, Lupe Velez, but stars played no real part in our Hollywood life.

Rex Evans, mentioned above as singing his own songs at the Café Anglais, a friend of young Rowley Leigh's, had left England to settle in Hollywood. Evans's songs proved too English, perhaps too subtly of their passing moment, for export, but he had found plenty of other things to do. Huge, plump, good-natured, always heaving with giggles, he took Hollywood's suburban atmosphere less seriously than most of its phrenetically inward-looking residents, a refreshing attitude.

Another couple who kept their heads in relation to their surroundings, very hospitable to us (a quality by no means so universal in those parts as elsewhere in my own experience of the US), were Stanley and Odette Logan. He was an English actor, now turned director; she French (having enjoyed theatrical success in London too), not only charming but an excellent cook. Logan had many stories of the Theatre, such as the producer of a 1920 revival of a wartime musical by Bruce Bairnsfather and Arthur Eliot called *The Better 'Ole* saying: 'It can't fail—there's not a new thing in it'; or recalling a night-out with C. B. Cochran: 'At the end of it CB was in a dilemma—he wanted to borrow his fare home, but he also wanted to try and sleep with Odette.'

The veteran English actor C. Aubrey Smith (created Sir Charles Aubrey Smith in his eighties, no doubt one of the stately Hollywood knights pictured in the opening paragraphs of Evelyn Waugh's *The Loved One*) had played in the dramatized version of Kipling's *The Light That Failed* in 1898, and was to appear in his *Wee Willie Winkie* in 1937 (of which more later) teamed up with Shirley Temple. Prototype of the Gentleman of the Old School, Carthusian, cricketer, Aubrey Smith was already getting very deaf. He had recently been present at an actors' dinner-party also attended by Stanley Logan. Conversation had turned on the subject of homosexuality. Seeing talk become animated, assuming the merits of some sport were being argued, Aubrey Smith suddenly leant forward and spoke with authority: 'Well, whatever you say, give me three stumps, a bat, and a ball.'

Through Mabel Leigh we met Freddie Bartholomew, whose laurels as Little Lord Fauntleroy had not long before been conspicuously renewed in Kipling's *Captains Courageous*, copies of which fans would bring the boy-hero to sign. Freddie Bartholomew lived with his aunt, a splendidly sensible and unassuming English woman, at that moment assailed with law-suits instituted by her nephew's parents, who, previously content that she should take on the expenses and responsibilities of their son's up-bringing, now hoped for a larger slice cut from the cake of his fame. Miss Bartholomew remained quiet, firm, unfussed, entirely dedicated to what she looked on as best—not solely with an eye to professional advancement—for her nephew; a lady of whose bearing in the circumstances any country might be proud.

Throughout these commotions, theatrical and legal, pleasant and unpleasant, Freddie Bartholomew himself remained in private life an attractive little boy, quite 'unspoilt' by all that was going on round him.

With charming candour he insisted on revealing to me the complex cat's cradle of delicate wires and filaments installed in the furthermost caverns of his jaw, purposed to remodel the back teeth in whatever form was regarded as most appropriate for a child-star of his eminence.

5

Sequestered in North Palm, our life was uneventful enough. After unavailing offers of my services during the day, I would return from the Studios in the evening to read *War and Peace*. It was at North Palm, under Violet's instruction, that I first attempted some primitive cooking.

Once in a way we would go to a film or play. The Mayan Theatre in Los Angeles, a low terracotta-coloured building, designed inside and out to resemble a temple in Yucatan, stood near the intersection of South Hill Street and West Eleventh. Here the trollies clattered past clumps of twelve-storey blocks, a wilderness of car-parks, disused lots, mean shops selling trusses, Panama hats, secondhand typewriters.

The WPA (Works Progress Administration, a governmental organization for dealing with unemployment) had mounted *Macbeth* at the Mayan Theatre with an all Black cast of over a hundred. This performance has always remained in my mind as an example of the fluidity characteristic of most great art. The play was also notable for the manner in which actors relatively obscure or even unsuccessful can sometimes put on a show scarcely at all short of the best.

The curtain went up on a tropical forest. A thunderous storm raged, giant cactuses spreading their spikes in a manner to make the luxuriant undergrowth all but impassable. The trembling foliage parted. Two big Blacks in ostrich-plumed head-dresses, carrying exotic broadswords and wicker shields, stepped through into a clearing. Their provenance was uncertain: Zulu warriors; knights of Benin; Ethiopian nobles; chieftains from the South of the Sudan; they might have been intended as any of these.

'So foul and fair a day I have not seen.'
'How far is't call'd to Forres?'

A sudden green glare above the warriors lighted up the three witches, cackling horribly in a neighbouring eucalyptus tree where they seemed to be practising the rites of Voodoo.

Most of the action of the play had the same palace or castle for background, the interior of an African mud fort, in the centre of which was set a deep archway leading to a gate and turret. In this tower Duncan, a short thickset Black, whitebearded, crowned with a high cylindrical cap hooped with gold, was murdered with his grooms. On either side, staircases led up to the ramparts, and the massive wooden door on which Macduff and Lennox knock from without.

This was one of the best moments of the play, for the porter was a fine actor, although his lines had been shamefully bowdlerized. He was the only member of the cast to allow himself the traditional accents of the Old South.

'. . . Knock, knock, knock. Whose dere i' de name ob Belzebub? . . . Knock, knock. Who's dere, i' de ober debil's name? . . . Knock, knock. Neber at quiet! What are you?—But dis place is too cold for Hell . . . Anon, anon: I pray you, remember de Porter.'

Lady Macbeth was small, slight, a good actress, but here perhaps the metamorphosis of presentation seemed not quite right. Macbeth and his wife are so essentially a British couple, her lines, especially, not intended for the favourite of the harem. In the torrid zone, one felt, weak-willed husbands and strong-minded wives would behave differently from the Macbeths, so Nordic in their moods.

The banquet, on the other hand, had with good effect been turned into a wild Harlem party, in which first dancers, then guests themselves, the thanes of Scotland and their ladies, palpitated backwards and forwards in frenzied rhythm, which, but for its peculiarly African grace, might have been a reel. When the dancing had subsided Macbeth and his Queen circulated among the company. Drinks were handed round.

'Here had we now our country's honour roof'd,
Were the graced person of our Banquo present;'

At that moment came a blinding flash, Banquo's head, some twenty times larger than life, appeared in the form of a giant mask, grotesque and terrifying, peering over the castle walls. This happened several times, throwing Macbeth into paroxysms of terror, which seemed to infect the rest of the party; indeed was frightening enough for the audience.

In the scene where the three witches (with their Voodoo men and Voodoo women) preside over the burning cauldron, American sensitiveness to such things—even at this period—omitted the lines:

> 'Liver of blaspheming Jew,
> Gall of goat, and slips of yew
> Sliver'd in the moon's eclipse,
> Nose of Turk, and Tartar's lips,'

With the exception of Duncan's murder, all violence in the play was acted out with fire-arms, Young Siward's failure—because 'born of woman'—to slay Macbeth being represented as missing with a pistol shot.

There was a final admonitory footnote to this excellent show:

The Federal Theatre project is part of the WPA Program. However, the viewpoint expressed in the play is not necessarily that of the WPA, nor any other agency of the government.

6

We went to hear Ernest Hemingway speak a commentary to *Spanish Earth*, the documentary about the Spanish Civil War made by Hemingway in collaboration with Joris Ivens, a professional movie-man. The film was to be shown at the Los Angeles Philharmonic Auditorium in Pershing Square, gardens where the bums clustered in the twilight under subtropical boscage. We called up in the morning to reserve seats for the performance, billed for 8:15 p.m., but were told booking was unnecessary. Nevertheless, on arrival at about seven, a brisk sale was in progress. Outside the hall neon lights shone:

HEMINGWAY AUTHOR
SPANISH EARTH

After what subsequently proved an indiscreet dinner of clam chowder, seafood à la Bernstein, Sonoma Valley Chablis, we took our seats. There must have been 3,000 or more people in the hall. Some committed socialists—with one gentleman announcing himself as a Cuban fascist— had to be unwillingly removed from seats reserved for other people. It was nearly nine o'clock before these dissident elements were sorted out,

you were close. I am very close to my sister, so I thought maybe she was your sister.'

The view that Violet's nose and mine, structurally speaking, had much in common, showed an unacademic approach to significant form, but I did not offer to dispute the matter aesthetically, especially as the young man seemed disposed to enlarge on his own relationship with his sister.

'I was so close to my sister at one time,' he said, 'that I used to suffer just the same sort of pains when she had her periods.'

'Did you really?'

'Sometimes when we were apart, for no reason, I would have cramps and headaches. Then I'd write to her and enquire, and that was always when she was having her period.'

Somebody came up and spoke to one or other of us at that moment, so we drifted apart, and I heard no more of this unusual, even fascinating, physiological phenomenon. Afterwards, when I tried to find out who the young man was, no one seemed to know anything about him, except that he belonged to the US Marine Corps, and had been bought a suit to appear at the party by whoever had there introduced him.

9

Through Rex Evans we met Elliott Morgan, a young man employed in the research department of Metro-Goldwyn-Mayer; now, I believe, in charge of research for all the film companies that survive that distant epoch. Morgan's family, emigrants from Wales in his father's generation, was now settled in Los Angeles, and, apart from himself, unconnected with the movie business. The Morgans were wine drinkers, a habit marking them out, and they were kind enough to ask us to dinner.

Elliott Morgan turned out to be 'researching' *A Yank at Oxford*, the film which I had once hoped would provide my own entrée into Hollywood scriptwriting. These activities had quite recently brought him into contact with Scott Fitzgerald, just arrived in Hollywood in an attempt to repair his fortunes, and assigned to work on that very script.

In these days it is hard to remember that in 1937 the name of F. Scott Fitzgerald as a novelist was scarcely at all known in the United Kingdom. *The Great Gatsby* had appeared in England in 1926, making no stir at all.

Indeed, when *Tender Is the Night* followed in 1934, the London publisher did not even bother to list *Gatsby* opposite the title-page. Fitzgerald's reputation, such as it was, rested on the recommendation of a few critics, of whom T. S. Eliot was one (though not, so far as I knew, in print), Cyril Connolly being responsible for drawing my own attention to a novelist for whom I at once felt enthusiasm.

In the US, though in quite another manner—an essentially American manner—Fitzgerald's position as a writer was almost equally unsatisfactory. This once famous figure, golden boy, prototype of the 'Jazz Age', was all but forgotten. That is not quite true, for when we reached New York on this same trip, at least one Fitzgerald first-edition, in a tattered paper wrapper, was on display in his publisher's (Scribner's) window, positively emphasizing how much its author belonged to the past; Fitzgerald's book confirming the historic traditions of the firm, like the ancient headgear on display in Lock's hat-shop in St James's Street.

There are several reasons for this collapse into oblivion. Fitzgerald—that rare phenomenon, a 'bad' writer who made himself into a 'good' writer—had lost much of his former appeal simply because he had begun to produce immeasurably better novels than his early work. In the years of prosperity he had lived recklessly, drunk too much, involved himself in acute financial embarrassments, which would pursue him, while in addition had suffered unforeseeable and tragic blows through the mental breakdown of his wife.

At the same time Fitzgerald had always managed to keep afloat by writing short stories, some accomplished, some less so. He had outlined his own sad tale in *The Crack Up*, a collection of autobiographical pieces which I had not read as the book was still unpublished in England. One could not fail to notice the tone in which people in Hollywood spoke of Fitzgerald. It was as if Lazarus, just risen from the dead, were to be looked on as of somewhat doubtful promise as an aspiring scriptwriter. 'Meet him? Of course Scott will be very pleased indeed to find an Englishman who knows his work. He says he's never gone over in England, and never will.'

So all was arranged. Elliott Morgan was to bring Scott Fitzgerald to lunch with us. For convenience this lunch would take place at the MGM commissary. I noted the engagement in my book for Tuesday, 20 July, 1937; as it turned out, a date of some consequence to Fitzgerald himself.

After undergoing the customary formalities demanded for entering the premises of a film studio—security precautions that might be deemed excessive for gaining access to a nation's most secret nuclear plant—we met Morgan standing outside the commissary, a hangar-like restaurant of no great charm. He found a table by the wall.

The luncheon break for the subordinate employees of the film world, such as writers, was not yet due, but a sprinkling of loiterers of one kind or another had begun to congregate in the neighbourhood of the commissary, most of them in ordinary clothes. Through this crowd was suddenly led a girl in a blue Louis xv dress, her make-up bright yellow, powdered and curled hair enclosed under a transparent bag, her sunburnt hands suggesting the beach at Santa Monica, rather than the parterres of Versailles. Meanwhile, at the central table of the dining-room, the senior executives, the 'moguls', to use a popular term, were beginning to gather.

These magnates looked just as might be imagined, a picture by some Netherlands master of the moneychangers about to be expelled from the Temple, or a group of appreciative onlookers at a martyrdom. In the manner of most people in Hollywood, they seemed to be passionately acting the part life had assigned to them, movie moguls to the point of inartistic exaggeration exemplified in one of their own films.

It should be added that a legend of the period representing every Hollywood waitress or usherette as a failed film-star of unimaginable beauty was without foundation. One might even have hesitated to affirm with any conviction that the Hollywood standard of looks, female or male—the moguls steeply diminished the average of the latter—sustained a good working average; certainly nothing to be compared with the likelihood of seeing a lot of pretty girls in the course of a morning's walk through (to mention a couple of cities at random where such abound) Cardiff or Madrid.

Suddenly, all coming into sight at exactly the same instant, a vast throng of employees emerged from the MGM offices, and surged in spate towards the commissary. I immediately recognized which figure was Scott Fitzgerald's. In an inexplicable manner he was quite different from anyone else. Then for some minutes he was lost to sight, re-emerging near our table from somewhere in the background. Morgan jumped up.

'This is Mr Fitzgerald.'

He was smallish, neat, solidly built, wearing a light grey suit, light-coloured tie, all his tones essentially light. Photographs—seen for the most part years later—do not do justice to him. Possibly he was one of those persons who at once become self-conscious when photographed. Even snapshots tend to give him an air of swagger, a kind of cockiness, which, anyway at that moment, he did not at all possess. On the contrary, one was at once aware of an odd sort of unassuming dignity. There was no hint at all of the cantankerous temper that undoubtedly lurked beneath the surface. His air could be though a trifle sad, not, as sometimes described at this period, in the least broken-down. When, years later, I came to know Kingsley Amis, his appearance recalled Fitzgerald's to me, a likeness photographs of both confirm.

Food and drinks were ordered. Talk began to flow at once. That is certain. Scarcely a moment was required for conversation to warm up, adjustments all but instantaneous. Fitzgerald, off alcohol at that moment, drank milk, ate 'cold cuts'. The rest of us had beer, and—Violet's fairly convinced memory—pork chops with spaghetti. Naturally *A Yank at Oxford* cropped up almost immediately. The question of dialogue: would an English undergraduate say a 'shiner' for a black-eye? Could the American public be made to understand that 'the Prog' and his 'bullers' meant the Proctor and his bowler-hatted 'bulldogs', the University police?

This opened up a delicate theme, obviously a favourite topic of Fitzgerald's, the differences between the American and British ways of life. It was a subject upon which he had reflected a lot, one felt, and loved discussing. I said—what I have so often thought—that Americans allow other Americans such small powers of comprehension. Surely, if American policemen are sometimes termed 'bulls', only a minimum of imagination would be required in the context to guess the meaning of 'buller'. After all, the British public, in days when all films were American, had been expected to essay far greater feats in mastering alien language and customs. Fitzgerald seemed delighted to find someone with whom to argue that sort of thing. In a moment he was well away with what Americans were like.

'At a party, some time, I used the word *cinquecento*. Donegall—do you know who I mean?—was present. He said how unexpected it was to hear that word on the lips of an American.'

From the way Fitzgerald spoke I had the impression that the party in question might have taken place a year or two before. Lord Donegall, a professional gossip-writer for the London papers, was a very unsurprising person for Fitzgerald to have run across. I did not know that Donegall was then in California, therefore the comment had almost certainly been made the previous Wednesday. The dating is not without interest.

Fitzgerald explained how this assumption—that an American was unlikely to employ the term *cinquecento*—had brought him up with a start. In the past, in his own grandfather's day, even in his father's, Americans had been noted in Europe for being well educated, properly informed, culturally aware; possibly even too much so. Fitzgerald said he did not deny Donegall's imputation that Americans of the present age were often none of those things, nevertheless the conjecture saddened him.

Fitzgerald took a pen from his pocket, and a scrap of paper. On the paper he drew a rough map of North America. Then he added three arrows pointing to the continent. The arrows showed the directions from which culture had flowed into the United States. I am ashamed to say I cannot now remember precisely which these channels were: possibly the New England seaboard; the South (the Old Dominion); up through Latin America; yet I seem to retain some impression of an arrow lancing in from the Pacific. The point of mentioning this diagram is, however, the manner in which a characteristic side of Fitzgerald was revealed. He loved instructing. There was a schoolmasterly streak, a sudden enthusiasm, simplicity of exposition, qualities that might have offered a brilliant career as a teacher or lecturer at school or university.

We talked of his books. Fitzgerald dismissed the notion that they would ever be read in England. Certainly there seemed small chance of that then; a good example of the vicissitudes of authorship, for within ten years (true a world war had taken place) everything Fitzgerald had written would be in print in a London edition of his works. Among other things he mentioned that the American diplomat in *Tender Is the Night*, who wore a nocturnal moustache-bandage, was drawn from life; and it turned out we had met the rackety lady whose rescue of a British compatriot from arrest in Switzerland had suggested a similar incident in the novel.

Fitzgerald's *Collected Letters* reveal him as not all averse from the *beau monde*, in his own phrase 'dukes'. He possessed a writer's love for categorizing people, but, his own experience of life in the UK limited, some judgments were less than wholly reliable. After praising the aristocratic picturesqueness of Napier Alington (a peer with claims to be so designated), he spoke of a lady (whose name, rightly or wrongly, had been coupled with that of a Royal Duke) as 'the wrong sort of English aristocrat'. Fitzgerald was disinclined to accept that, whatever other characteristics the lady in question might possess, she could not by any stretch of terminology be thus defined. This trivial talk is recorded only on account of its repercussion.

An interruption took place at that moment in the shape of two film stars, Spencer Tracy and James Stewart, moving round from table to table in the dining-room. James Stewart had come to rest not far away from us. Fitzgerald indicated him.

'A Princeton man, I believe.'

That was to move into a more tangible realm of social surmise. Fitzgerald watched Stewart with the fascination of one Princeton man examining another; then (synthesis perhaps suggesting antithesis) he remarked that 'Ernest' was in Hollywood. At that time, unaware of the complicated love-hate relationship which professionally raged between Hemingway and Fitzgerald, I was interested to know that they were on first-name terms. We talked about the *Spanish Earth* performance, which I think Fitzgerald had not seen.

It has to be admitted that all this time Fitzgerald and I had been hogging the conversation, hardly allowing a word to Violet or Elliott Morgan. Fitzgerald must have become aware of this. In a good mannered effort to adjust the balance, make conversation less of a monopoly between the two of us, he brought back the subject of American and British degrees of difference. The Morgan parents, as mentioned earlier, were first generation in the US. Fitzgerald posed a question:

'Now what about Elliott? British or American?'

Eliot? I made a great mental effort. At that time I had never met T. S. Eliot. My knowledge of his works was limited to no more than the poems anyone living in a fairly literate world was likely to know. The Sitwells talked of him sometimes, but I couldn't remember other friends in common. I had given little or no thought to the question of Eliot's nationality. That was something not much bothered about in so accepted a figure, who, even if born an American, was now an essential feature of the British intellectual landscape. This was certainly an occasion for a lucid exemplification. The brilliant phrase utterly failed to materialize.

'You mean his poems?'

'Does Elliott write poems? I wasn't aware of that.'

Fitzgerald found the revelation amusing. I felt myself getting into increasingly deep water. Were there sides of T. S. Eliot that made his poetry a comparatively minor matter? I played for time.

'*The Waste Land*, and all that . . .'

A good deal of laughter followed the clearing up of this confusion in identities. Its echoes sounded loud, even embarrassing, in the silence that had now fallen on the commissary. A change had come over that grim room, which was now all but empty. Time had passed so swiftly, talk been so animated, that I was unaware of the transformation—noted by Violet—that had taken place round about us.

First of all the lesser executives had hurried back to desks or sets. Then some of the scriptwriters, probably uncertain about renewal of their contracts, made some pretence of showing keenness on their job. One by one executives of a somewhat superior sort, though not the highest, had drifted away. Gradually even the most undisciplined slaves of The Industry returned to their labours. In short, except for the exalted, the group of 'moguls', only our own table reamained occupied.

Worse than that, not only was the luncheon-break being grossly extended, but we were talking and laughing as if nothing mattered less than the making of commercial films. A gloomy silence had fallen on the moguls' table, as they puffed at their cigars. Like the patrolling cops glaring at an unexpected picnic among the yuccas, the same fishlike stare was beamed towards us. The moguls looked puzzled; not so much angry as hurt. Perhaps some of them had heard tell of Fitzgerald, even spelled out his early books. It was unlikely that any of them would know him by sight, but one never could tell. This climax was undoubtedly an indication that our party should break up, that we should all make a move.

I had brought with me to Hollywood one copy of each of my published novels. I asked Fitzgerald if I might send him *From a View to a Death*. That was the sort of question he knew how to answer very gracefully. I posted the book that afternoon. A couple of days later a reply came. The reference is to those British social categories adumbrated in the commissary.

Metro-Goldwyn-Mayer.
Corporation Studios.
Culver City.
California.
July 22, 1937.

Dear Powell:

Book came. Thousand thanks. Will write when I have read it. When I cracked wise about Dukes I didn't know Mrs Powell was a duke. I love Dukes—Duke of Dorset, the Marquis of Steyne, Freddie Bartholomew's grandfather, the old Earl of Treacle.

When you come back, I will be in a position to have you made an assistant to some producer or Vice-President, which is the equivalent of a Barony.

Regards,
F. Scott Fitzgerald.

10

Two or three days after this meeting with Fitzgerald we drove down to Mexico ('south of the border', a phrase sung by marching men to reverberate on the ear in a couple of years' time), before making for home via New York.

On the road to Ensenada we lost the way, and, owing to faulty timing, found ourselves towards nightfall in desolate country with nowhere to lay our heads. At one moment a cortège of sombrero-wearing riders on mules appeared on the horizon, bandits of silent film days, but, like the sequence of a film, the cavalcade disappeared into the sunset. Coming to an abandoned race-course, we decided to turn back on our tracks, suddenly arriving at a vast hotel standing by itself beside the Pacific.

This was Rosarito Beach. The gambling rooms next door to the hotel were the size (and architecture) of a cathedral, but Prohibition was now at an end, and Cardenas, Mexico's puritanical president, had forbidden gambling. The place was scarcely less deserted than a Mayan temple, and goodness knows how things were kept going, because there were only one or two other guests.

Nevertheless the manager was in the highest spirits. He came from Yucatan, a province producing men superior to all other Mexicans, he assured us, saying he had given out that we were Edward VIII and Mrs Simpson (by then, in fact, Duke and Duchess of Windsor), and presented me with a box of Mexican cigarettes rolled in black paper, lethal for those unprepared for their kick. The difference in wine from vineyards undisturbed for perhaps a century and a half was at once noticeable, and I at once took to the national drink, tequila.

We pressed on to Ensenada, a resort much frequented by Americans during the Prohibition era. The chief hotel looked expensive, so we put up at a decidedly sleazy establishment, where, one presumed for the better security of guests, a member of the staff slept across the outer threshold of our bedroom door.

Thirty or more years later, fifteen hundred or more miles from these parts, we undertook an archaeological tour of Mexico. The tourists' beaten track was then very different. Wine was no longer cheap, tequila made up into cocktails, food depressingly Americanized, though I believe in this last respect an excellent Mexican *cuisine* is to be found. The Mexican past is awe inspiring, sinister to a degree, but I am glad also to have seen that small corner of the north with its Prohibition Age associations.

In those days flying from coast to coast was regarded, with its risk of hitting the Rockies or Alleghenies, as quite an adventure, and entailed three descents for refuelling. In New York an American friend I had first met with Elizabeth Bowen, Tom Howard, was very kind and took us round. No to-do was made at that time about visiting Harlem if you were white. We attended a 'dance-in' at the famous Savoy Dance Hall, a night when new members were accepted only after showing their skill on the floor, followed by initiation ceremonies. With the exception of one American lady (evidently an habituée), our party of three or four represented the entire white element present at the Savoy, among a sea of Harlem residents. There was not the smallest sense of embarrassment or resentment.

Early in the evening on one of these New York nights I spoke in praise of what were then a novelty to me, glass swizzle-sticks in drinks. Tom Howard urged me to take a couple, no one would mind. We did a round of night-spots, where further swizzle-sticks were pressed on me. After return to London I did not wear a dinner-jacket for some weeks (strange to think that one changed for such informal occasions in New York), and, putting on the coat when next used, was surprised by the abnormal weight of the right side, which sagged down. Unnoticed in packing pervaded by a hangover, a dozen or more swizzle-sticks had remained in the breast-pocket.

We sailed for Plymouth by the French Line, the old *De Grasse*, a leisurely barque dating from the days of the Boom, manned entirely by Bretons. Our cabin had been originally designed to accommodate six persons. The first three nights out of New York were the hottest I have ever known in any circumstances. The *Normandie* passed us twice, once on the way to Plymouth, once returning to New York. Wine flowed, a bottle of red and a bottle of white on every table at every meal, *vins d'honneur* with the officers, Bretons with resounding multi-particled Breton surnames. On enquiry from the chief steward if any special *plats* were favoured, I expressed a taste for *bouillabaisse*. Not only was a splendid *bouillabaisse* cooked for us, but a whole string of dishes followed, individual to our table, as reward for appreciation of *la cuisine provençale*.

We landed at Plymouth in the middle of August, 1937. The security officer glanced at my passport.

'Author? Where's your pipe?'

II

Scott Fitzgerald's good manners, a niceness that went side by side with less attractive traits undoubtedly on record, had been notably shown by finding time to acknowledge *From a View to a Death*. I discovered only much later that a lot was happening in his own life which would have excused forgetfulness. Some of this is set down in *Beloved Infidel*, the autobiography of Sheilah Graham.

On Wednesday, 14 July (the night before the Hemingway film, when we had ourselves been watching the Black *Macbeth*), a party had been given to celebrate the engagement of Miss Sheilah Graham, a renowned Hollywood gossip-columnist, and the Marquess of Donegall, equally celebrated in London for the same vocation. This was no doubt the occasion when Donegall had been surprised by Fitzgerald using the term *cinquecento*. Here, too, Fitzgerald had first been introduced to Miss Graham. They had liked each other. Meeting somewhere else in Hollywood two or three days later, Fitzgerald had asked Sheilah Graham to dine with him on Tuesday, 20 July, the day he was lunching with us at MGM.

That same afternoon, so it appears, a telegram from Fitzgerald's daughter was delivered to him, announcing her own imminent arrival in Hollywood. Fitzgerald, accordingly, sent another telegram, excusing himself from keeping his dinner-date with Sheilah Graham. On receipt of this she telephoned, holding him to the invitation, and suggesting that he should bring his daughter too. The evening, so Sheilah Graham reports in her book, was not a success. At the end of dinner Fitzgerald drove Sheilah Graham home. That night was the beginning of their love affair. It lasted throughout the years, not many by this time, which remained to him.

Fitzgerald was forty-four when he died. I heard of his end, nearly two months after, on 21 December, 1940 (my birthday, as it happened), when I was in the army. By that time Fitzgerald, Hollywood, films, writing itself, all seemed a long way away, but that luncheon at Culver City Studios came back very clearly to my mind.

IV

Chester Gate

The Hollywood expedition set a dividing line across the pattern of early married life. On return to England one settled down to the fact that sooner or later there would be a war.

> The southern wind
> Doth play the trumpet to his purposes,
> And by his hollow whistling in the leaves,
> Foretells a tempest, and a blust'ring day.

The two years that followed were of ever increasing menace, as possibility became probability, probability turned into the real thing. I had never supposed another war inconceivable—quite the contrary—but that made no easier the question how best, both as an individual and a writer, to deal with the developing crisis. Meanwhile, even if circumstances were far from ideal for settling down to a new novel (except for those writers actually stimulated by uncomfortable pressures) nothing much could be done about work but carry on as usual.

If war came I knew that, however inadequately adapted to the military profession, I should feel dissatisfied with myself unless in the army. In any case the Services, for a writer in times of war, seemed to offer infinitely the most advantageous viewpoint. Nevertheless, thought of all the tedium of military training, especially demands made on spare time, brought reluctance to join the Territorials straight away with a view to getting a commission, so that when the Territorial Army was doubled soon after Munich (September, 1938) I was a few months too old for that.

I had, however, been accepted on the War Office's register of an Army Officers' Emergency Reserve, made up of those (over thirty, I think) possessing certain rather vague civilian qualifications.

We prepared a gas-proof room in the basement at Chester Gate, and both of us enrolled in the Air Raid Precaution Service, attending lectures twice a week on that unentertaining subject. I was one of those deputed to take an ARP census of the neighbourhood for distribution of gas-masks, a duty irksome in itself, though not without all reward through the insight thereby acquired into how people live. Those answering a door-bell are apt to assume confrontation will mean either a demand for money, or threat of sexual assault. On my own side, I was struck by the anonymity in which so many persons exist. Many of the houses in Albany Street contained a lodger or two, and to discover the exact number of residents, with their names, was not always easy.

'Then I have here a complete list of all tenants who'll need a gas-mask?'
'That's the lot, I think.'
'Thank you.'
'Wait a moment—there's the old lady on the top floor. I forgot her.'
'Then I'll add her name. What is it?'
'Oh, I don't know her name.'
'She must have one for a gas-mask.'
'Never heard her full name—we always call her Mary.'

2

Professionally speaking, I was in lowish water at this period. Finding the atmosphere of Hollywood totally inimical to writing, I had returned to London without even the germ of a book in my head; nor had I a job. In due course I managed to procure a novel-reviewing column once a fortnight for *The Daily Telegraph* (a book page then edited with less enlightenment than in later years), also doing notices of autobiographies and memoirs fairly regularly for *The Spectator*.

Connolly has rightly written with horror of the task of having to review several more or less unrelated books at the same time within a small space, a labour particularly unalluring where novels are concerned. I have known a few novel-reviewers—R. G. G. Price, for example, on *Punch*—skilful at this humble, yet necessary and by no means contemptible craft, but it is not easy to be at once brief, informative, fair, readable. The matadors of reviewing risk as serious injury from the leather cushions hurled in by the spectator-readers as from the usually crumpled horns of the novelist-bulls plunging round the arena for criticism.

'Are you mad to have recommended such-and-such a novel?' friends would say. 'The book's unreadable.'

There was usually little or no defence, beyond stating the fact that a novel-reviewing job cannot be held down (mine was not anyway) by writing week after week that the whole depressing batch lack the smallest merit.

So far as getting to work on my own fifth novel was concerned, some sort of a recovery took place—though perhaps three mornings a week might be spent gazing at a typewriter—*What's Become of Waring* reaching completion towards the end of 1938 or beginning of the following year. The manuscript was first offered to Duckworth's, who (on the whole to my satisfaction, because I wanted a change) refused to pay the modest increase of advance asked. The novel was published by Cassell (why I can't now remember), a firm with which for some reason I never managed to establish at all a close relationship, and published no subsequent book of mine.

Since *Waring* has been described in print as a more or less blow-by-blow account of my own days as an employee of Duckworth's, it is relevant to add that Duckworth's former director, Tom Balston, read the manuscript (commenting that the plot was 'most ingenious and amusing, beautifully worked out', together with a hope that the novel would sell 'like hot cakes'), while the current directors of the firm raised no objection to the theme, merely showing disinclination to offer more money.

What's Become of Waring finally appeared in March, 1939, just at the moment when Hitler was sending troops into Memel (then governed as an international free port), a juncture at which many people, not without reason, supposed that the war, due in September, had already arrived. With such vibrations in the offing, the Spring publishing season that year was not a favourable one for book sales. *Waring* achieved a circulation of just 999 copies, resembling hot cakes only later, when, like King Alfred's, the remaining stock was burnt to cinders in the blitz.

Re-reading *What's Become of Waring*, I am struck—even more than in

Agents and Patients—by a sense of nervous tension that seems to underlie a superficially lighthearted tone of voice. The working out of its 'situations' seems at times even over-meticulous (after all the book was not a detective story), using that epithet with its pedantically correct implication of fear. This brooding anxiety is hard to pinpoint—to some extent expressed perhaps by an almost railway time-table approach to chronology —but the racking international atmosphere of the epoch seems to me pervasive, even if never explicitly mentioned.

3

For some little time before we left London for Hollywood, plans had been set on foot to launch a new comic weekly, to be called *Night and Day*. Graham Greene, who was closely involved in this venture, had suggested that I might become a contributor. In the event the paper did not appear until we were in California, from where two pieces of mine (basis of what has been said here about the Hemingway film and Black *Macbeth*) were sent, under the heading *A Reporter in Los Angeles*. A few very minor odds and ends followed on return to England.

Although Greene had been only a year senior at Balliol, in the Balliol tradition of everyone living his own sort of life, we spoke together there only once, I think. At least I have a sole memory of Sligger's (F. F. Urquhart's) rooms, Greene one of a crowd of undergraduates in dinner-jackets, no doubt a Balliol dining-club ending the evening by a call on the Dean. We had come to know each other in 1933 or 1934, when Greene was editing a volume by various hands called *The Old School*, and used occasionally to dine together. The Greenes were then living on Clapham Common, one of the fine 17th century red brick houses, later, he told me, destroyed in the blitz.

Night and Day was designed to dislodge *Punch*, long regarded by the Young Turks of Fleet Street, many people elsewhere too, as the quintessence of tameness, tapering off into an insipid philistinism. To judge from such 19th century rivals of *Punch* as I have seen—the aim of displacement being by no means a new one—competitors offered much the same entertainment at an inferior level, certainly never rising to the standard of great comic artists like Leech, Keene, Du Maurier, Tenniel, who always eclipsed the reading-matter. The present departure was contemplated by its founders as getting away from the built-in stuffiness of the *Punch* tradition, producing something altogether more sophisticated, with *The New Yorker* to some extent as model.

The *New Yorker* format was, indeed, rather too much in evidence, when the first number of *Night and Day* was put on sale in July, 1937, though the contents showed an undoubted freshness and style, which was kept up during the brief six months that the magazine was to survive. Graham Greene was not, I believe, operating as editor of the paper (which was marketed by the publishing house of Chatto & Windus), but one had the impression that he played an active part in its life. Peter Fleming wrote the opening editorial notes (signed Slingsby), and his younger brother, Ian Fleming (later to beget Bond), may have helped to raise money for the enterprise in the City. Glancing through a bound copy of *Night and Day* in its entirety, I am struck by Fleming impact on its tone.

At this time I had not met Ian Fleming, Peter Fleming only very casually. After the war I saw something of both of them, though never knew either at all well, the elder brother the better of the two. Ian Fleming was one of the few persons I have met to announce that he was going to make a lot of money out of writing novels, and actually contrive to do so. Peter Fleming used very obligingly—always most valuably—to read the proofs of the war volumes of my own novel before publication to check correctness of military detail and army jargon.

At the *Night and Day* period Peter Fleming, already renowned for explorations in Brazil, with more recent adventures in Tartary, was a great favourite with retired generals and the like, as almost singlehanded consoler of all who shook their heads over the decadence of Youth. In his own person he demonstrated that unquestionably the Younger Generation was 'all right'. He was often tipped as future editor of *The Times*, but I think any such routine would have irked him; besides, he was not really interested in politics.

A brave man both in peace and war, prepared to take on bleak feats of endurance, as well as flashy acts of daring, Peter Fleming had a preoccupation, almost an obsession, with not appearing to 'show off'. This self-consciousness about avoiding anything in the least resembling Hemingwayesque bluster, might in itself have become a form of showing off, had not the characteristic been balanced in Fleming by a profound inner melancholy. A strong sense of duty also went hand in hand with a certain puritanism. Peter Fleming's conversation, as befitted a man of action, was laconic yet pithy, ornamented with his own individual figures of speech, such as when he was heard excusing himself from some invitation with the words: 'Got to help a friend give a hot meal to the Queen.'

Night and Day's book review 'lead' each week was written by Evelyn Waugh, on the whole less testy than might have been expected, anyway than he became after the war, Aunt Sallies of the Left being knocked about from time to time, but in a balanced manner. Waugh's opening review in the first number of the paper begins with praise of the painter (his pictures 'by no means bad') David Jones, whose war autobiography, *In Parenthesis*, had just appeared, describing service in the ranks with the Royal Welch Fusiliers, with whom Jones was in action and wounded. Waugh speaks highly of *In Parenthesis*, a book which did not make a great stir at the time, though now recognized as not much short of a classic. 'Not a novel', Waugh said, so much as a 'piece of reporting interrupted by choruses . . . as though Mr T. S. Eliot had written *The Better 'Ole'*.

Graham Greene reviewed films, his approach in marked contrast with the man-about-townish understating Fleming manner. Greene, on the other hand, fulminated like a John Knox of movie-criticism, sometimes demanding maiden tribute, sometimes denouncing the sins of the flesh. Every phrase was forged in a white heat of passionate feeling, emotive images abounding, such as von Stroheim 'climbing a ladder in skin-tight Prussian breeches towards an innocent bed'. This calling of fire down from heaven—and up from hell—on the cinema and all its works, did not remain unanswered, but retribution was still several months ahead.

Among other regulars in the critical columns were Elizabeth Bowen's rather staid notices of plays; sometimes varied by Peter Fleming's (who had dramatic status himself as an ex-OUDS actor), and the novelist Antonia White's. Osbert Lancaster (whose drawings would have suited the *Night and Day* style, but was perhaps inhibited by other contracts) wrote on Art. I did not know Lancaster in those days, though we were to become friends soon after the war. John Hayward (of whom more later), scholar and bibliographer, cast an eye over Broadcasting in those pre-Television days. Constant Lambert wrote an occasional article on Music. Architecture was given more of a look in than usual by Hugh Casson (later President of the Royal Academy) and John Summerson (who would rehabilitate the Soane Museum). A. J. A. Symons (*The Quest for Corvo*, Food & Wine Society) discussed Restaurants. Less expectedly, the poet Louis MacNeice wrote on the Dog Show; the literary critic, Walter Allen, on Football.

There were several serial features: John Betjeman's compendium of his own aversions, Percy Progress; Cyril Connolly's middlebrow family of Arquebus, viewed through their daughter Felicity's diary; pilgrimages by Hugh Kingsmill and Malcolm Muggeridge (HK & MM) to former homes of Victorian writers. Among the novelists and short story writers also occurring in *Night and Day* were Rose Macaulay, Christopher Isherwood, Pamela Hansford Johnson, T. F. Powys, V. S. Pritchett, R. K. Narayan, Gerald Kersh, Dennis Kincaid, Nigel Balchin, Hans Duffy (pseudonym of Mary Pakenham). Poets included Walter de la Mare, Stevie Smith, William Plomer, Herbert Read, William Empson, the last three contributing, in fact, prose pieces.

This strange mélange synthesized pretty well. Dennis Kincaid's contribution was posthumous. After Balliol (where, he a year junior, we had not met) Kincaid had gone into the ICS; written a couple of promising novels and a book about British social life in India; then died in a bathing accident.

Gerald Kersh, at this period occupied with gamy novels about the London prostitute/ponce world, made some name when the war came with *They Died With Their Boots Clean*, and other novels about service in the ranks of the Coldstream Guards. Kersh, bearded, rampageous, immensely prolific, eventually emigrated to the US, where he died at no great age. When I met him once at El Vino's in the 1950s I had the impression that a little went a long way, but he was certainly funny teasing a pompous journalist (using the pseudonym Cassandra, and obnoxious to P. G. Wodehouse at the time of the unhappy wartime broadcast), Kersh pretending to bite Cassandra in the leg, while both were drinking in the bar.

Contributors to *Night and Day* from abroad included Paul Morand and James Thurber. Morand, who was to be French Minister Plenipotentiary in London in 1940, later became one of Vichy's ambassadors, but he rode the storm, and Violet found herself sitting next to him at a luncheon party in 1968, given at the Ritz in connexion with the French 18th-

Century Exhibition at Burlington House. Morand was then in his eightieth year, but unsubdued. We talked afterwards of English friends eternally taking him to the Thames-side pub, The Prospect of Whitby, as somewhere he would never have heard of.

Thurber, who wrote and drew for *Night and Day*, did both without any loss of quality in change of public, but his presence undoubtedly emphasized the paper's already over-close similarities to *The New Yorker*.

A good comic artist, more or less ushered into prominence by *Night and Day*, was Roger Pettiward (drawing, quite why I don't know, under the name Paul Crum), Eton and Brazil pal of Peter Fleming, his pictures absolutely in the mood of the paper. Pettiward was later killed serving with the Commandos. Had he survived (though in quite a different manner from either), he would have been a cartoonist in the company of Osbert Lancaster and Mark Boxer (Marc).

I met James Thurber, not through *Night and Day*, but the year following the magazine's demise at a party given by Alice (Astor) von Hofmannsthal, as she then was. Thurber was in London with his second wife. They lunched with us at Chester Gate, the other couple present being Tommy and Betty Phipps. There seems no doubt that Thurber was sometimes an awkward guest, drinking too much, and insisting on singing 'Bye-bye, Blackbird' at inappropriate moments. He certainly put back a fair amount of wine at luncheon, but could not have been more agreeable, leaving behind him in our Birthday Book a tiny example of one of his dogs.

Just twenty years later, in 1958, we met again, when Thurber was invited to the *Punch* 'table'. By this time, possessing at best throughout most of his life the use of only one eye, he was now blind. Those present at the luncheon were led up and individually introduced. It is hard to express how immediately Thurber took in—gaily replied to—the word of explanation as to our having met ages before. Thurber's method of dealing with his food was masterly. He would lightly touch the contours of what had been set before him on the plate. Once that was done no one sitting round the table would have guessed for a moment that he was a blind man. One grows to respect in the highest degree such self-management.

4

In October, 1937, *Wee Willie Winkie*, a film distantly based on a story of Kipling's, a tale his admirers prefer to pass over quickly, came to London. In it the small boy originally hero underwent a sex change, the little girl he became being played by Shirley Temple, in later life pillar of the US Diplomatic Service, then, aged nine, among the top child film stars of the era. The cast also, as it happened, included C. Aubrey Smith, mentioned earlier.

In reviewing *Wee Willie Winkie* for *Night and Day*, Graham Greene commented with even more than his usual verve. The film evoked in him a string of striking images. The article is good reading even to this day. Lawyers' letters were by no means unknown at the *Night and Day* office, but the one which arrived after the *Wee Willie Winkie* notice was of quite exceptional protest. A libel action ensued.

The case came up before the Lord Chief Justice, Lord Hewart, in March, 1938, Sir Patrick Hastings, KC, representing Shirley Temple. Sir Patrick (less sanctimonious at his own table, where I had dined as a young man) described the libel as one of the most horrible that could be imagined; he would not read aloud the words complained of, as it was better that those who had not seen them should remain in ignorance of what was hinted.

Lord Hewart (author of a sage book about civil service encroachment on personal liberty, but evidently a man for whom Freud had lived in vain) agreed as to the depravity of the review. He asked if the whereabouts of its writer was known. The answer—Greene being by then in Mexico—was in the negative. The Lord Chief Justice observed: 'This libel is a gross outrage, and I will take care to see that suitable attention is drawn to it.'

I suppose in those days a case might exist for considering Greene's notice 'bad box-office', but, even at that distant period, the notion that children neither had nor could express sexual instincts was, to say the least, an uninstructed one. The puritan's obscurantisms of one period provide the pornographer's extenuations of the next.

The magazine was already in ·a parlous financial condition. Shirley Temple delivered the *coup de grâce*—what a scene for her that would have made in a film. A six months' run concluded in December, 1937. Nothing became *Night and Day's* brief existence as a comic paper better than the exquisitely comic climax which terminated its publication.

5

Not long after the passing of *Night and Day*, Gerald Reitlinger, meeting us with his car at Robertsbridge station for what was always a perilous drive to Woodgate, where we were spending the weekend, suggested making a detour to call on the Muggeridges, recently come to live at Whatlington, a village a couple of miles away from Battle. I do not recall how, if at all, Reitlinger characterized these new neighbours, but (earlier than the *Night and Day* literary pilgrimages written with Hugh Kingsmill) I had been struck not long before by an article on Russia in the *Evening Standard* with Malcolm Muggeridge's name as by-line. This piece, full of wit and acuteness, had been quite different from what was usually reported about the USSR at that period. I felt curious as to the personality of the writer.

First sight of the façade of the Muggeridge house called to mind pictures of the home of the Old Woman Who Lived in a Shoe, children swarming all over the steps, children's faces looking out of every window, yet more children, one felt, concealed in the garden at the back. In fact there were only four Muggeridge children, possibly reinforced at that hour of the morning by auxiliaries from the village, but the effect was as of a dozen or more.

Kitty Muggeridge, welcoming, though plainly overwhelmed by domestic duties, dislodged two boys grappling together on the floor, so that we could pass into the house; then, her husband appearing, hastened away to further duties in the kitchen. Although we had called without warning (probably not at the most convenient moment on a Saturday morning), Malcolm Muggeridge displayed all the air of having been impatiently awaiting our arrival.

'Come upstairs,' he said. 'We'll have a talk.'

Years later, on my asking a girl whether she knew Malcolm Muggeridge, she replied: 'Yes—he always looks *blue* with cold.' There was, anyway from time to time, a certain felicity in this image. Muggeridge, then in his middle thirties, had the physical trait of sometimes appearing much older than his age (a man already getting on in life), sometimes much younger (almost a boy still). These transformations, which could take place from one minute to the next, were no doubt one of several outward expressions of an inner duality quite exceptional in the violence of its antitheses.

The exterior mutation between Youth and Age was to be observed, with others, as long as I used to see Muggeridge pretty regularly. On the one hand ('blue with cold'), he could seem waiflike, undernourished, a coenobite agonizing over sins for which there was no forgiveness; on the other, any such first impression (if given at all) was likely to be denied almost immediately by a glowing warmth of manner, outgive of nervous energy, passionate response to any new idea.

Sudden intrusion of visitors is commonly a sign for abandoning whatever may be on hand in favour of at least a few moments' conversation, nevertheless, when Muggeridge spoke of 'a talk', talking was undoubtedly accorded by his tone of voice a somehow inviolable status. That was one's reaction, no mistaken conjecture. The special meaning was, in one sense, far from the slightly ominous 'Shall we have a talk?' of schoolmasters, clergymen, and the like (though even at this date pietistic echoes were not to be absolutely ruled out), because Muggeridge *causeries*, except to the extent of cant of all sorts being in general excoriated, were unlikely to be morally improving in any popular sense; even if worldly pleasures, in certain forms, might (if not personally abjured) anyway be deprecated. Unlike most good talkers, Muggeridge needed as a rule not the smallest warming-up process. As he began to talk, I felt here was a man I should like.

So pervasive is the latter-day Muggeridge public *persona* that it seems extraordinary—even to myself—that we did not already know about him; extraordinary that there should ever have been a time when the Muggeridge 'image', Muggeridge *obiter dicta*, were not familiar literally to millions. Yet such celebrity was in those days not merely an unaccomplished fact, but—so at least the circumstances seemed to me, something I cannot too strongly insist on—very few people seemed ever to have heard of him.

Muggeridge being a journalist, his name naturally appeared in print from time to time. To that extent some might agree they remembered the name under an article. Nothing more than that. In contrast with scores of nonentities whose names and personalities were common currency in various worlds, conventional or bohemian, in which I myself maintained some sort of a foothold, no one ever appeared to know anything about this—to me—manifestly gifted and unusual man. The extent of his obscurity I found astonishing.

No doubt the impression that Muggeridge was so little known rested to a large extent on my own ignorance of the byways of Fleet Street, where plenty of editors and others must have been by then alerted to the existence of a journalist of such promise. Even so, journalistic reputations are precarious, made one week, forgotten the next, and Muggeridge's whole approach to life seemed remote from those determined to achieve that sort of ephemeral fame as quickly as possible. Obviously he had strong convictions (at least that seemed obvious, even if definitions might be less easy), but, except so far as such convictions had to be reconciled with earning a living, he showed not the least concern with personal ambition. To this was added an utter self-confidence.

I may seem to labour the point, but in those days Muggeridge's relaxed attitude towards 'getting on' (short of keeping afloat) appeared almost his salient characteristic. It was an attitude as surprising in the light of his endowments as his inconspicuousness in the world round about him, and, one supposed, the latter consequence was to some extent related to the former standpoint.

I can think of no close parallel among my other contemporaries in this particular respect. Several of these moved from being comparatively unnoticed into the condition of having made some name for themselves. None in quite the same manner straddled the gap between an early personal privacy, more or less deliberately chosen, and an equally volitional relinquishment of that privacy in exchange for publicity on a multitudinous scale. In short, I find an almost complete contradiction in Muggeridge as he appeared to me when we first met; Muggeridge as the generally accepted end product.

Muggeridge has himself, with brio, related the outlines of his own career. His memoirs contain no particular suggestion of making a change of direction in middle-life; on the contrary, if anything emphasis is placed on continuity. I do not demur at this, experience convincing me that individuals do not greatly change in character, though they may modify or develop what is there already. In other words I am struck (as not seldom) more by the imperfection of my own early judgments, especially in relation to people known fairly well. Muggeridge was to play some part in my professional as well as personal life, yet I am not at all sure that I ever got the hang of him.

A few years before we met ('with weeping and with laughter still is the story told') Muggeridge had gone to Moscow full of Left Wing enthusiasm, as correspondent for the *Manchester Guardian* (now *The Guardian*), to return utterly disillusioned with Communism and the Soviet régime. In happening first on his name in connexion with Soviet Russia, I had struck Muggeridge's chief preoccupation of that moment, one to some extent always so to remain. India, Egypt, Fabianism, other current infections, might be examined by him under the microscope for their morbific bacilli; the USSR remained the favourite tissue for expert if intermittent research.

Disillusionment with Communism, dismay at the methods of the Soviet Union, are nowadays such familiar themes that the force of Muggeridge's virtually one-man onslaught in the 1930s is hard to grasp for those who did not experience those years. The Muggeridge impact, for its cogency to be appreciated, must be understood in relation to the intellectual atmosphere of the period. At that time many people were apt to think of what was happening in Russia as no worse than a few rich people being relieved of their surplus cash, a proceeding of which some approved, some disapproved. True there were awkward stories about executions, torture, forced labour, government-engineered famine, but the analogy of omelettes and eggs would often be invoked by those who approved; while those who disapproved were suspected of doing so for the wrong reasons, that is to say, desire to keep their own money.

When, from time to time, those now called dissidents, having escaped to the West, described what was happening in Russia, no great impression was made on Left Wing intellectuals, who by now had invested too much moral capital in Soviet collectivism to adjust their portfolio without considerable loss of face, compassion being unevenly balanced against *amour propre* in most branches of life.

Muggeridge has some claim to be the first writer of his sort to disturb this Left Wing complacency in a lively manner. Hitherto detractors or reassessors of the 'Russian Experiment' had caught the ear only of those already interested in Russian affairs. Muggeridge, informed, readable, witty, convincing, was also an authority on the vulnerable side of Left Wing intellectuals themselves. Not only had his father been a Labour MP, but Kitty Muggeridge was niece of the Sidney Webbs, main British apologists for what Muggeridge denounced as a ghastly tyranny, an evil way of life, deserving abhorrence as much from the Left as the Right.

The Russian experience, and its effects, comprised certain essential Muggeridgian ingredients: moral issues—enthusiasm—disillusionment. An interest in both politics and morals is not uncommon, but Muggeridge brought to both elements a degree of objectivity, a curiosity about the way things happen, comparatively rare in moralists and politicians; both inclined to market their own panaceas without being much concerned about human behaviour for its own sake. Indeed, those groups tend to dislike anything in the nature of objectivity, admittedly unattainable as that aim may be.

If a distinction is drawn between 'having politics' (as most people do, of one sort or another), 'being interested in politics' (as quite a lot claim to be), 'knowing how politics work' (comparatively rare, even among political commentators), Muggeridge, so it has always seemed to me, 'knew how politics work'. This is a gift altogether separate from how its possessor may lean politically, or the ultimate value of such leanings. Politics had permeated the manner in which Muggeridge had been brought up, become an integral part of him, in the manner that others might be musical, mechanical, have an instinct for horses or jewels. He could make the most prosy parliamentary measure sound an absorbing topic.

In contrast, Muggeridge was altogether indifferent to the arts. Like most journalists, he might from time to time invoke a famous name in painting or music to hammer home a point, but in private he made no bones about being unable to distinguish one picture from another, and existing quite happily in that unacquaintance. Indeed, he was not merely indifferent, but possessed an active puritanical dislike for any approach remotely to be described as aesthetic. Writing was the only one of the arts which he was forced up to a point to recognize as such—having himself exceptional fluency and ear for phrase—but even in writing he would become impatient when emphasis was laid on form for form's sake, or over much to-do made about polishing up an article, or even a book.

This disapproval of the arts (which went so far as reprobating the idea of a house too pleasing architecturally) may, in the first instance, have been vested in a need to excel in whatever Muggeridge himself touched, the arts not offering in that respect a congenial field. It was essentially different from, say, the execration aroused by suspicion of pretentiousness in aesthetic areas (in fact sympathetic to the writer himself on his own terms) to be found in some of Kingsley Amis's books. Muggeridge was the only close friend I have known over a longish period of years to be thus orientated. After this first meeting we soon began to see a good deal of each other.

6

There had been domestic anxieties too, as well as those caused by the becalmed state of professional employments, overcast skies of international affairs. In August, 1938, Violet suffered another miscarriage, this second mishap suggesting something might be physically amiss that needed to be put right by medical means. To other stresses were therefore added those connected with gynaecological superintendences aimed at improved hopes of having a baby. In spite of disquietudes, we were determined, while circumstances still allowed before the storm broke, to enjoy for the food and wine, if possible at least one holiday in the Bordeaux area, one in Burgundy.

We had intended to make the journey to Bordeaux by sea, but troubles about the miscarriage prevented that. Instead we went first to Pilat Plage near Arcachon, then moved about in those parts, including a stay in Bordeaux itself, on first sight grim and grey, then revealed as a delectable city. In those days wine put on the table *en carafe* there was likely to taste better than a relatively expensive claret in a London restaurant. At the Chapon Fin, the wine-list the thickness of the telephone book, a Pomerol '22 (in principle a despised year) remains in the mind as one of the pleasantest bottles I ever drank.

Meanwhile, during meals that were delicious without being as a rule either heavy or expensive, the radio would sometimes be switched on by the restaurant proprietor to hear the latest regarding threats of war, sometimes releasing over the air Hitler's own horrible shrill screech.

Then those French call-up posters, their crossed flags and antique lettering scarcely altered since the 18th century, began to appear on walls, announcing categories of conscripts mustered to the colours.

By this time we were on our way home, with a pause at La Rochelle. Two twin towers of mediaeval date on either side of the harbour housed British prisoners of war during the Napoleonic wars. The interior walls are studded with names, quantities of them, carved by the prisoners. One day they should be transcribed for genealogical purposes.

At Nantes, while we were looking round the Castle, a workman, on his knees in one of the dungeons, appeared to be installing electric light there. A gendarme appeared. He said a word to the workman. The man listened carefully, then rose from the ground, put on his coat, began to collect his tools. The gendarme moved on to further duties. An old woman, who had been chatting with the workman, commented: '*On appelle le fascicule huit.*' The man's call-up had been issued by the gendarme. We all wished him a word of luck. He went on his way, leaving the dungeon in darkness.

From Nantes to Dieppe we travelled by auto-rail, a kind of express tram that ran along railway lines, rattling and shaking unceasingly as it sped down the track. This very unideal form of transport, almost empty except for ourselves, started about six in the evening, reaching Dieppe at midnight. The hotel had provided us with a packed meal, a bottle of wine, but no glasses or cups.

The galvanic judderings of the compartment when en route made drinking from the bottle almost impossible, so opportunity to do so was immediately taken on a brief pause at Rennes. The curtains of the window were drawn, but our figures must have been silhouetted against the lights of the carriage, because, when Violet raised the bottle to her lips, a resounding cheer came from a gang of French workmen standing outside on the line, just where the auto-rail had stopped.

This was 29 September, 1938, the day of Neville Chamberlain's return from Munich, and his talks with Hitler about Czechoslovakia. The following morning news of the settlement was in all the papers. There was not going to be a war, as had seemed very possible. Back in London, volunteers, Constant Lambert among them, had been digging trenches in Regent's Park, as hastily constructed air-raid shelters; a scene emblematic of the country's unpreparedness.

For many years the cartoonist Low (later Sir David Low) had depicted the obese and ludicrous figure of Colonel Blimp, clad only in a scanty towel, advocating rearmament from his Turkish bath. Perhaps Low's only memorial is in this invention. Blimp's absurdities were often contrasted with the benevolence and good humour of Stalin. These cartoons were by no means unrepresentative of a considerable body of public opinion, yet in later years it was those who had most vigorously opposed rearmament, who also most bitterly complained that the country did not go to war in 1938. At some moment, between Munich and the outbreak of war, Gerald Reitlinger wrote to the paper, asking if it were now agreed that Colonel Blimp had, in fact, been right. I recall no reply.

7

By now fairly inured to the day-to-day business of novel writing, I felt clear about at least one aspect of the work: if war came, and I myself survived, that would not be in the state of comparative inner calm required for writing a novel. A thorough reintegration of essential elements would have to take place. Even before war arrived working conditions were already becoming less than tolerable owing to recurrent crises, so that it seemed wise to abandon the Novel for the moment— perhaps no bad thing to give those faculties a rest—and set out on a book which would require application rather than invention; one not likely to be finished before war broke out, and—should one still be extant— providing a nucleus to play about with on return to normal routines.

Possibly even as far back as undergraduate days I had been interested in John Aubrey (1626—1697), antiquary, biographer, folklorist, above all writer in whom a new sort of sensibility is apparent, the appreciation of the oddness of the individual human being. Aubrey's real originality in this respect is often dismissed as trivial observation, dilettantism, idle gossip, by those who have skimmed through his writings superficially. This mistaken view is not only on account of Aubrey's own extreme modesty and unpretentiousness, but because, in the case of Aubrey's *Brief Lives*, readers often fail to grasp that most of what is now published was intended only as rough notes.

Aubrey, it is true, was incapable of running his personal affairs in a coherent manner, accordingly, as he himself pointed out, never had an opportunity to work consistently for a long period at any of the subjects which preoccupied his mind. That did not prevent him from contributing to English history a very fair proportion of its best character sketches and anecdotes; or, by first drawing attention to the magnificence of the prehistoric temple site of Avebury, laying the foundation of that branch of archaeological research in this country. Aubrey's essentially new approach was vested in the manner in which he looked at things with an unprejudiced eye; an instinct for what his contemporaries, or historical figures, were like as individuals; his mastery of the ideal phrase for describing people.

No adequate biography of Aubrey had ever been put together, only a few scrappy summaries of his life, often full of inaccuracies of fact. When *Waring* was finished I began to assemble Aubrey notes with the idea of writing a book about him, which might see me through a war. There was a good deal of material, both in his own manuscripts and elsewhere. An additional circumstance which made Aubrey's background sympathetic to work on was that his family, like my own, was associated with the Welsh Marches, and he himself had passed some of his days in Wiltshire, a county where I too had lived at one time or another.

In February, 1939, Violet and I undertook a tour through what Aubrey calls the 'campania of North Wilts', looking at the place of his birth, the villages and country from which he drew so many examples in his writings. In spite of the troublous times, as Aubrey himself remarks somewhere, *juvat haec meminisse.*

8

That August we set off once more for France, this time making for Dijon, with the aim of moving about Burgundy, as the previous year through the Gironde. At Beaune, the Hôtel de la Poste (I record, at the risk of being a wine-bore), we drank an Eschezaux '23, about third or fourth on the list of burgundies, priced at 7s 6d in English money, providing one of the only two occasions when I have experienced the vinous exhalation spoken of in wine manuals, the bursting from the newly opened bottle of the scent of violets.

The second occasion when this redolence was noticeable took place a couple of years later, when wine, unreplenishable in Great Britain, except for a little Algerian seeping in from North Africa, was quickly being drunk up. Alick Dru was dining with me at The Travellers, and we had the same experience with one of the club's last remaining burgundies. The name and year I have shamefully forgotten; probably another '23, possibly a Corton.

Summer in France was hotter than usual that year. One of our intentions was to cross the Swiss frontier for a day to see the pictures from the Prado, which had been taken to Geneva to avoid risk of destruction in the bombardments of the Spanish Civil War. We moved up to the mountain lake of Nantua for a day or two, for cooler weather, to sample the *quenelles* and Arbois wine. Passing through the hall of our hotel at Nantua I though I must have made a good impression on a girl wearing a short divided skirt, as she stared rather hard, then looked quickly away. That night, while we were having dinner, I noticed another girl of somewhat similar appearance sitting at a table by herself.

'It's extraordinary how all the girls in Nantua look like your sister Mary. I saw one this afternoon. There's another over there.'

Violet gave the matter her attention.

'That particular one not only looks like Mary, she is Mary.'

Mary Pakenham had suddenly decided to set out from England on a solo bicycle tour across France, a trip also to take in the Spanish pictures at Geneva. She had not mentioned this expedition to anyone. For no particular reason Nantua had been included in the route. We saw her off to Switzerland the following morning, while we ourselves made for Bourg-en-Bresse.

This meant a return to sweltering heat. News in the papers was becoming ever more disturbing, but we continued to eat, drink, sightsee, with as much composure as could be summoned up. In Bourg's vast church, the Église de Brou, Burgundian accomplishment in sculpture, a regional tradition, reaches peculiar splendour in the attendant figures, Les Pleureuses, on the tomb of Philibert, Duke of Savoy. They were only too appropriate at that moment of European history.

The announcement of the Molotov/Ribbentrop Pact burst one afternoon. Soviet Russia had become the ally of National Socialist Germany. Hitler and Stalin were one in facing the rest of the world. War now seemed certain. We discussed what was best to be done in our circumstances. Violet put forward a proposal: if Parliament were recalled, we would start for home at once; if not, stay on and see our holiday out. Parliament was recalled. We set off for England immediately, 24 August, St Bartholomew's Day.

9

The following week was spent making hurried provision for coming events. At the time it was popularly supposed that on declaration of war (possibly even before that) London would be assailed by heavy air-raids. Members of the Emergency Reserve like myself thought—as it turned out mistakenly—that they would be called up forthwith for military training. Violet was a volunteer nurse in the Port of London Authority River Emergency Service (where the standard of female looks was unusually high), a body designed to undertake evacuation by water of casualties suffered during anticipated attacks from the air.

There was another consideration, a rather special one. It seemed possible that Violet was pregnant again. Medical tests were being taken. If these proved positive, she would leave London, and, in an attempt to avoid another miscarriage, lie up throughout the whole of the nine months. This eventuality had been foreseen. Violet's aunt, Margaret Dynevor (her mother's elder sister), had suggested, should this precaution be necessary, that Violet should come to stay in Carmarthenshire.

The Pakenhams' Longford grandmother had been daughter of an earlier Lord Dynevor (family name Rhys, spelt by some branches Rice), and, cousins abounding, Violet knew the place well. In the 9th century Dynevor had been one of the royal capitals of Wales. The Old Castle, a ruin, was a former stronghold of The Lord Rhys (though the Dynevors themselves descended directly not from Rhys ap Gruffydd, but Sir Rhys ap Thomas, Henry VII's powerful ally at Bosworth), the present owners living in a castellated 17th century house in the park. Spenser's *Faerie Queene* speaks of the 'woody hills of Dinevowre', and, even if uncertainties about Violet's condition created another anxiety, we were very lucky to have such a refuge to rely on.

Finally remained the problem of what to do about Bosola and Paris, a world-war postulating no future on which to set out with two Siamese cats as part of one's entourage. Enquiries were instituted as to catteries, so that they might be at least temporarily accommodated. We were recommended to a Mrs Perkins (with whom, in the event, Bosola and Paris were to reside permanently), whose establishment was not far from London.

On Sunday, 3 September, 1939, Neville Chamberlain made an announcement over the air that war with Germany had been declared. The day was spent undertaking a thousand last-minute arrangements, packing things away as best that might be done. At last, pretty tired, far from cheerful, we retired to bed.

Some time not long before midnight the telephone bell rang. Violet answered it. The call was from her doctor. He had completed the pregnancy test. The findings were positive. She was with child.

The following day Violet left for Wales. It was a sad and upsetting moment when the train steamed out at Paddington, one I don't care to dwell on.

10

I remained at Chester Gate. The next three months constituted a strange unreal interlude, combination of the remnants of pre-war life, working on Aubrey, unwonted routines like ARP duties. There was still no sign of the Emergency Reserve call-up. Fellow members of the AOER, making enquiries, were told the War Office envisaged no immediate need of their services. This state of suspended animation was not well adapted to concentration on Aubrey or other work, though one could read and take notes. A few friends of my own age were already absorbed into the Services. It was possible to feel a pang of envy when they appeared in uniform, or their names figured in the Gazette.

Some of the time Wyndham Lloyd, as a doctor now working with the Health Service, stayed at Chester Gate for company. Constant Lambert reported that he had received a long patriotic poem from Aleister Crowley (engaged during the first war in making pro-German propaganda in the US), entitled *England—Stand Firm!*, for which he requested from Lambert a musical setting. A dream Lambert described may also belong to this period: he and I were at a party, where Virginia Woolf (whom I had never met, but Lambert might have known slightly) was also present. I went up to her and said: 'How now, bluestocking, what about the booze?'

During the first week in October the telephone rang one evening. A man's voice asked for me.

'Speaking.'

'This is Captain Perkins. We haven't met, but my wife is looking after your Siamese cats. I thought you would like to know they are well.'

'That's very kind of you.'

I was overcome with fear that he might go on to say that his wife was unable to undertake further care of the cats, but he continued to another subject at once.

'I'm at the War Office, in AG 14 [or whatever the Section was], the branch dealing with the AOER. I've just seen your name there. Do you want to be called up?'

'Very much indeed. That is what I most want.'

'You'd like me to put your name forward?'

'Certainly, if you can.'

'What regiment would you like to join?'

I had not thought about that, expecting the whole Emergency Reserve process to be quite other than this.

'My father was a regular officer in The Welch—why not them?'

'Easily get you into a funny regiment like that,' said Captain Perkins. 'Everyone wants to go into London units.'

My father would not have been pleased by Captain Perkins' estimation of The Welch Regiment (made up of the old 41st and 69th Foot), with its long roll of Battle Honours, phenomenal record for winning the Army Rugby Cup. Wellington had been an officer in the 69th, who had served as marines on Nelson's Flagship at St Vincent, but this was no occasion for taking offence. I suggested that Captain Perkins should lunch with me, when he could give if possible further details of what might be in store.

When we met, Captain Perkins (who wore ribbons of the first war) said I should be called up within the next week or ten days, medically examined, gazetted, probably sent a week later to the Regimental Depot at Cardiff, trained for about a month, then posted to one of the Welch Regiment battalions short of an officer. A condition of this candidature was possession of Certificate A, a military diploma, acquirable usually at school or university, attesting the holder's sometime proficiency in a few elementary principles of drill and tactics.

I mention this because it often used to be said that 'Cert A' would be of no value whatever, if war came, since the army would require all potential officers available, whether they held Certificate A or not. In this case the qualification was *sine qua non* of being accepted, and (although I could have falsely claimed it without much likelihood of being detected), as things turned out, I should have been in an extremely awkward position later, had I never drilled a squad on a parade-ground.

Another requirement for immediate call-up was to be passed as medically A.1. The examination necessitated attendance at Millbank Military Hospital (Jocelyn Brooke, rather eccentrically rejoining after the war, served in the VD branch not here but Woolwich), a gloomy red-brick accretion of buildings behind the Tate Gallery. All went well until the ocular test. I have a long-sighted eye and a short-sighted eye. A young RAMC officer set me in front of the usual row of letters descending in size.

'Put your hand over your right eye and read the smallest letter you can.'

I did so.

'Now do the same with your left eye.'

Without thinking, I had pressed so hard on my short-sighted right eye that, with a hand over my left, all ahead was blurred. I could hardly see at all.

'I can't pass you A.1. You're almost blind in one eye.'

I tried to explain. He seemed doubtful, but yielded under persuasion.

'All right, put your reading spectacles on, and try again.'

This time I got through.

Uniform and equipment had to be acquired. My father, who showed no particular enthusiasm about the whole undertaking (being unable to attain re-employment himself), handed over two well-worn khaki service-dress uniforms, blue patrols of even earlier date, a Sam Browne belt and revolver-holster, both of which had been through the South African as well as First World War. He was a shade larger than myself, but after trifling alterations the uniforms fitted tolerably well.

It seemed wise to practise wearing them after being gazetted, though I was uncertain whether such procedure was correct, and hoped no contretemps would arise with a prowling APM. There were embarrassing moments. Leaving Chester Gate one morning a squad of about fifty men were marching towards the Household Cavalry Barracks in Albany Street. The NCO in charge gave 'Eyes right'. I felt the last line of *Hamlet* might be adapted: 'Go bid the soldiers salute.'

About three weeks after my first contact with Captain Perkins on the telephone, an order arrived from the War Office instructing me to report for regimental duty on 11 December, in the rank of second-lieutenant, not to the Depot at Cardiff, but to the 1/5th Battalion, The Welch Regiment, at Haverfordwest, Pembrokeshire; as it happened, a familiar name, the Powell family having been associated with that neighbourhood at the end of the 18th and beginning of the 19th centuries.

Monday, 11 December, was a brisk winter morning. The train to Haverfordwest (a matter of two hundred and fifty miles from London) left Paddington at some such hour as 8.44 a.m. There were five other second-lieutenants in the compartment, all bound for different units and destinations. No one talked much, so far as I can remember. It was a long journey, one leading not only into a new life, but entirely out of an old one, to which there was no return. Nothing was ever the same again.

V

What's the Drill?

At Haverfordwest an army truck was waiting, driven by a white-haired lieutenant, one of those veteran military types, leading a more or less freelance existence, to be found all over the place at the beginning of the war. We made our way through steep streets towards the Castle Hotel, where officers of the 1/5th Welch were billeted. I had stayed for a night or two in the town ten years before. It was too dark to see the Norman keep and battlemented walls.

A French invading force, landing in Pembrokeshire in 1797, had been captured by the Fencibles of South West Wales, predecessors of the local Territorials, some of their units bearing the only indigenous Battle Honour, *Fishguard*, throughout the whole British army. The 5th (Glamorganshire) Battalion, The Welch Regiment, had also known a unique distinction in the first war, on Turkish surrender of Jerusalem, having mounted the first British guard in the Holy City since the Crusaders. In 1938 (after winning the Territorial Cup), the unit had been expanded into two battalions, explanation of its apparently fractional numbering.

Territorials in Wales were very much a family affair, sons following fathers, father and grandfather of the 5th Welch's Commanding Officer having held that same command. The Colonel himself was a solicitor, but by long tradition nearly all the rest of the officers came from banks, few living more than a few miles from Cardiff. The 'other ranks' were from the Valleys, coal miners whose connexion with regiment and neighbourhood was no less close, the four Companies being recruited respectively from Pontypridd, Mountain Ash, Aberdare, and Merthyr with Treharris. At all levels of rank brothers-in-law and cousins abounded.

This strongly regional background, close consanguinity, did not, as might have been expected, result in the faintest expression of coolness towards someone like myself coming in from outside. I cannot imagine being received with greater cordiality that night, when (no 'treating' allowed in the Mess) a certain amount of beer was consumed in the bar of the Castle Hotel.

The Commanding Officer, more than a little appalled at being sent an untrained second-lieutenant in his middle thirties, could not at the same time have been nicer about my manifest drawbacks. It came at first as rather a surprise to be regarded as elderly to the point of senility, but with many other unaccustomed things, I soon became used to that rôle, one not without all validity in the circumstances. Gazetted at the tail end of a score of local subalterns commissioned from the ranks of the Battalion a few months before, ranging in age from nineteen to twenty-three, I was in fact next in years to the Second-in-Command.

I had brought a sleeping-bag, but no camp-bed, so something or other was fixed up for the night (perhaps I slept on the floor), with orders to buy one in the town as soon as the shops were open, then come out on training. This I did, after purchase of the camp-bed, finding my way to the training area of the Company to which I was attached. From that moment it was necessary to pick up as expeditiously as possible such military skills as were to be acquired by taking notice, while off duty a sergeant-major taught me how to 'strip' a bren; a weapon not yet invented in days with the Eton OTC, when the Lewis gun had been in use. Since then changes had also taken place in drill. In the past soldiers had formed-fours; now they fell in at once in three ranks. In due course my Company Commander demonstrated the elements of double-entry for keeping Company accounts; no mystery to those accustomed to the routine of banks, though one I myself never wholly mastered.

Three or four days after joining the unit I was changing guard as Orderly Officer; the second Sunday I had to march the Company to church, back past the Brigadier's saluting-base. There was no disaster, but I had not shouted out commands such as were required for more than sixteen years. Many officers away on courses, I would find myself sometimes in charge of two platoons, forty or fifty Welsh miners to be taken into the country and taught how to attack a hill or 'lay down smoke'. Such training was naturally carried out with the support of NCOs, even

97

so all sorts of decisions were required in an altogether unfamiliar sphere of action. Only by experience, for example, does one learn the impediments of an apparently simple undertaking like disembarking thirty men —especially Welshmen—from a truck with reasonable speed.

The immediate requirements of such duties, the physical fatigue at the end of the day, were preferable to anxieties suffered before being called up, but suddenly to become a soldier in this manner made considerable demands on the will, especially in recognizing the expediency of not contemplating too analytically the metamorphosis that had taken place. Complete forgetfulness was needed of all that had constituted one's life only a few weeks before. This condition of mind was helped by the anonymity of uniform, something which has to be experienced to be appreciated; in one sense more noticeable off duty in such environments as railway carriages or bars.

A powerful factor in this new existence was the ambience of the South Welsh (as distinguished from the North Welsh, almost a different race), a people by nature talkative, good-natured, witty, given to sudden bursts of rage, unambitious, delighted by ironic situations. The South Welshman's lack of desire for promotion made the finding of NCOs difficult, hesitation almost always existing as to accepting authority which meant giving orders to relations and butties, thereby arousing not so much antagonism as derision. Violence of feeling, passionate need to express at once in words what was felt, however solemn the occasion, necessitated discipline of a rather different order, one more flexible than that required for English troops; something noticeable when later the Battalion took in drafts from Lincolnshire and Leicestershire.

At this embryonic stage of the war the atmosphere was still much that of Territorials in peacetime, friendly, easygoing, a certain amount of ragging (in which, except mildly at Christmas, I was never expected to do more than look on), with none of the friction between officers and men that some wartime writers, for instance J. Maclaren Ross, have recorded. Maclaren Ross was both amused and astonished when told that, after the platoon-sergeant at morning parade had called the platoon to attention and I advanced to inspect them, my batman, Ellis, G. O., was likely, rather embarrassingly, to give a friendly smile from the front rank.

As I never served at regimental level with an English battalion I cannot speak with certainty, but my impression is that Welsh officers, close

98

temperamentally to their men, probably understood their men's pre-
dictability better, while at the same time were utterly without what
might be termed an Orwellian sense of guilt in being set above what was
in general an overwhelmingly different class.

I do not mean that English officers minded giving orders (which would
have been absurd), but some were at times conscious of the complexity of
their authority, how mixed in composition could be the ranks subordinate
to them. In Wales, although there might be less 'public school' divisive-
ness, there was also complete acceptance of such divisions, class or
military, as did exist. I have heard suggested that in Wales is found,
relatively speaking, no sense of class. I can see what is meant by this view,
but the judgment seems to me unsubtle. The Welsh, like all Celts, have a
very strong adherence to certain forms of social hierarchy. Good relations
between officers and men seemed to me akin to that of the 'free tribesmen'
of Cambro-British society as described by historians, when (unlike the
never clearly defined English social categories) hard and fast lines were
drawn according to certain well understood rules.

The limited extent of Welsh surnames often necessitated the use of
initials after a man's name, even then reduplication taking place, in which
case the first three numerals of the soldier's army number would be used
as alternative. In South Wales biblical given-names like Levi, Abraham,
sometimes minor prophets such as Habakkuk, had over the centuries
become surnames, but on the whole a few ordinary Christian names
predominated, names in any case looked on as an unimportant adjunct of
the individual in Welsh daily life. A man in my platoon was sometimes
addressed as Stone, sometimes as Stones. To the question which should
be correctly recorded, he replied: 'Well, sir, I don't rightly know. Some
call me one, some the other.'

An interesting sociological process (occurring in South Wales no
doubt since prehistoric times) was quick absorption of the Irish. In
England—one might perhaps generalize—the Irish tend to keep their
national identity; the Welsh to lose theirs. In South Wales the contrary
was true. I have asked men undivergent from the rest in my platoon
named, say, Daley or Crowley, whether they were not Irish, receiving
the answer: 'Why, funny you should say that, sir. I do believe I once
heard my grandfather did come from Ireland.'

In South Wales (not, I think, in the North) the Williamses probably outnumber the Joneses. An officer I ran across, who had served with one of the battalions of The Welch Regiment in the first war, told me that his unit, then stationed in the United Kingdom, was required to furnish a draft of two hundred men for another unit of The Welch at, I think, Dieppe or Boulogne. Some regimental vendetta existed, so, to cause the maximum of administrative trouble, the two hundred men sent were all named Williams.

2

When I wrote about Welsh troops in *The Valley of Bones* and *The Soldier's Art* (books that throw more light on the experience than can be achieved in memoirs) some demur was made among reviewers as to the phrasing of the Welsh-English spoken by certain of the characters. Techniques for dialogue in a novel have always greatly interested me, and I shall say a word about this complex subject in that particular connexion.

Welsh officers, joking or arguing with each other, would sometimes deliberately assume a consciously stylized Welsh sing-song, not much short of stage-Welsh, a mannerism intended to be comic or teasing, not their normal talk, even if that too had something of Wales about it. This exaggerated Welsh-English, as a form of humour, was by no means unknown among the men too, especially if covertly pulling the leg of an NCO, though abrupt heightening and a Welsh lilt in speech among 'other ranks' was much more likely to be brought about by excitement or anger.

The peculiarities (to an English-conditioned ear) of Welsh-English are vested in the fact that the speaker (sometimes as a race memory, not linguistically, the Welsh language being unknown) is thinking 'in Welsh' rather than 'in English', therefore using Welsh turns of phrase. I found an example of this a few years ago in the Regimental Magazine. An NCO, writing an article about some operation in which he had taken part, referred to another NCO as 'this worthy gentleman', a designation with strongly facetious overtones in contemporary English. In Welsh, the phrase might be found in translation of almost any document of three or four hundred years ago, implying scarcely more than 'this man', and, curiously enough, 'worthy gentleman' is the term Mortimer uses for Glendower in Shakespeare's *Henry IV*.

In short, to arrive at a satisfactory literary convention in a novel for rendering Welsh-English, especially in its varied inflexions of mood noted above, is not easy. Since my own method has been adversely criticized, I consulted the Welsh actor and dramatist Alun Owen (whom I did not know personally, but had spoken kindly of an earlier work of mine), asking if, as an impeccably authentic Welshman, he thought revision was required in the dialogue of these two volumes in the novel sequence.

I record Alun Owen's reply because (apart from its reassurance, later supported by other Welshmen of incontravertibly Welsh background) I believe it to embody an important, perhaps essential, principle in writing dialogue in a novel. Owen said that, on rereading *The Valley of Bones*, he agreed that a tape-recording of Welsh soldiers talking with one another might give a rather different result from what was put down in my book. At the same time, he saw no objection to that. He found nothing inherently wrong in the interchange of talk, nor in the rhythms and inversions of speech. Above all, he said, the dialogue reproduced 'what the Narrator heard'.

Owen's definition seems to me to embody a required precept for novelists aiming at naturalistic dialogue, one always to be borne in mind. Unconvincing dialogue in novels stems not so much from being ascertainably correct or incorrect in what would actually have been said by the character concerned, as whether or not the sound of the person talking, remembered or imagined, has echoed in the ears of the author. This is a test probably no less necessary in a novel not related in the first-person. I do not put such a concept forward as magical solution for all problems in writing dialogue in all novels, but it is certainly a test always to be applied, sentence by sentence, phrase by phrase.

3

This new world was in some ways like moving through a musical performance, a voice almost always singing in barrack-room or yard as one passed through, the Company very tired if hymns and songs died down on the march. Many of these were common to the whole British army, the Company Sergeant-Major growing tomatoes on his chest, rats as big as cats in the Quartermaster's store, but in the Welch Regiment the leitmotiv of the opera was always *Cwm Rhondda*, as it were national anthem of South Wales (a better one than *Land of my Fathers*), refrain against which all life was lived, all events set.

> Guide me, O thou great Jehovah,
> Pilgrim through this barren land.
> I am weak, but thou art mighty,
> Hold me with thy powerful hand,
> > Bread of heaven,
> > Bread of heaven,
> Feed me till I want no more.

Just before Christmas, 1939, the 53rd (Welch) Division (to which the 1/5th Welch, with Territorial battalions of the Royal Welch Fusiliers, the South Wales Borderers, other associated regiments and corps belonged) was ordered to Northern Ireland, a move I did not at all welcome. The Battalion was first stationed in Portadown, a town politically reliable, if scenically unromantic.

In February I was sent from there to a course at Aldershot, 169 OCTU, a training unit designed to give elementary instruction to those who had already become officers but needed polishing up in such matters as square-bashing trench-digging barbed-wire erecting, together with more theoretical sides of army training. Army food is on the whole justly reprobated, so that it seems worth remarking that the Army Catering Corps can do perfectly well within its own lights when it tries. One would rise from the table at Aldershot all but intoxicated with huge helpings of the lightest sultana roll steeped in golden syrup, a refinement of luxury for those who had hitherto austerely known either suet-pudding-and-treacle or spotted-dog, never a Lucullan combination of both.

One of the instructors at the 169 OCTU, a charming old boy with a VC (a Lancashire Fusilier, I think, though he did not wear uniform), gave talks on his experiences in the first war. He had been in the Gallipoli landings, and described how his regiment, after coming ashore, all began to clean their rifles with their toothbrushes.

'Don't be surprised,' he said, 'if you're moving down a trench past a half-buried corpse with an arm exposed, and every man in the platoon shakes the dead man's hand in passing.'

9. The Tranby Croft case at Woodgate: Violet (doubling
Lady Brooke and Mrs. Wilson), John Lloyd (Prince of
Wales), AP (Sir William Gordon Cumming), Francis Watson
(Capt. Wilson), about 1938

10. Violet and Rex Evans in front of North Palm, 1937

11. 357 North Palm Drive, Beverly Hills, California

12. AP buying tequila in Ensenada, Mexico, 1937

13. The Oakland car

14. Violet in t[
Red Cross (Po
London Auth[
River Emerge[
Service) endi[
exercise at Alb[
Bridge, Chelse[
1939

15. AP on leave at
Dynevor, 1940

There were naturally lectures on the German army. The old VC observed: 'They teach you here about the composition of the German Division. I never can see the use of that. After all, you can't alter it.'

On return from Aldershot to Northern Ireland everything was in a state of flux. The Battalion's Commanding Officer (whose health had not been good) was replaced by a Regular, Lieutenant-Colonel W. G. Hewitt, a somewhat younger contemporary of my father's in the Regiment. Bill Hewitt had a high reputation for personal courage in the first war. He is mentioned in Robert Graves's autobiography, *Goodbye to All That* (1929), Graves having done a short attachment to one of The Welch Regiment's battalions in France before joining the Royal Welch Fusiliers.

Soon after this change in Commanding Officer the 1/5th Welch marched out of Portadown on the road to quarters in Newry, a town twenty miles south, nearer the Border. Unlike Portadown, most of the Newry people were anti-British. Corner-boys (in parody of the song: 'We're going to hang out the washing on the Siegfried Line') used to sing: 'We're going to hang out the washing on the Maginot Line'. Their friendly feelings for Hitler and his army might well have been carried a stage further, as a German attack on Southern Ireland was officially regarded as very much on the cards.

At Newry, shabby though less architecturally unprepossessing than Portadown, Hewitt began gingering up the Battalion; getting rid of older less efficient officers, promoting the younger and livelier to command Companies.

The requirements of a Company Commander are simple in the sense that (with the exception of creative imagination in the arts) they demand almost every good quality a man can possess: energy; initiative; conscientiousness about detail; capacity to delegate authority; instinct for retaining the liking and confidence of subordinates, while at the same time making them work hard, and never develop the least doubt about who is in command; all these combined with a sound grasp of handling weapons, and practical application of the theory of small scale tactics. Off duty the Company Commander must spend most of his spare time coping with the personal problems of his men, such as having got a girl with child, or receiving news that a wife is being unfaithful at home; not to mention minor matters like being reduced to one pair of socks too shrunk to wear.

When I was on leave at about this stage of the war, I ran into an MP

(Lab), known very slightly at Oxford, who said he had just left the army (which MPs could do at whim), an infantry battalion, because 'there was nothing to do'. This seemed to me a surprising conclusion to have arrived at, because, if a full training programme is imposed by higher authority, time is never sufficient to undertake much else; but, if higher authority imposes no such pressure, the onus is even heavier on the junior officer to keep his men in training to the best of his ability, and reasonably well amused off duty.

I list these ideal qualities in a Company Commander, because very few persons (even those capable of becoming MPs) give much thought to the matter; certainly not because I had the smallest claim to them myself. Indeed, though I came back from the Aldershot course with a goodish report, it was clear to me that, unless I soon found myself some other employment, I ran the risk, with other middle-aged subalterns possessing no great turn for leading men (the absolute essential in an infantry officer), of exile to the Regiment's Infantry Training Centre; whence one might only too easily descend to the *bas fonds* of the military ant-heap.

At one moment it even crossed my mind to try and exchange into the Intelligence Branch of the RAF Volunteer Reserve, where friends had found niches at once interesting, at times even reasonably exciting. Hewitt, who had plenty of down-to-earth common sense, together with much experience of the exigencies of soldiering (after dashing exploits in the first war, condemned to years of limbo commanding the Regimental Depot as a major), grasped my situation pretty well. In his streamlining of the Battalion it would not have been in the least unreasonable to have got rid of me, but he did not do so.

4

In private life an important event was about to take place in Oxford, where Violet was spending the latter part of the pregnancy. Her doctor was working in a hospital there, and could therefore personally supervise the birth when that took place. There were various false alarms, but delay could not be extended much longer.

One morning in April, 1940, I was crossing the parade-ground at

Newry (where, a former garrison town, the Battalion was in barracks, rather than the flax factory at Portadown), when two subalterns came out of the Orderly Room together. They advanced towards me. At range of about thirty yards one of them shouted: 'It's a boy.' That was the announcement of Tristram's birth. Leave was granted for such occasions, and I got off right away. All had gone well. There was a day or two of a new sort of domestic life. I found that becoming a father had a profound effect upon the manner in which one looked at the world.

On return to Northern Ireland my Company (under the command of Captain Horace Probert, a peppery but not disagreeable character who, surprisingly, served later in Madagascar) was sent 'on detachment' to the Divisional Tactical School, to provide 'security' and a demonstration platoon.

The Tactical School was quartered in Gosford Castle, Co Armagh, an 1820 neo-Gothic pile (said to be the first mock-Norman castle built in the British Isles), surrounded by a fine park. The castle replaced a former burnt-down Georgian mansion belonging to the Earls of Gosford, the house and grounds having associations with Jonathan Swift, one spot still known as the Dean's Seat. In consequence of high living in Edwardian days, the Gosfords, short of cash, had abandoned their castle, which by this time had lain unoccupied and unfurnished for twenty years or more.

An air of inexorable gloom hung over Gosford, undissipated by the crew of seedy bad-mannered middle-aged officers who made up the staff of the Divisional School. The place figures as Castlemallock in *The Valley of Bones*, one of the paperback covers of which was designed by Osbert Lancaster, who, though he had never seen the Castle, brought by instinct an extraordinary verisimilitude to Gosford's keep and turrets.

Later that summer a change took place in my army circumstances, which, as things turned out, removed me for good from the Battalion. Headquarters, 53rd Division, at this moment stationed in Belfast, required an assistant Camp Commandant. This is one of the least distinguished jobs in the army, but its holder is required to be less than utterly uncouth in habits, being responsible, among other duties, for the Defence Platoon guarding the Divisional Commander's Tactical HQ in the field, accordingly a member of the Major-General's Mess.

Unknown to myself I had been marked down for this employment. I was posted to Belfast as one of two (subsequently three) officers in charge

of HQ troops: that is to say the Defence Platoon, clerks, drivers, bat-
men, cooks—in military parlance the odds and sods—who made up
'other ranks' at Div HQ. Pretty well all administration of Headquarters
interior economy was undertaken by the Camp Commandant's office,
when the formation was not out on an exercise. This unglamorous
appointment was perfectly appropriate to a second-lieutenant of mature
age—in any case the army rank most buggered about—and in many ways
I was not sorry to make a change, being by now aware that (possessing
few if any of the qualities listed above) I was unlikely to be given a
Company, and, to tell the truth, little equipped to command one.

The picture of a Divisional Headquarters offered in *The Soldier's Art*
projects, broadly speaking, what I have to say about this interlude of
army experience. Instead of the office work being 'A' matters (personnel,
courts-martial, etc), as in the book, duties in Belfast ranged from respon-
sibility for distribution of vehicles to the disposal of ash and swill. My
rôle on exercises is also touched on in those pages.

A Divisional Headquarters tends to fall between the companionable
atmosphere that a battalion at any rate should possess, the snug compact-
ness of Brigade HQ (if the Brigadier himself is tolerable), while at the
same time lacking the variety, comparative closeness to High Command,
of a Corps HQ or above. I got on well with immediate colleagues; the rest
of the staff, with one or two exceptions (the General was not at all unen-
lightened), a crowd one would never wish to see again. At first I messed
with the dregs; later being shifted, through some administrative re-
organization, to the Royal Artillery Mess, which was greatly preferable,
Gunners having a sound tradition of looking after themselves in a civilized
manner.

Alick Dru was fond of the expression *la merde surnage*. The GSO 1
(normally known as G 1, the Colonel acting as chief-of-staff to the
Divisional Commander) was an excellent example of that law. He also
rather fancied himself as a wit. The Divisional concert (as set out in
The Soldier's Art) was an annual entertainment traditionally organized by
the officer in charge of the Mobile Bath Unit, in this case a man of
sympathetic humour. G 1 sent anonymously to Bath certain lyrics he had
written, and supposed suitable to the concert, no doubt banking on Bath
recognizing his handwriting. Bath did indeed recognize G 1's handwriting,
but his reaction was not that expected. He consigned the lyrics to the

waste-paper basket, and publicized the story throughout the formation.

'Other ranks' were here drawn from all units of the Division, which, as well as the South Welshmen of The Welch Regiment, included men from the Marches in the South Wales Borderers (one of whose Territorial battalions was designated The Herefords), and North Welsh, of whom the Royal Welch Fusiliers was principally composed. All these differing elements liked doing things their own way. When Div HQ was 'in the field' the Defence Platoon had its cooking arrangements, the Royal Signals theirs, while at least one other group ate separately from these two.

Obviously all three—possibly more—groups would be more easily served by one cookhouse, but all passionately clung to their own Messing. The army authorities—sometimes more understanding in such matters than civilian ones—did not press the matter. Three or four private picnics remained. This seems to me a not unimportant point, something increasingly disregarded by contemporary governmental and municipal officials: the fact that human beings like doing things their own way with their own associates. Politicians and bureaucrats might well ponder this.

Variation of North Wales and South Wales temperament was well illustrated my first morning at Division inspecting breakfasts. The Orderly Sergeant, a Royal Welch Fusilier, remarked: 'The porridge is very good this morning, sir.' I was by this time so acclimatized to the irony of the South Welsh that, at once supposing some fearful slop full of cockroaches had been served up, I asked with apprehension: 'What's wrong with it, Sergeant?' The North Welshman (not one of the dour sort, and an excellent soldier) meant no more nor less than what he said; the porridge was indeed very good.

5

Meanwhile, though air-raids had not yet begun in Belfast, the Battle of Britain was being fought out over the south of England. Sussex, where Violet, with Tristram, was now living, represented one of the most vulnerable areas. The question arose whether or not it would be best for her to cross to Ulster. Wives were in certain circumstances allowed to join their husbands in Northern Ireland, having arrived there might return to England, but, once that second move had taken place, were no longer eligible to come back across the sea.

Accommodation was far from easy to find in Belfast, especially as army duties gave little or no time to search for a furnished flat or small house. Either of these alternatives, even if available, was likely to be expensive. It was also possible that Div HQ might at any moment be transferred to some more or less inaccessible spot in a part of the country without housing for camp followers.

Notwithstanding these uncertainties the increasing vehemence of the blitz in the south of England seemed to make a move advisable for a mother with a young baby. Violet arrived in Belfast before any very satisfactory arrangements could be made to receive her there, putting up for a time at a boarding-house in fairly dispiriting surroundings. In the end, after a good deal of searching about, we managed to rent a small house, one that might indeed have been worse in a city not famed for its charm; perhaps even rather unjustly disparaged, some of the University quarter being not without all distinction.

Up to this time Northern Ireland had been free from air-raids. Now, as if planned to coincide with the new presence of one's family, they began with some heat. Belfast had settled down to a state of mind in which attack from the air was scarcely contemplated, and Civil Defence preparations were minimal. In consequence much confusion was caused. The Luftwaffe's visits, unlike those to London, where a stray plane would sometimes make a lone flight, were usually in force, if Belfast was thought worth the journey at all. For a time I had orders to turn out the Defence Platoon, mount brens as practice for anti-aircraft cover, but, no dive-bombing taking place, this routine was after a while abandoned.

Meanwhile, the only promise my army future held was that, after expiration of eighteen months, all second-lieutenants became lieutenants, automatically promoted. The prospect was not inspiring. Then an altogether unexpected thing happened. In January, 1941, a War Office telegram arrived at 53 Div HQ, instructing 2nd Lt. A. D. Powell, Welch Regt, to attend the 3rd Politico-Military Course at the Intelligence Training Centre (Cambridge Branch). This signal caused a certain flutter among the colonels of the Divisional staff, the G 1—he of the rejected lyrics, beneath whose chariot wheels one was infinitely less than dust—being not above showing envy, even a certain mean-spirited respect.

The order surpised me at least as much as the colonels. I have never discovered what interlocking of army machinery brought it about, though later I remembered that the contemplated establishment of some such course had been mentioned by David Talbot Rice, perhaps even before I had been in the army. Talbot Rice, owing to his knowledge of the Near East as an archaeologist, had been commissioned (ending as lieutenant-colonel) into Military Intelligence early in the war, possibly even before its outbreak. He may have been responsible for putting my name forward. This temporary move to England entailed leaving Violet and Tristram in Northern Ireland, but raids did not begin until my return.

VI

Cambridge Waters

I had lived in Cambridge for a short time in 1916, when my father was instructor at the Staff College, then quartered in the University, otherwise full of officer-cadets. More recently, in 1936, Violet and I had spent a night at Cambridge in order to see *Rosmersholm* performed there during an Ibsen season at the Arts Theatre. This expedition had been set in motion by George Kennedy (the architect in whose office Violet's sister, Pansy Lamb, had formerly worked), who was accompanied by his cousin, Margaret Kennedy, married to a judge, though on this jaunt both cousins left their respective spouses at home.

Margaret Kennedy's novel, *The Constant Nymph* (1924), had on first impact bowled over not only the circulating-library public, but (see, for instance, Cyril Connolly's undergraduate *Letters* to Noel Blakiston) captivated a great many of the highbrows too. Later the highbrows furiously backpedalled. Nevertheless, as best sellers do, especially those of a superior sort, *The Constant Nymph* in some unerring manner hit off to perfection the particular forms of romanticism and self-pity belonging to its own moment of appearance. (Interviewed some years ago for a New York paper, I remarked how self-pity is an all but invariable element of the bestseller; an observation subsequently sub-edited as: 'No one wants self-pity.')

The Constant Nymph had been brought into being by a chance visit on the part of its author to the house of Augustus John. In Margaret Kennedy's novel the bohemian patriarch is a musician rather than a painter, with a heterogeneous retinue of wives, children, mistresses. One of his adolescent daughters, Tessa (progenetrix, in her own right as a novel-character, of a countless offspring named after her), falls in love with a young man called Lewis Dodd, also a musician. After making an ultra-respectable marriage, Lewis Dodd elopes with Tessa (barely within the age of consent), but she—the constant nymph—dies before their love can be consummated.

None of the Johns was greatly pleased by such discernible approximations as existed in this narrative to their own conditions of living (which they did not regard as being in the least unconventional), and (Margaret Kennedy possessing none of the quiet but contagious geniality of her cousin, George Kennedy) they were additionally piqued that so unostentatious a guest should achieve this sudden phenomenal success by use of material which might be looked on, so to speak, as John property.

For Violet and myself *The Constant Nymph* had the special relevance that its anti-hero, Lewis Dodd, was supposedly modelled on our brother-in-law, Henry Lamb. This alleged identification had long been adumbrated—indeed Pansy Lamb herself, on describing to Mary Pakenham a first meeting with her own future husband, had alluded to Dodd 'being' Lamb. The chief resemblance between Lamb and Dodd was not in any parallel incidents having taken place in their lives, so much as the fact that Lamb was musician as well as painter, undeniably frequented the Augustus John circle, above all might be seen from time to time wearing several waistcoats simultaneously.

These cases of novelists' models, in which a few trivial likenesses to the original are lumped together with much disparity, are often of more interest in the subsequent effect they have than in themselves. When *The Constant Nymph* was dramatized, the part of Lewis Dodd was played by Noël Coward. Coward, off the stage, could hardly have looked less like Lamb, nor talked less in Lamb's manner, but, in the scene when Coward was acting Dodd at the piano, Pansy Lamb herself conceded that he had just the appearance of her husband in the same circumstances.

George Kennedy had Bloomsbury associations—indeed could be looked on as Bloomsbury's pet architect—and, after *Rosmersholm* was ended, we had supper at the Arts Theatre restaurant with Maynard Keynes and his Russian wife, the ballerina Lydia Lopokova (her name usually accented by English friends on the third syllable), who was for a change playing Nora in this Cambridge production of *The Doll's House*.

Keynes, who had been instrumental in bringing the Arts Theatre into being, was unusually tall, heavily moustached, magisterial, giving the impression of regarding himself as always on duty. Lopokova, on or off the stage, had a unique charm. In 1921, still a schoolboy, I had watched her in Diaghilev's ornate but splendid *The Sleeping Princess* (where she had danced the pas de deux), subsequently in many other ballets.

Lopokova remained quite independent of the Bloomsburyishness with which she was surrounded most of the time. Her unorthodox employment of the English language was famous, one of her most felicitous phrases having been to surmise that the Sitwells suffered from 'undeveloped arrestment'. In the course of this Cambridge supper, conversation turned to her days in the Imperial Russian Ballet School at St Petersburg before the Revolution. She said that, contrary to what might be supposed, French was hardly ever spoken at the Ballet School. Keynes urged her to amplify this matter of rarely talking French. Lopokova laughed.

'We only used French when we wanted to go to the lavatory. We had to ask: *Puis-je aller là-bas?* The invariable answer was: *Oui—vous-pouvez aller là-bas.* Once we were down the stairs we would all collect together and chatter.'

Keynes, though he must often have heard the story, listened with evident approval. The picture invoked of little gossiping ballet girls pleased him, made his manner momentarily less portentous.

2

The Politico-Military Course, each one of which comprised about twenty officers, and lasted eight weeks, did credit to British self-assurance as to the eventual outcome of the war. At that moment victory did not seem very probable. Germany, having overrun Europe, would soon feel strong enough to attack the Soviet Union, her own ally in the devastation of Poland; while Pearl Harbour, bringing about US declaration of war on the Axis Powers, was still nearly a year away. The blitz was in full swing; invasion of the British Isles apparently imminent. Notwithstanding the sunlessness of the strategic horizon, the Politico-Military Courses had been organized with the object of training a nucleus of officers to deal with problems of military government after the Allies had defeated the Axis.

The concept of setting up the PM courses was mainly due to Colonel (later Brigadier) K. V. Barker-Benfield, then Commandant of the Intelligence Training Centre and Inspector of Military Intelligence. The principle of these Cambridge courses was that the greater part of the instruction should be undertaken by the University, officers living more or less as undergraduates (two in a room, eating in hall), billeted in Trinity, most of the lectures in St John's. Other army courses were also taking place in the colleges at this time, notably one for languages, designed for interpreters and personnel likely to be infiltrated behind the enemy lines.

Colonel Barker-Benfield, regarded in the army, I believe, as rather an eccentric, a big man with a bald bumpy cranium, had a DSO and Bar from the earlier war, which he must have won as a very young officer. He looked at first sight like one of the retinue depicted in a 19th century Academy picture of Attila and his Huns (a race to be studied on the Course), and had served as military attaché in various capitals (Vienna, Budapest, Berne), peacetime employment of considerable interest, though not regarded by professional soldiers as likely to pave the way to very senior rank.

Barker-Benfield was, in fact, one of the kindest of men, something I discovered not so much at Cambridge as later in the War Intelligence Course at Matlock, where, as Inspector of MI, he would turn up from time to time, always prepared to take trouble about subordinates. At Matlock, where he would mix with the students in the bar, he asked me to produce a short report on the PM Course. While discussing the brief notes I jotted down on this subject, he remarked: 'One's in this world for such a short time that it seems best so far as possible to do the work to which one's most suited'; a view by no means universal, especially in the army.

The teaching side at Cambridge was organized by Professor (later Sir) Ernest Barker, Emeritus Professor of Political Science (a school he had been largely responsible for establishing), and, among many other distinctions, Honorary Fellow of Peterhouse. Over and above these academic appointments, Barker, in his late sixties, was a fairly famous Cambridge figure. His exuberant personality, public and private, belonged to what is popularly thought of as Oxford, rather than Cambridge, tradition. Barker had indeed been up at Balliol, a college he never ceased to panegyrize, though love and respect were tempered with sorrow (rather than anger) that Balliol, unmindful of her sons, had never offered him a Fellowship.

Barker, in an era when claims to humble birth were less widely boasted than today, was always determined to emphasize the extreme modesty of his beginnings, the fact that he had made his way entirely by winning scholarships. Cheerful, dominating, egotistical to a degree, he had lost none of the Victorian optimism, sense of a career open to talents, which had brought him where he was, and, apparently prepared to lecture on all subjects, was free from many donnish caprices. As another Balliol man, he was predisposed towards me, at post-lecture discussions always encouraging the putting forward of what he called the 'Balliol paradox'. I am glad these unlikely circumstances gave me a chance of observing Ernest Barker gyrating, enthusiastically and excursively, within his own academic orbit.

3

Notwithstanding the supposed frigidity of Cambridge manners, the dons there were exceedingly hospitable to members of the PM Course; indeed showed themselves more anxious to entertain the army than their counterparts of my own University, when later in the war I briefly found myself in Oxford; though perhaps that is hardly a fair parallel owing to different circumstances.

Among my Cambridge hosts was A. S. F. 'Granny' Gow, a former Eton master, now Fellow of Trinity. Andrew Gow (who died in 1975 at the age of ninety-one) could hardly have been in greater contrast with Ernest Barker. Barker was the sort of don who would these days be familiar on the 'media', while Gow, with his muted humour, somewhat Jamesian manner, taste for cultivated bachelor life, preferred an absolute personal privacy; tempered with great concern for the arts, expressed through the National Art Collections Fund. He left 'my French things' to the Fund for presentation to the Fitzwilliam Museum. Gow's 'French things' included a couple of dozen drawings by Degas, perhaps fifty more by such masters as Boudin and Toulouse-Lautrec.

The Eton instinct for penetrating nicknames had not gone astray in appending 'Granny' to Gow's name, in spite of the fact that he was by no means an old woman, and had been firm rather than the reverse in school. He had taught me Greek for one term at a lowish level, and been George Orwell's 'classical tutor'. When Gow kindly sought me out at Cambridge, and asked me to dinner, we did not talk of Orwell, who had not yet come into my life, but I believe Connolly had already mentioned to me that Orwell kept up to some extent with his former tutor.

Such discriminating dons of the old tradition had no doubt always been something of a rarity with their collecting (though Gow was not a rich man) and good claret. A few years before this, Gow had produced a memoir of A. E. Housman, whose friend he had been, a book with moments of dry humour, but chiefly bibliographical in aim, intended to assemble together a record of Housman's academic writings, rather than dwell on his poetry and idiosyncracies.

Gow gave me his Housman book, inscribing it. In return, at the first opportunity, I sent him *Agents and Patients*. He wrote in acknowledgment that he 'found its frivolities a suitable solace for the weary hours spent this week at the [air-raid] warden post where it alternates with professional matter and a book on the equally frivolous habits of the cuckoo.'

One night, dining I think at Jesus high table, I found myself next to Sir Arthur Quiller-Couch, 'Q', sometime Professor of English Literature, another celebrated Cambridge figure. Q's books are now not much remembered, but he left an indelible mark on two generations by editing *The Oxford Book of English Verse* in 1900, 1910 and 1939, thereby netting three miraculous draughts of wartime readers of poetry, war producing conditions when the gauge of poetry consumption rises steeply. Quite why Quiller-Couch should have been chosen for this job, even in the first instance, was never very clear. On the second round, a change would have done no harm, but, as things fell out, for forty years Q pretty well laid down what verse ought to be given a chance to survive.

Quiller-Couch, then approaching eighty, extremely spry, gave the impression of thinking not too badly of himself. He told me he had just received a letter from Marie Stopes (apostle of birth-control), trying to enlist Q's help in keeping Lord Afred Douglas off the rocks financially. I had met Douglas when John Heygate and Evelyn Gardner were married and living at Brighton, and not been greatly taken with him. He had curious movements, entering a room almost as if about to turn a cartwheel.

I do not know whether or not Q and Marie Stopes between them solved Douglas's money crisis.

On one of these high table evenings a don asked: 'What's T. S. Eliot's brother-in-law like?', thereby disclosing the fact that a fellow student on the PM Course, a captain in the Manchester Regiment with first war ribbons, M. H. Haigh-Wood, was brother of Eliot's first wife. I was interested to learn of this relationship, since it wafted some faint redolence of what must have been the poet's early married life, always so indistinct. I was able to offer no information, Haigh-Wood being the reverse of talkative, indeed rather exceptionally silent, nor was there any outward indication of why he had been nominated for the Course.

Personal anonymity of that sort was in itself not at all uncommon among the variegated assembly of officers at Cambridge, where a Regular major, who had done a pre-war attachment to some foreign army, might be sitting next to a second-lieutenant without the smallest military experience, but some claim to a working knowledge of Central European politics. Unrevealed qualifications were not necessary qualifications in default.

I know little of the subsequent careers of most of my fellow-students, either in the short term of second war military service, nor long term fate in life. One of them settled down to be a permanent official in MI 5; another ended as an ambassador; a third (with some name already as writer of thrillers) was involved in a tremendous army rumpus a year or two later, regarding the abduction from a military prison (by use of false documents) of a Pole, a professional gambler of shady connexions, thought well adapted by SOE to their purposes in German-occupied territories.

4

Among those students whose potential qualifications were plain enough on hearing them was a white-haired captain, whose appearance struck me at first sight as indefinably strange. He wore first war ribbons, and was rather incongruously listed with his Oxford degree on the roster of names: 'Captain G. P. Dennis, MA, Intelligence Corps'. In the manner of much duplicated typewritten documents, in which misprints inevitably occurred throughout an eight-weeks course, MA would occasionally appear as MC.

It immediately struck me—by a means which he himself would certainly have looked on as occult—that this officer with an odd air about him might be Geoffrey Dennis, author of a couple of novels I had read years before, *Mary Lee* (1922) and *Harvest in Poland* (1925). I had got hold of these books not so much because the reviews they had received were wholly favourable, as on account of the obvious bewilderment of the reviewers.

Captain Dennis, then about fifty, agreed almost with emotion that he had written these two novels. He seemed quite startled. His manner suggested that no one had ever heard of these early works of his. 'I'm a very *highbrow* writer,' he said. 'You understand that, don't you? A much more *highbrow* writer, for instance, than Aldous Huxley.'

This comment was made in a tone not in the least conceited, in fact almost apologetically, with a note of anxiety in his voice, nearly chronic, so I discovered, when Dennis spoke about himself. His novels had seemed not so much highbrow (whatever that epithet, undoubtedly at times convenient, might be held to cover), as outpourings of an exceptionally uninhibited personality, highly strung, even tortured, obsessed with a sense of aggression against himself on the part of those around him.

The heroine of *Mary Lee* was a girl brought up (as Dennis himself had been) among the Plymouth Brethren. *Harvest in Poland*, related in the first person, apparently autobiographically, an account of an Oxford undergraduate going to Poland, during the vacation just before the outbreak of war in 1914, to teach English in the house of a Polish prince. *Harvest in Poland* ended with the hero becoming the victim of diabolical possession. Both novels had perceptibly sadistic undercurrents running through them.

Dennis had written several books I had not read, including *Coronation Commentary* (1937), which dealt with Edward VIII's abdication, and landed the author in libel troubles, no doubt adding to his sense of persecution. Although the earlier novels were weakened by wild writing and lack of coherent form, they could not be called without all talent. One felt that Dennis had something to say, but the novel was not the right medium for his self-expression.

Dennis himself, who possessed a considerable gift for picking up languages, had lived for many years at Geneva, working in the Secretariat of the League of Nations. Speaking of this turn for languages, he would insist that an enormous amount of hard work was also required before anything like perfection could be attained. He said he would go to the same play for perhaps twenty or thirty nights running to improve accent and enunciation.

An amusing talker when not oppressed by anxiety, Dennis had many stories of incidents at the assemblies of the League of Nations. One delegate (whose nationality I forget) had a beard from which he would pluck imaginary hairs while he delivered his speeches, moving his hands at the same time in bizarre gestures. This bearded delegate made an official complaint that what he said was not being adequately rendered in translation. Accordingly the translator whose work had been criticized, when next on duty, scrupulously reproduced all this plucking and gesticulating, but doing so with an imaginary beard.

On another occasion, the Japanese delegate spoke for several minutes in an utterly unknown tongue. When the Japanese had made an end, each supposing himself responsible for the translation, both English and French interpreters leapt simultaneously to their feet.

Novelists have a way of bringing with them the distinctive characters and typical situations of their own novels. This law, so it seemed to me, even with uncertain memories of Dennis's books, was borne out by an unhappy incident reported by him halfway through the Course, a vexation that could well have been visited on one of his heroes. His usual state of mild worry was thereby increased to desperate agitation. If the facts were indeed as he described them, the annoyance was reasonable enough.

Dennis said he had a patent medicine in his room to cure some minor ailment (named, but now forgotten), and this pot or tube had caused someone to approach the Assistant-Commandant (not a regular officer, but keen to maintain a high standard of military discipline in the relaxed atmosphere of a university) with a complaint that Dennis was treating himself for venereal disease. Dennis had a strongly developed capacity for self-justification, and for some time the rumblings of this unpleasantness beneath the surface disturbed the harmony of the Course. Finally peace was restored. I never knew the name of the supposed troublemaker, nor what amends, if any, were made to the outraged Dennis for an unwarrantable allegation. Somebody told me that years later the Assistant-

Commandant was still complaining of the time Dennis had given him on the subject.

If this incident could easily have come out of one of Dennis's novels, I have to concede that another one, in which Dennis was also involved, pertained to my own books, at least to the extent that I subsequently made use of it. The scene in question took place on the last night of the PM Course, after a dinner at which no doubt a certain amount had been drunk.

Just as I was about to retire to bed, a fellow-student told me to come with him up another staircase to see some practical joke that had been played on Dennis. I had been in no way associated with this prank myself, probably expression of a general feeling that Dennis was an odd fish; a conclusion that may have been further interpreted—wholly erroneously—as indication that he was therefore homosexual. I could be paying the organizers a compliment in conjecturing anything so comparatively thought out, however wide of the mark. The joke, such as it was, consisted in having arranged a dummy in Dennis's bed.

The mock-up of the dummy was quite well done. In the company of its constructors I was admiring the body's convincing outlines, when Dennis himself appeared. The scene then took place which is reproduced in *The Valley of Bones*, where brother-officers plan to rag Bithel (a character in every respect unlike Dennis), a drunken middle-aged subaltern of dubious sexual tastes. The manner in which Bithel turns the tables on the raggers might be thought implausible in a novel, but Bithel's behaviour, and its consequences, exactly coincided with Dennis's at that moment in the Trinity bedroom.

No doubt Dennis, like the rest of us, had drunk a certain amount, but he was in complete command of his wits. He glanced at the recumbent dummy, at once grasping the inferences. Without the least warning he began to perform a complicated dance round the bed. While he danced, hands raised above his head, he sang. This stately pavan continued for a minute or two, at the end of which Dennis collapsed on the bed, clasping the dummy in a passionate embrace.

A consciousness of awful embarrassment descended on all around. In spite of having myself taken no part in the planning of the affair, I had not been immune to a touch of inner uneasiness while Dennis went through the formal evolutions of his dance. The perpetrators of the frolic were altogether discomforted in their own terms. They crept off silently to bed. I don't think I have ever witnessed a similar hoax carried off by the intended victim with such unexpected éclat.

5

Among those who had withdrawn from the London blitz to work in Cambridge, where air-raid warnings were heard only rarely, was John Hayward, who had himself been up at King's. Hayward, invalid man of letters, bibliographer, editor of such poets as Rochester and Donne, was about the same age as myself. I had met him in very early Duckworth days at a tea-party of Edith Sitwell's, but—through friends of Violet's— it was only latterly that we had known him at all well. At Edith Sitwell's, although already attacked by the incurable muscular disease which brought an end to his life in 1965, Hayward could still walk, though with difficulty. Now for years he had been confined to a wheelchair.

Hayward, who faced his condition with the greatest courage, did not allow this dire state to stand in the way of enjoying the strenuous social life to which he was absolutely devoted. His shrunken body, part of the toll taken by disease, was sufficiently light in weight to be lifted, wheelchair and all, into a taxi, and, provided a party was held on the ground-floor, John Hayward was more likely than not to be one of the guests.

Suffering had left its grim marks on Hayward's features, turbid lips, and an expression of implacable severity, making him look like a portrait of Savonarola. In fact nothing could have been less puritanical than Hayward's lively talk, always expressed in carefully chosen phrases, somewhat Augustan in diction. A cluster of pretty women were usually standing round about his wheelchair at parties, doing their best to entertain him. In dealing with well-wishers of both sexes (men would push his chair, otherwise attend to his physical needs). Hayward, whose temperament was at once nervous and dominating, could at times approach the positively tyrannical. Indeed, holding court at a party, he had much about him of Ham, the seated autocrat in Samuel Beckett's *End Game*, regal yet immobile, continually dispensing a rich flow of comment, imperious, erudite, malicious.

Hayward's condition of health, if not positively necessitating a companion (before this Cambridge interlude he had lived on his own in Bina Gardens, South Kensington), was much ameliorated by having a housemate. He was now sharing Merton Hall (an ornamental house belonging to Lord Rothschild) with another notable figure unwontedly in Cambridge, Lord Gerald Wellesley. Lord Gerald, by profession an architect, was now a major in the Grenadiers, instructing at one of the army's courses for languages.

Hayward could comfortably continue his literary work at Cambridge, and he also taught once or twice a week at a girls' school in the neighbourhood. Anthologies of verse were immensely popular during the war years, and, not long before my own arrival in Cambridge, Hayward had produced one of these: *Love's Helicon*, a volume arranged under headings to illustrate the myriad aspects of Love, ranging from successful seduction to hopeless despair.

After the war John Hayward, who had long been not only a close personal friend of T. S. Eliot, but a valued critic of his poetry before publication, set up house with Eliot in Carlyle Mansions (where Henry James had lived at the end of his life) on the Chelsea Embankment; a household which continued, until brought to a close by Eliot's second marriage in 1957. During this period Eliot might often be seen pushing Hayward's chair, sometimes as far afield as Battersea Park. Their companionship under one roof was looked on as an undoubted success, though one of its anomalies particularly remarked was that suggested by Hayward's boundless relish for stories, contemporary or historical, with a strong tang of sex about them; Eliot's notorious distaste for anything of that kind.

So far as was known, contretemps had never arisen over this disparity of humour; the same antithesis in what might be thought amusing certainly not arising during his co-tenancy with Lord Gerald Wellesley. Wellesley was to become 7th Duke of Wellington within two years, on his nephew's death in action serving with the Commandos, and it will be convenient to call him by the title he was soon to inherit.

Gerry Wellington, then in his middle fifties, distinguished in appearance, a connoisseur in the arts, a courtier, possessed a keen sense of his own exalted position, which made him the subject of many stories even before his unexpected accession of rank. Indeed, his touch of haughtiness was scarcely, if at all, augmented by becoming a duke. No amount of ragging on the part of his own contemporaries, say, Osbert Sitwell, Harold Nicolson, Malcolm Bullock (long in the House of Commons, great purveyor of badinage), could undermine this lofty demeanour, maintained as much in bohemian circles—where Gerry Wellington did not at all mind making occasional forays—as in the *beau monde*.

Mere pomposity, however splendid, would never have brought Gerry Wellington his fame if he had not possessed many other qualities too, one of which was a powerful capacity for counter-ragging his raggers. In that respect he could perfectly well look after himself. His preoccupation with the mystique of his great ancestor, the 1st Duke of Wellington, might cause jocular friends to refer to him as the Iron Duchess, but he was a personality to be reckoned with, whose amalgam of gifts and idiosyncrasies are not easy to outline with justice to both.

As a younger son, who had to make his own way in the world (a starting point which, as much as Ernest Barker, he liked to emphasize), he had been in the Diplomatic Service, to the end of his days capable of making a stylish speech on any public occasion in French or German. He retired from Diplomacy as a comparatively young man to become an architect, the profession he had always wanted to follow. His knowledge of the visual arts was wide, and, although in principle he liked what was 'classical', quite uninfluenced by fashionable pedantries. In reading he was unpredictable, quoting from unexpected poets like Dyer or Alfieri, but unable to get on with Proust, within whose pages he himself might have figured congruously enough.

Devoted to ceremonial, Gerry Wellington equally disliked fuss, making a habit of carrying his own suitcase downstairs at hotels, perfectly prepared to do the washing-up, if circumstances imposed that liability. He possessed energy, kindliness (allied to a hot temper), an immense sense of personal obligation in performing duties he regarded as incumbent on his position, and, sixty in sight, was to leap into the sea with the British invading force undertaking the Sicilian coastal landings.

Gerry Wellington (who had two strikingly good-looking children) was separated from his wife, Dorothy Wellesley, a poet much admired by W. B. Yeats. According to Osbert Sitwell, the two chief causes of marital discord had been Dorothy Wellesley's impatience with her husband's incessant plugging of the glories of the first Duke, together with his taste for highly spiced stories, cited above as a bond with John Hayward.

Osbert Sitwell asserted that, at an attempted reconciliation between husband and wife, the former had arrived carrying an enormous brown-paper parcel, a present. While Dorothy Wellesley was undoing the string her husband had time to recount an anecdote of startling pungency; when the paper was removed, the gift turned out to be a gigantic bust of the 1st Duke of Wellington, executed in terracotta.

6

These legends about Gerry Wellington proliferated not only because we had friends in common before meeting, but through living opposite his house in Chester Gate, one not large but with a notably elegant façade. He had set a bust of his fellow architect, John Nash, designer of most of Regent's Park terraces, on a niche overlooking the little garden, which stood on one side of the house.

Unfortunately the porch of the house had the look of an alcove intended for a moment's rest on the journey of life, which made the steps a favourite staging-post for children returning from play in the Park; the weary of more mature years to be seen from time to time sitting—even lying—on them. Miscreants would indulge in runaway rings, and, when painting took place, leave the imprints of their hands on the front-door. These goings-on provoked the strongest reactions from the owner when he arrived home in the middle of them, constantly causing the cry: 'Come quickly—Lord Gerald's having one of his rows!' Perhaps the best of these took place just before the outbreak of war, when he was already wearing the black-and-gold cap of the Brigade of Guards, his vis-à-vis on this occasion a child about a foot high.

After the war we came to know Gerry Wellington quite well, often staying at Stratfield Saye in Hampshire, once at La Torre, the Wellington property in Spain, granted when the 1st Duke was created Duque di Ciudad Rodrigo. Gerry Wellington's great literary passion was for Jane Austen, a novelist on whom Violet is expert, and for some time the two of them maintained a correspondence, purporting to be exchanged between Austen characters, carried out in the language of the novels, though more ribald in strain. He also liked Violet to check some of his family papers (the First Duke having married Kitty Pakenham), and a firm tradition grew up for us to come to Stratfield Saye once a year to attend the annual meeting of the Jane Austen Society, held in the gardens of Chawton House (bequeathed to Jane Austen's brother), the novelist herself having lived in that Hampshire village.

Stratfield Saye, formerly belonging to the Pitt family, had been bought by the nation for the 1st Duke of Wellington after Waterloo, the proposal being to pull down the existing house, to be replaced by a more palatial affair designed by Benjamin Wyatt or at least in that Regency manner. The Duke had preferred to retain this dignified mansion of mellowed walls, with its attractive stable-block in the Dutch style, though friends and relations demurred at its lack of pretension. The victor of Waterloo had installed an altogether exceptional abundance of water-closets for those days, and amused himself by pasting, with his own hands, engravings on the walls of many of the bedrooms, their sole mural decoration to this day.

My own feeling is that some of the First Duke's liking for Stratfield Saye must have been vested in its park's striking resemblance to a conventional battlefield. With a river running through the grounds, clumps of trees set about haphazard over the low open contours of grassland (not at all in the contrived manner of Capability Brown), an occasional small house or cottage to provide Advance HQ, or a strongpoint to be defended, the terrain offers a large-as-life tactical table for use with or without troops of any period.

La Torre, not far from Granada, a plain white building set on a hill, had something of the charm of a large old-fashioned English rectory, especially its interior, but a rectory set in a country of vineyards and tobacco plantations. When we stayed there Gerry Wellington brought off a feat unheard of among most visitors to Spain who have tried to watch Flamenco dancing, that is to say keeping the Gypsies waiting, instead of vice versa, the almost invariable experience well into the small hours.

By happy chance for one so preoccupied with that epoch, Gerry Wellington, as a young diplomat, had been *en poste* in St Petersburg in 1912, the year of the centenary celebrations for the battle of Borodino, regarded by the Russians as the turning point of the defeat of the *Grande Armée*. As souvenir of this centenary he possessed a photograph of a Russian peasant, aged one hundred and four years, alleged to have been held up as a child when Bonaparte and his staff had made a public appearance on the balcony of some building. The old man in the photograph, standing between two officers or court officials, had been questioned.

'And what did the French Emperor look like?'

'A very tall man with a fair beard.'

7

Gerry Wellington had himself appreciably added to the relics of the First Duke at Stratfield Saye, the interior of the house belonging wholly to that period. The place had at times suffered neglect, but luckily not the sort of renovation to destroy the atmosphere. One of its owner's keenest convictions was that his ancestor had never uttered the opinion that the battle of Waterloo had been won on the playing-fields of Eton, offering a standing remuneration of a hundred pounds to anyone who could prove its authenticity; the First Duke having been by no means a dedicated Old Etonian, the earliest coupling of the names of Waterloo and Eton (recorded by a Frenchman in 1855) making no mention of playing-fields.

Francis Needham, the librarian at Stratfield Saye, a tall scholarly figure, also no longer young, became increasingly crony rather than retainer as Gerry Wellington (after eighty commenting 'now I'm between eighty and ninety') grew older. When Needham had been librarian to the Duke of Portland he had written to me about a comment in *John Aubrey and His Friends*, where I had suggested that Aubrey's patron, Lord Thanet, had composed a deliberately disdainful letter for Aubrey to use as credential against imprisonment for debt. Needham, perhaps a little sensitive about noblemen's dependents, declared Thanet's letter no more than a formality, but I retain doubts.

The parallel suggested, however, by Francis Needham's relationship with Gerry Wellington—though neither had the least taste for fox-hunting, nor at all physically resembled Leech's drawings of their prototypes—was more like that mutually existing between the Earl of Scamperdale and Jack Spraggon in the novels of Surtees—always a rich mine of English types—for example, in Lord Scamperdale's chronic indecision whether or not to lend Spraggon his silver spectacles. Needham had a traumatic fear of cows, at certain seasons cropping the grass of the fields between the house and the church (situated in the park), so that on such Sundays the Duke had to drive his Librarian to morning service round by the road; a characteristically Scamperdale/Spraggon contingency within its own terms.

One of Gerry Wellington's strongest addictions was to the detestable spelling-game, Scrabble (similar pastime to that played by the film people at Teddington), and it was hinted that, when alone together in the house, he and Needham would play tête-à-tête games of Scrabble, using combinations of letters of shocking impropriety.

A fellow-guest at Stratfield Saye of the annual Jane Austen meetings was usually the novelist L. P. Hartley, a younger contemporary of Gerry Wellington's, friend of ours too and country neighbour. Leslie Hartley lived at Bathford, a suburb of Bath, in Avondale, a house with something oddly Italian about it, on one side the main road thick with traffic, on the other a quiet garden sloping down to the river. Hartley used to take a boat on the water, where he had a continuous war with hostile swans. He did a great deal of entertaining at Avondale, employing a dynasty of truly extraordinary valet-butlers, each one seeming more bizarre than his predecessor.

Hartley did himself—and his guests—extremely well so far as drink was in question, the wine always first-rate. One butler made a point of refilling a guest's glass after every sip, moderation thereby difficult for the most abstemious. The food at Stratfield Saye was always in the best tradition of good English cooking, but neither wine nor spirits by any means flowed. The host was himself not interested in wine, such as provided coming from the Spanish estate and in no great abundance at that. To remedy this alcoholic deficiency Hartley used to bring his own supplies, sufficient to see him through the weekend—or, as Gerry Wellington would have insisted on terming that efflux of time, Saturday to Monday.

During one of those two days, sometimes on both, there was likely to be a largish luncheon-party, followed invariably by a personally conducted tour of the house for those who had never seen its historical treasures. The rest of house-party inclined to join in the sightseeing, the owner loving nothing better and more often than not producing little-known stories about personalities of the First Duke's period. For instance, someone once speaking disparagingly of George IV, Gerry Wellington said at once: 'But we must be grateful to him for introducing boots shaped to right and left foot. Before the Prince Regent thought of that, no distinction was made by shoemakers between the two feet.'

Tours of the house included the principal bedrooms, but, after inspecting these, did not usually stray from the main upstairs passage to an area somewhat further on, where bachelors were likely to be accommodated, and, in fact, Leslie Hartley was generally given a bedroom. For some reason on one occasion, when even more guests than usual had been at the table, Gerry Wellington, contrary to habit, altered the routine.

'You don't mind if we see your room, Leslie?'

Hartley, always somewhat involuted in speech, uttered a faintly deprecatory affirmative. The long crocodile of guests trooped into his bedroom, too many to be included all at once. The chief object for admiration in the apartment was a newly opened half-bottle of gin, standing in front of the looking-glass on the dressing-table. The sightseers gazed round and withdrew. The tour continued. 'Gerry didn't see, thank God,' Hartley muttered to me, as we proceeded to another wing of the house.

8

To return to wartime Cambridge, the PM Course: John Hayward, as I have said, used to teach once or twice a week at a girls' school. Not long after this work had begun he was horrified to receive a letter one morning, signed by the Headmistress of this school, saying she must at once terminate his employment. She could not possibly expose her pupils to contact with a man responsible for editing a book of verse which had just fallen into her hands, a farrago of lascivious obscenity, a collection altogether unfit for the eyes of a young girl. Hayward's presence must never again pollute the precincts of her school.

Hayward, who could be easily rattled, was not unnaturally very upset on reading this onslaught, the intemperance of the phrasing particularly disturbing him. It was true that *Love's Helicon* contained poems not specially adapted to a school textbook, but he had never attempted to introduce the anthology to the attention of any of the girls, nor included even a selection of the poems in their instruction. Much disturbed, he set the letter aside to read again later in the morning, while trying to think out what would be the best answer.

A renewed reading of the Headmistress's letter some hours later revealed a certain familiarity in the handwriting, at the same time one he did not somehow connect with earlier letters received from the same source. Examination of previous correspondence showed, in fact, that the writing was quite different, nevertheless still encountered not long before. Then the truth was apparent. The letter was a forgery, plainly the work of Gerry Wellington.

Hayward took no action immediately, neither did he mention the matter to his housemate. He merely put the letter away in some private place. A day or two passed. Then a telegram arrived at the house: *Lord Gerald Wellesley* stop *Am in rather a fix* stop *Coming to stay next week* stop *Paddy Brodie*.

Of Paddy Brodie (now deceased) it is necessary to say no more than that his surname had been made use of by Evelyn Waugh to create the composite character, Martin Gaythorne-Brodie (whose other two in-gredients were also not far to seek), who appears in the first edition of *Decline and Fall*, but, owing to threat of legal action (from Brodie himself, I think), was reissued in subsequent printings as The Honourable Miles Malpractice, a figure who also occurs in *Vile Bodies*. When *Decline and Fall* was republished in 1962, together with the replacement of certain words and phrases in the manuscript omitted from the first edition, Miles Malpractice maintained his supplanting of Martin Gaythorne-Brodie.

After receiving this ominous telegram Gerry Wellington mentioned to John Hayward that, very inconveniently, urgent family business had forced him to put in for a week's leave. This request had been granted. He would therefore be absent from Cambridge the following week. There, so far as I know, both the matter of the Headmistress's letter and the Brodie telegram rested; neither subject being ventilated to each other by the two occupants of Merton Hall.

9

The Politico-Military Course was extremely well organized. I cannot picture a more inclusively concentrated account of conditions, historical, political, social, economic, of Europe between the wars, than was given there. So far as my own subsequent employment was concerned this instruction turned out very handy, and has since been useful in all kinds of ways. At the time there was inevitably a certain amount of derision as to contemporary history being traced back to, say, the Golden Horde (crushed by Tamerlane in the 14th century), but the roots of racial relationships, accordingly of all foreign policy, are likely to be found at least as far back as the Middle Ages.

One item I brought away from Cambridge was some smattering of information about that interesting nation, the Khazars, apparently of Turkish origin, inhabiting the Volga and Crimean area in the early Christian Era. The Khazars, under pressure on one side from Christians, on the other from Mahommedans, to avoid compromising themselves with either, adopted the Judaic religion. Arthur Koestler, in *The Thirteenth Tribe* (1976), has put forward the plausible and fascinating theory that most of the Jews of Eastern Europe are accordingly of Khazar rather than Jewish derivation.

The Cambridge don lecturing on the peoples of Russia, and the border countries, required his students to write a short essay on The Slav Character. He endorsed mine: 'Well and brightly written'. A summarized report at the end of the Cambridge Course stated: 'Able, but with no very obvious qualifications'. Barker-Benfield recommended application for exchange into the Intelligence Corps.

As a matter of routine all students were for the moment posted back to their units. Divisional Headquarters now moved from Belfast to Castlewellan in Co Down. This was another neo-Gothic pile, built by the Earls Annesley, and inhabited until that moment by an offshoot of the Annesley family. Lodgings were found for Violet in the neighbourhood at an extortionate rent. The lumbering army machinery of exchange to the 'I' Corps now came into slow motion, seeing me into my second pip after eighteen months' service.

When transfer from The Welch Regiment took place, I was sent as a preliminary on the War Intelligence Course, a six weeks' affair at Matlock in Derbyshire. Students of the WIC were quartered in an Italianate Victorian edifice looking rather like a monastery, Smedley's Hydro, built by a philanthropic textile merchant, anxious to transform Matlock into a spa for the neighbourhood's thermal waters. The country round about was of striking beauty, and in the immediate vicinity of the Hydro all sorts of ornamental pools and grottoes had been constructed. John Smedley had also built himself a neo-Gothic castle high on the hill above the town, at that time more or less a ruin (said to contain government reserves of food); later, I believe, transformed into a zoo. I do not remember these exotic features of the landscape playing much part in the humdrum weeks of military instruction, though a welcome break in routine was a day with Osbert Sitwell at Renishaw.

For some weeks after Matlock I was consigned to the Intelligence Corps Depot at Oxford, quartered in Pembroke College, at that moment full of Spanish-speakers, in case it was decided to anticipate German invasion of the Canaries. During this period took place the interview (described more or less word for word in *The Military Philosophers*) when I was considered for the job of liaison officer, at battalion level, with the Free French in the Near East, turned down on account of insufficiencies of language. That was rather a blow to me, as I was told that otherwise I was what was being looked for, but I recognized the decision as just. A short time later I was posted, on probation, to a Section in the War Office.

VII

Kierkegaard in Whitehall

Life in an infantry battalion, or at a Divisional Headquarters, is sufficiently stereotyped to be given generic implications when reproduced in a
novel. Former infantrymen, who did not serve with Welsh troops, have
told me *The Valley of Bones* and *The Soldier's Art* record plenty of their
own military experience. Such banalities require little recapitulation in
memoirs. My employment in the War Office was rather different. There
the highly specialized duties, varied colleagues engaged on them, sometimes need amplification of what appears in *The Military Philosophers*,
though I hope so far as possible to avoid too much ground already
traversed.

For the artificially created world of the novel, the War Office, as a stage
on which the actors performed, was in one sense so limited, in another so
extended, that all sorts of technical problems were posed in harmonizing
the actual individuals, especially those who composed the Section, with
parallel characters to be absorbed into the pattern of the novel. In earlier
army routines, as I have said, autobiographical components could be
generalized. In the War Office that was much more difficult. Besides, I
particularly wished that the unusual nature of the duties should not play
a disproportionate part in the action of the narrative. Certain persons,
therefore, who occur 'as themselves' in *The Military Philosophers* (though
essentially not pivots on which the novel's action turns) inevitably
reappear 'as themselves' in these memoirs.

2

Military Intelligence (Liaison) had a room on the first floor of what is now known as the Old War Office, at the Trafalgar Square end of the passage, facing on to Whitehall, though the windows were all but entirely bricked up in wartime. Work was concerned in principle with most of the army's foreign contacts in Great Britain. These were made chiefly through the military attachés resident in London (not British military attachés in foreign capitals, who were separately administered), both Allied and Neutral.

In peacetime (as the Neutrals on the whole remained) the military attachés (sometimes covering air duties or *vice versa*) were merely members of their embassy staff keeping an eye on the British armed forces. Now, in the case of Allies with troops in the UK, the military attaché was the main channel through which the greater part of all communication with the War Office was routed.

MIL was very decidedly not involved in any activities of the Secret Service (MI 6), nor Special Operations Executive (SOE). When, very rarely, administrative dealings with these organizations were in question (for example, transfer of Allied personnel for secret duties) negotiations were kept to a stringent minimum, so that liaison relations with Allies should be recognized as existing only in the sphere of open dealings.

Vichy, although naturally without an embassy in London, was recognized as the legal government of France (unlike the puppet régimes set up in German occupied territories), the Free French under General de Gaulle being approached through a special mission, by officers of which I had been interviewed for the battalion liaison job with the Free French overseas. When, after invasion by Germany, the Soviet Union perforce joined the Allies, a special mission also came into being to deal with Russian military affairs, particularly the huge supplies of *matériel* shipped by British convoy to Archangel. After the United States entered the war they too had a special mission (already in embryonic form, I think) owing to the large volume of work, though the American and Russian military attachés, as such, continued their routine contacts with MIL.

Among the Allies only Poland had a sizeable concentration of troops in the UK, the 1st Polish Corps numbering some 20,000 men, mostly stationed in the Lowlands of Scotland. When Stalin agreed to release the (still brigaded) units of the Polish army, held prisoner in Central Asia after the Soviet Union's invasion of Poland in 1939 (to become the 2nd Polish Corps), MIL was concerned with the arrangements made, and on certain other occasions with Allied overseas matters.

The Free French, Czechoslovakia, Norway, Belgium, Holland, each had a few thousands, Luxembourg (the Grand Duchy's military personnel at first cadred with the Belgians, later a separate entity), a few hundreds. These were the foundation members of the club, of which Greece, Jugoslavia, other Powers, were in due course to become members.

The numerical establishment of MIL, varying slightly from time to time, consisted usually of nine or ten officers under the command of a lieutenant-colonel. The foreign military attachés (whose rank might range from major to perhaps even as high as lieutenant-general) mustered at this period a corps of between twenty-three and twenty-six. An Allied military attaché and his staff would be in close touch with MIL all day long, but some of the Neutrals, for example, certain Latin-American states who ran to a military attaché, might appear at the War Office only once in several months; kept in mind only by an occasional routine report from MI 5, stating that some Neutral had without notification, travelled beyond the area permitted in wartime, to spend the night at Maidenhead with a tart.

For some reason fluency in foreign languages seemed combined comparatively rarely with the characteristics required in a proficient liaison officer, and, in the early days of MIL, a fairly brisk turnover took place of officers who spoke various languages with skill, but proved otherwise unsuitable for the work. Among those who remained, some were multilingual to a remarkable degree, some capable in one additional tongue, some—like myself—offering no more than a scrap of French.

At first, as one on probation, I was assigned all sorts of odd jobs with both Allies and Neutrals, useful experience of those very different areas of work, then allotted as assistant to the officer dealing with the Poles. Within a few weeks (after sudden conjunctions when it seemed I should be posted first to Iceland, then to the Middle East) I was taken on the permanent strength of MIL as GSO 3, and promoted captain. My colleagues, greatly varying in type throughout my two spells with the Section, an uncommonly nice crowd *en gros*, included three or four individuals to be regarded as altogether unusual personalities in any assemblage of human beings.

3

As already indicated, some—though not all—of the military attachés who appear as characters in *The Military Philosophers* are drawn directly from life. The British officers of MIL, few in number, were less easy to handle in a novel, even those to some extent delineated requiring substantial remodelling. Colonel Carlisle, in charge of the Section, possibly from its inception, certainly from the earliest stages of the war, holding the appointment until his own demobilization in 1945, created a particularly tricky problem.

Any character shown in the position of MIL's Commanding Officer would, unless firm steps were taken on my own part to circumvent any such thing, inevitably be identified with Carlisle. For several reasons I wished to avoid that, the chief being that Carlisle's own personality was too marked to represent him as a shadowy figure—which would in any case give a false impression of the Section, one with a distinct flavour largely due to Carlisle himself—while any attempt to invest an imaginary character with Carlisle's complex temperament would have risked the prototype overweighing the rôle demanded by the narrative.

Accordingly, I devised a scheme for avoiding any projection at all of Carlisle as model for the Commanding Officer of the Section described in the book, while at the same time not abandoning MIL for Carlisle's replacement. The second-in-command (deceased by the time I was writing the novel) was far from a nonentity, but, in a novel, would at the same time not complicate relations with the other characters.

The Commanding Officer of the Section in *The Military Philosophers*, therefore, instead of bearing some approximation to Lieutenant-Colonel J. C. D. Carlisle, DSO MC, is Lieutenant-Colonel Lysander Finn, VC, who (apart from certain invented civilian associations) is a fairly authentic portrait-sketch of Major A. E. Ker, VC. The reason for going into this Carlisle/Ker transference in some detail will be seen later.

In practice Ker (whose middle name was Ebenezer) never exercised the seniority that made him second-in-command more than by deputizing in the Colonel's room when Carlisle himself was on leave or sick. In no other sense did Ker take charge or give orders. A solicitor by profession (Writer to the Signet before the Court of Session in Scotland), he had stayed on in the army for several years after the first war (in which his Victoria Cross was generally agreed to have been an Homeric one), and, in spite of comparatively advanced age (b. 1883), managed to find early army employment in the second war too; somehow throughout its course always dodging the superannuation which would certainly have descended on most officers of his rank and years.

Ker was one of the nicest of men, which may have played some part in this easygoing attitude of the military authorities, though that quality does not always yield a dividend, either in the army or elsewhere. He had often been offered promotion, but preferred to remain a GSO 2 in MIL, where, with two captains to assist him, he looked after the Neutrals, some of whom from time to time were elevated into Allies.

The Neutrals included certain delicate components, such as Jugoslavia and Portugal, not to mention Turkey. The Portuguese military attaché, for example, was so highly strung that he could not bear to be kept waiting for two minutes. As it happened, the Portuguese colonel's routine weekly interview took place immediately after Carlisle's similar routine weekly interview with the Director of Staff Duties, a major-general, preponderant in War Office affairs, and not to be hurried. Every week the Portuguese military attaché nearly had a stroke in Carlisle's room, on the assumption that he had been forgotten. Ker was adept at calming him down.

Deafness was a handicap from which Ker suffered, but was prepared to put to good use when that suited him. He was smallish, immensely broad, with a huge nose like Punchinello. Normally he would wear a peaked cap and General Service badges, but, if he had to take a foreign officer on an expedition, he would assume the first-war rig of a field-officer in the Gordon Highlanders, glengarry, tartan breeches, top boots —or Gertie Millar boots, as they were sometimes called by older officers, thereby commemorating a famous Edwardian Gaiety Girl. Pressures of work would sometimes discompose Ker, but on the whole he seemed to extract a good deal of enjoyment out of the devices and desires of the Neutrals, particularly when they blossomed into Allies.

It would be hard to imagine two men more consummately different from each other in outward appearance, temperament, background, approach to life, almost everything else, than Ker from Carlisle. In civil life Carlisle was a City figure, banker and businessman, who had served with distinction (as his decorations indicated) in the first war with Queen Victoria's Rifles, a London Territorial unit. Though now officially in the Intelligence Corps, he always wore the black buttons of a Rifleman.

Jack Carlisle, in his early fifties, tall, slim, good-looking, with candid blue eyes that looked straight at you, possessed a charm of manner of which he was himself not at all unaware. He worked immensely hard, found delegation of duties difficult, indulged in a good deal of intrigue, especially as to his own longed-for promotion. Imbued with an overwhelming respect for his superiors in rank, he rapturously longed for the red capband and red tabs of a full colonel; even a 'local' unpaid full colonelcy. He was always telling senior officers how 'rank conscious' were foreigners. In fact, foreign officers always seemed to me to make less heavy weather about rank than in our own army, though in exile they were no doubt to some extent (General de Gaulle always excepted) on their best behaviour.

Carlisle's promotion would have been well deserved in the light of the responsibilities which fell on him, often far beyond those coming the way of most lieutenant-colonels. Red tabs would not have been inappropriate in the light of some of the exalted personages with whom he had to deal, considering, too, some of those who sported them, anyway until 1942, when 2,000 Regular officers were put on the retired list. Perhaps Carlisle overplayed his hand. The favour was never conferred by those who disposed of such sugarplums.

4

The postscript to my scrupulous substitution of Ker for Carlisle came in 1968. Not long after *The Military Philosophers* appeared in that year, Carlisle, then in his eighties—rather to my surprise, as he used to make some play with the fact that he rarely read a book—wrote saying he had greatly enjoyed the novel, and would like me to lunch with him when I was next in London.

The date was arranged. I had expected—indeed slightly feared—a tête-à-tête, but Mrs Carlisle (of whom her husband stood in the deepest awe) decided this was a good opportunity to work off certain social commitments of her own, so that in the event, at a comparatively large luncheon-party which included both sexes, Carlisle had little or no opportunity to talk privately with me at all (it was his own invariable practice to speak of talking 'with', rather than 'to', someone), much less discuss the book in detail. When I left the party, however, he grasped my hand, and, moving a little aside, spoke in a low tense voice:

'You know, Tony, you *oughtn't* to have given me a VC.'

It was clear (even more so when he played me a return at lunch) that he had accepted Finn as an exact portrait of himself.

5

The officer to whom I was apportioned as assistant was listed on the door of the MIL room as *Captain A. Dru, Intelligence Corps.* He wore spectacles, General Service badges, a blue side-cap. His manner was precise, perfectly agreeable, but not in the least forthcoming.

Alexander Dru (who married Gabriel Herbert, sister of Laura Herbert, Evelyn Waugh's second wife) makes an appearance in *Messengers of Day*, though scarcely anything is said there of a friend of extraordinary brilliance and subtlety, met not through any of the many people we turned out to know in common (until then I had never heard Dru's name), but quite fortuitously when thrown together in the army. A faint projection of Alick Dru's personality (as David Pennistone) is also given in *The Military Philosophers*, because (short of attempting something on the lines of the Carlisle/Ker transference) the fact could not be evaded that Dru and I were at that period the only two War Office liaison officers with the Polish army authorities in London. The lightly pencilled outline of Pennistone leaves immensities unhinted about Dru's nature and gifts, though I hope some spark survives of his wit and style.

Alick Dru, about eighteen months older than myself, not yet married, had been up at Cambridge, afterwards briefly at the Sorbonne in Paris. His father was French (a family to have provided *présidents* of the pre-Revolutionary *parlements* of the Franche Comté, the province on the Swiss frontier); his mother (who had been dead for some years) coming from one of the Lancashire Roman Catholic families.

I never met Dru's father, who lived in England, but I believe remained a complete Frenchman to the end of his days. His son, an only child, had been brought up as an Englishman, but an Englishman habituated from the start to Continental life. Alick Dru could remember a birthday in pre-Revolutionary St Petersburg, when, wanting an iced cake, he had been disappointed with one covered with cream and wild strawberries. He used sometimes to recall this cake with nostalgia in the war years. He had been guest at shooting-parties in remotest Ruthenia. France was known as a second country, together with an abiding attraction towards Swiss intellectual life, as if nearness of family origins still exerted some hold.

Dru, speaking French as easily as English, was only a shade less fluent in German. To say that one met in him a Frenchman translated into an Englishman is tempting, but not wholly true. In some ways he could be very English. When, on his father's death after the second war, he inherited some house property in Paris, Dru insisted on paying the legally required—though rarely discharged—tax on its sale. The French solicitor protested that, if such British whimsicality of behaviour was demanded from him, another firm must be sought. The upshot of Dru's conscienciousness turned out that, not only was the tax rendered, but a fine was also imposed for being a month or more late, delay consequent on finding a new solicitor in delivering the amount.

Dru was fond of saying that all rows in England were because someone thought he had been unjustly treated; all rows in France, because someone supposed he had been treated as a fool. He was always irritated by the cliché that English education produces a type; French education an individual. He insisted that precisely the opposite was true. English education did not bother with 'ideas' as such; 'ideas' in French education being regarded as of the very first importance. Accordingly, an English boy leaving school might or might not be adequately instructed, but he had an open mind. Dru asserted that a French boy was not only taught 'what to think', but—if judged the sort of boy likely to be 'in opposition' —what to think 'in opposition'. Nevertheless Dru always loved the French mind, and would comment on the pleasure of returning to Balzac after much reading of the Russian novelists, the clarity of the Latin after the obfuscations of the Slav.

Perhaps one might compromise by describing Dru as looking at things from an English standpoint, while pondering them in a French manner. His jet black hair (never grey even in later life), powerfully lensed spectacles (not inhibiting an air of elegance), something about the suits he wore (though unquestionably cut in London), contributed to an exterior in some manner distinctly French, but it was the line along which Dru's thought moved which made the inner Frenchness most manifest. His mind (in my own experience equalled in speed at reaching the essential point only by Constant Lambert's) was of lethal quickness. This instantaneousness of energy in speech—and action—was sometimes counterbalanced by bouts of *je m'en fichisme*, these contrary elements warring within him perhaps recognizable as a not unusual French amalgam.

Dru, after coming down from Cambridge, worked for a time in an oil company, spending a year or more in the US, a sojourn he hardly ever spoke of, one which seemed to have left surprisingly little impression on him. He possessed to a high degree the capacity for shutting himself off from all round about, if so disposed, and he may have done that in America. The work (which he described as 'easy') had bored him. He disengaged himself from oil. When I asked if no parental objection had been made to this abandonment of all visible means of support, Dru had laughed a lot, agreeing certain pressures had been brought to bear. Finally his father (with whom he was on the best of terms) made no great difficulties about allowing his son to go his own way.

In the years before the second war Dru represented to most of his friends the ideal 'spare man' for concert or dinner-party (Violet, who had met him then, says he danced beautifully), attending musical evenings (he played the piano rather well himself), reading much and promiscuously, with a leaning towards works in French and German on the subject of religion and philosophy. A Roman Catholic of profound—though incessantly searching—belief, he was on the whole inclined to frequent Catholic circles (no doubt one of the reasons we never met), a relatively enclosed world; though Osbert Sitwell, who knew Dru slightly, told me he associated him with the T. S. Eliot environment.

Such amorphous studies as might seem to engage Dru's attention in this pre-war period were not taken with undue seriousness by most of his friends. Throughout his life it would have been possible—though perhaps not very perceptive—for a fellow-guest to have spent an evening in

Dru's company without carrying away much more personal impression than an uncontrollable *fou rire* when amused, and (though Dru was no wine snob) a taste for vintage claret. A certain aura of mystery—not wholly dissipated even when one knew him well—was vested in Dru's unwillingness, indeed almost total inability, to be explicit about himself or anything that had happened to him.

In the course of all this apparently desultory pre-war reading Dru had come on the works of the Danish philosopher and theologian, Søren Kierkegaard (1813—1855), by then translated fairly widely into German. Kafka, for instance, notes in his Diary for 1913 that he had been reading Kierkegaard; in a letter four years later writing: 'Kierkegaard is a star, although he shines over territory that is almost inaccessible to me.' In the English-speaking world Kierkegaard was still little known and to Dru was a *coup de foudre*. Dru's Catholicism did not at all preclude being carried away by a Protestant theologian, who, though greatly dissatisfied with the Lutheran Church of Denmark in his day, had himself planned to become a pastor.

Dru at once set about learning Danish with a view to translating Kierkegaard's *Journals* (Dru's selection from which appeared in 1938), later also the satirical essay, *The Present Age*, in other respects pioneering the philosopher's recognition in English. He remained absorbed in Kierkegaard all his life, writing about him intermittently, though never producing the major study probably once planned. Dru always said the name phonetically in English, and in the War Office we produced a limerick celebrating this usage, and also Dru's habitual disregard for his own surroundings:

> In the Mess on the staff of a Corps,
> To avoid seeming pedant or bore,
> Dru pronounced the 'd' hard,
> When he spoke of 'churchyard'
> In Danish—that is 'kierkegaard'.

Dru often complained that critics insufficiently emphasized Kierkegaard's aesthetic side. He insisted that the philosopher should be thought of in terms of a poet or novelist, say Baudelaire or Dostoevski. All the same one has to admit that Kierkegaard never managed to weld into any supreme form of literary expression the three archetypal figures that obsessed him: Don Juan (sensuality), Faust (doubt), Ahasuerus the Wandering Jew (despair).

Kierkegaard, like Blake, is claimed as an early Existentialist, and Dru, believing passionately in individual choice, shared existentialist distaste for abstract thought, philosophies advocating what is outside ordinary human experience. Like Kierkegaard (in whom religious life was the aim), or Nietzsche (with a very different goal), Dru held that mysticism could be approached—was perhaps best approached—through the arts. To non-Christian Existentialists, religion, philosophy, ordered morality, are merely methods of avoiding the issue in solving the disastrous predicament in which man finds himself, and—as I understand it—their sense of absurdity, their despair, is all they have in common with the Christian Existentialism attributed to Kierkegaard.

Dru would have enjoyed the American poet Delmore Schwartz's observation: 'Existentialism means that no one can take a bath for you', and I should have liked to hear Dru's judgment on Schwartz's short story in which a character remarks: 'Kierkegaard . . . thinks there are three fundamental attitudes to existence—the aesthetic, the ethical, and the religious. Probably as good an illustration as any other would be a situation in which you wanted to kiss the wife of a friend. If you were aesthetic you would kiss her without compunction, and like it very much. If you were ethical, you'd take a sedative . . . if you were religious, you'd neither kiss the lady nor take a sedative.'

In fact, Kierkegaard's own sole involvement with a woman was a painful broken engagement, an experience to make him victim of much psychological investigation. Dru found that side intensely boring, the very term 'subconscious' irritating him. Nevertheless, many of the writers in whom Dru was himself interested were close to the sources of modern psychology. Dru's own attitude towards sex was an enigmatic one. He was not in the least averse from bawdy jokes—would laugh a lot over them—but, where he himself was concerned, possessed an armour-plated withdrawnness, a way of being aloof from the small-change of army badinage in that respect which seemed to be granted in a surprisingly universal manner as if by common consent.

Although Dru could scarcely have been less Scandinavian in outlook (differing from Kierkegaard in many other ways too), he did perhaps accept a touch of self-identification in concentrating on this peculiar and tormented figure, who, in the popular mind, has become prototype of intellectually pretentious name-dropping. In fact, so far from being an austere hermit, Kierkegaard (inheriting some capital when a young man) was for a time (in the Baudelairean sense) a dandy, a wit, a gourmet, a tease, who liked leg-pulling and getting tight. He himself says somewhere 'the humorist, like the wild animal, walks alone', and there is perhaps no real paradox in the fact that Kierkegaard was also desperately exercised about his own spiritual state. I do not suggest that Dru existed in any such agonized condition (nor was he, as in Kierkegaard's more worldly aspect, a tease), but something was shared in love of religious contemplation, while at the same time being regarded by those round about as a *flâneur*.

Dru's outward attitude to his own Catholicism differed considerably from that of many of his Communion, especially most of the converts who were contemporaries. He agreed that it might be said of himself *Yes, we have no Bernanos*, and would remark: 'Of course it's quite absurd to suppose that some sort of Reformation would not have taken place sooner or later', or 'I find such-and-such as difficult to believe as in a Future Life.' I once asked Dru if he had ever thought of going into the Church himself. He laughed, and said: 'No—but perhaps I wouldn't have minded being a very political bishop.'

I have dwelt rather long on the side of Dru fascinated by Kierkegaard, but something of that must be understood to appreciate what Dru himself was like to work with in the War Office.

6

Even those of Alick Dru's friends with clearer notions than others of his intellectual potential never guessed that the war would transform him into a staff-officer of exceptional ability. Something of the sort must, however, have crossed the mind of the major-general (an acquaintance through some merely social contact) responsible in the first instance for recruiting Dru into the army a few months before the outbreak of war. This senior officer, at that moment Director of Military Intelligence at the War Office, answered a request for an additional assistant at the British military attaché's office in Paris by causing Dru to be gazetted an immediate emergency commission and posted to the appointment.

The General in question must be admitted thereby not only to have shown admirable disregard for bureaucratic procedure, but remarkable prescience in respect of Dru's hidden capabilities, outward military qualifications being nil. Naturally this period was one of the greatest activity in Paris. Several officers who came across Dru during that turmoil emphasized to me how well he kept his end up, one Regular using the phrase 'the earthiness of his [Dru's] logic in military matters'. It was the perfect justification of Admiral Lord Fisher's precept: 'Favouritism is the soul of efficiency'.

After the Fall of France Dru was sent on one of the early (Minley Manor) War Intelligence Courses, serving briefly at a Corps HQ, then going to the War Office, where he remained in liaison with the Poles throughout the war, being promoted major soon after my own arrival there.

In the ever varying, sometimes quite delicate, duties of MIL, Dru was habitually good mannered, taking immense pains to sort out intricate and tedious liaison problems, but, not at all given to military brusquerie, he was equally free from too much of that English liking to be thought a good fellow. In the War Office the vast majority were efficient and courteous, at worst grumpily correct. If Dru, in matters that seemed to him of prime importance, came up against obstruction or blockheadedness in an officer (or civil servant), he could be inflexible, use the sort of phraseology that got home. He did not at all mind making people angry, which he certainly contrived to do from time to time, and was not in the least impressed by rank.

The work Dru and I shared was chiefly transacted with the Polish military attaché, Major-General Bronislaw Regulski (Bobrowski in *The Military Philosophers*) and his staff. Regulski's office at 53 New Cavendish Street later housed the surgery of my immediately post-war dentist, in whose dental chair I would sit in a room where formerly I had discussed Polish military affairs. MIL also had close contacts with Polish GHQ in London (The Rubens Hotel, Buckingham Palace Road), where Major-General Klimecki (pronounced Klimetzki) was Chief of Staff. After working with Dru for more than a year Klimecki expressed utter astonishment on learning that he was not *officier de carrière*. Klimecki died in the disastrous plane crash which deprived the Poles of an irreplaceable leader in General Wladislaw Sikorski.

The Poles, high spirited, gallant, ever unfortunate, were stimulating to work with. By the time I arrived in the War Office there was already great uneasiness as to whereabouts of 15,000 Polish officers deported after the Russian invasion of Poland to the Soviet Union, and not identified as among those Polish units known to have been transferred to Central Asia. At this period it was thought by the London Poles that the missing officers had been exiled to distant camps within the Arctic Circle. Their atrocious massacre by the Russians at Katyn was to emerge only later.

After about nine months of Polish liaison I was sent on a week's tour of duty in Scotland to make contact with the British Liaison Headquarters attached to the Polish Corps there, and see something of troops known only on paper. Rationing, I found, was not taken with undue seriousness north of the Tweed (the west of England later turned out to have an equally relaxed attitude), the London area throughout the war being by far the most meagre source of food and drink, which, when lacking, come to play an almost obsessional part in daily life.

The chief medical officer at Polish Liaison HQ, Colonel Archer Irvine-Fortescue, was a personality whose visits to the War Office always brightened the day. He was equally amusing—and hospitable—on his own ground (where further north Fortescue was a laird), when he accompanied me to some of the Polish units. 'Among four British lunatics,' he said, 'three are perfectly easy to deal with, one impossible. Among these people that is different. Of four Polish lunatics, one is easy to deal with, three impossible.'

Fortescue (who sometimes announced himself on the War Office telephone as Fortèscu, a Rumanian officer) kept alive, like Ker, first-war turnout of breeches and boots for field-officers (majors and above), in Fortescue's case not merely for special occasions. With crimson capband and tabs of an RAMC full colonel, a row of foreign decorations, he was a picturesque figure. He had served at one time or another in all sorts of obscure campaigns and exotic corps, including the Persian Cossack Division.

When (November, 1944) we moved back into Chester Gate, and the Drus for a time lodged with us, Colonel Fortescue, at that moment stationed in London, would visit us, sometimes, flu very prevalent, in a professional capacity, on which occasions he would always address Violet as 'Matron'. All that was a long way ahead.

7

Dru and Carlisle had a complicated relationship, which in itself would have ruled out the possibility of using a projection of Carlisle in a novel; a whole volume scarcely sufficing to do justice to its psychological implications.

Carlisle's respect for Dru's judgment made him unwilling to incur his subordinate's displeasure, but, if up to a point Dru dominated Carlisle, Carlisle's manner of looking at things (and implementing them) was in such absolute contrast to Dru's approach to life that sheer philosophic bewilderment at such deviousness would momentarily cause Dru to lose his hold. Dru could be shrewd enough, but what he thought and did was always based on strong principle. Carlisle could astonish by a perpetual willingness to abandon principle for the pragmatic.

As already remarked, Carlisle did his job uncommonly well, working unremittingly, taking decisions (as indeed did even majors and captains of the MI directorate) exceeding what might be thought normal to his rank. At the same time his obsequiousness to superiors (he would enrage Dru by a grotesque habit of addressing senior civil servants as 'sir'), his extreme resilience under setback, were all things to be discussed unendingly. He became a kind of cult to Dru and myself, and one could feel a real affection for him. Carlisle was, indeed, a near-Shakespearian figure, who would have been superb proclaiming in blank verse, like Polonius, his personal rules of conduct in life.

8

My own normal War Office routine was to arrive at half-past nine, knock off as a rule at seven or soon after in the evening, if nothing special in the way of work had arisen. That was the usual day for captains and majors (between which ranks no distinction was made, that being chiefly a matter of what 'establishment' had been laid down for a particular Section), though some heads of Sections, like Carlisle, would keep later hours, senior officers often working long into the night. There was one free day a week, which most people saved up to make two at the end of a fortnight, so that if possible they could get away for the weekend.

After a certain amount of moving about in an effort to find a place to live, Violet, with Tristram, finally went to Shoreham in Kent, about twenty miles south of London, a house called Dunstall Priory belonging to Lord Dunsany, the writer, who had married her mother's younger sister. The Dunsanys themselves had retired to Ireland, where they had a castle. Most of the rooms at Dunstall, not large, but rambling, were out of commission in wartime, just enough being left open to make living there possible.

Shoreham, much painted by Samuel Palmer (giving a name to Blake's disciples the Shoreham Ancients), was still the scene of astonishingly Palmer-like cloud effects in the northern sky at evening. At the end of a summer day the black smoke of London would drift south, then, as it were, stop dead in the heavens at a given point towards the setting sun, recalling the extravagant colours spoken of earlier over the Cretan mountains. There was in any case something strange about the Shoreham landscape, which caused foreign visitors to Dunstall in wartime—Polish, Belgian, French—all to insist that the wooded hills and water meadows that surrounded the house strikingly recalled their own country.

Although there was no strategic target in the immediate neighbourhood, the RAF station at Biggin Hill was not far away, so that at one moment Shoreham was proclaimed by the BBC as the 'most bombed parish in the United Kingdom'. This may also have come about because, as anti-aircraft defence put up an increasingly hot barrage, German bombers jettisoned their cargo some way short of London, more quickly to return home. For whatever reason, the place was much blitzed. The only occasion during the war when I descended to a cellar during a raid was at a Dunstall weekend. We had managed to get hold of an onion or two, and, a great treat, just sat down to a curry. Then a fierce raid began, which went on right above the house. This continued for at least forty minutes. It seemed wise to move Tristram from the room upstairs, and, following Sir George Sitwell's advice to Osbert Sitwell, then in the army during the first war, if a bombardment took place, 'retire to the undercroft', for the moment abandoning the curry.

In one of these raids a direct hit caused wholesale tragedy at a farm of people known to us on the hill just above Dunstall. Incendiaries especially used to hail down. When the Belgian military attaché, Major Kronacker (of whom more later), spent a Sunday with us, we went for a walk in the afternoon through fields which seemed to have been sown with dragon's teeth, incendiary bombs, exploded and unexploded, lying every few yards, including a whole basketful which had failed to ignite.

In June, 1944, the flying-bombs (V-1s) came into action, the first of such raids persisting night and day, every few minutes without cease, for seventy or more hours on end. These were perhaps the most trying form of attack from the air. They were followed by the V-2 rockets—the 'dull deferred explosion' of Eliot's *Four Quartets*—which, descending without warning, were less hard on the nerves. Shoreham subsequently turned out to be on the direct route of the flying bombs' course to London.

The day's work over at the War Office (the building itself hit by bombs more than a dozen times, but never seriously damaged), I would as a rule take bus straight to the Lord Nelson, a pub just by the Chelsea Palace music-hall, not far from where I lived; at first a flat in the King's Road, then one in Sloane Avenue. Dinner at The Lord Nelson was tolerable by wartime standards, a lively couple, husband and wife, waiter and waitress there. Some of the husband's *mots* are embedded in my novel. Once he remarked: 'I worry too much—Shakespeare's dying words.'

After dinner I would return to my one-room flat, get into bed right away with some book likely to be useful in writing the Aubrey biography. In this manner a good deal of fairly operose 17th century material was painlessly absorbed; war lending attraction to the prosiest aspects of the past, works like Toland's *History of the Druids*, or Hearne's *Remarks and Recollections*, calming to the spirit while the blitz was reverberating through the night air.

The worst of the blitz—short of being hit—was the manner in which its detonations murdered sleep. One's windows would occasionally be blown in, flying-bombs were undoubtedly disagreeable when they floated over, three at a time, just before one rose from bed in the morning, cutting out their buzz (prelude to explosion) immediately above (as it always seemed) the block of flats, but the chronic burden, as time went on increasing attrition, was trying to concentrate on work after a series of sleepless nights.

Sometimes I would draw my rations, and eat in the flat. Behind the block was a small Italian shop (apparently unaffected by Italy fighting on the other side) where I used to go once a week for butter, bacon, cheese. A very pretty Italian girl, Nina, dispensed these. She was possibly Cypriot, a race then British subjects, which—so my restaurateur friend, Castano, had told me—had taken over many outwardly Italian businesses. Some weeks, without a word, Nina would put double rations on the counter. Nothing was ever said on either side. I have always thought this a poetic relationship; one to have been adumbrated, in their different manner, by Stendhal or James.

9

One reads of 'literary life' in wartime London: Connolly and *Horizon*; a younger generation, mostly on leave from the Forces, dredging the Soho and Fitzroy Street pubs for cultural contacts. These last ports of call were in general off my own beat even in leisure hours, and, although more than once Connolly exhorted me to produce something just to 'get my name into the Index' of his magazine, I never found a moment (or theme) to do so, seeing him very rarely during this period, reading *Horizon* not much more often.

After the war, reviewing the selection called *The Golden Horizon*, I was able to appreciate the good work Connolly did (between Christmas, 1939, and New Year, 1950) of a kind no one else could have achieved in quite the same manner. 'I fall an easy victim to political quacks and neurotic journalists', he wrote of himself, such leanings keeping the magazine from becoming too officially respectable; while the editor exercised his own particular mixture of enthusiasm, irritability, humour, romanticism, self-pity, attention, inattention, and finally boredom with the whole affair. The image of Connolly's editorship in the closing years of *Horizon* was of a kind of Pentheus in reverse, a man held together by Maenads, rather than torn asunder by those ladies.

After my first meeting with George Orwell at the Café Royal (*Infants of the Spring*) we used to see each other on and off, but, drink in short supply, anything like a night out was a rarity. In any case fairly chronic fatigue at the end of the day kept one from seeking out those with whom something of the sort might have been envisaged. As remarked, my chief memory of the war is feeling consistently tired; and perfectly awful on mornings-after, when quite exceptionally, some sort of a carousal had been celebrated.

Such an occasion happened soon after my arrival in the War Office, which coincided with Malcolm Muggeridge's preferment from Field Security to the Secret Service. Muggeridge, after we had dined together, took me to see an old friend of his from Cairo University days, Bonamy Dobrée, a Regular soldier turned Eng. Lit. professor, now, like the man in the Kipling poem, back to the army again. Dobrée produced several bottles of Algerian wine. Muggeridge and I left at a late hour, both able to walk, but got lost in the blackout in the wilds of Camden Town. No one was about. Then miraculously—or we should have perished utterly— a car came out of the darkness and slowed up.

'Are you a taxi?' Muggeridge asked.

'No,' said the man. 'I'm a taxi-driver.'

One night Alick Dru and Osbert Sitwell dined with me at the Travellers Club, afterwards both of them witnessing a will I had just made: Dru recording his profession as 'Major, General Staff'; Sitwell as 'Poet and Justice of the Peace'.

Dru said how much he had always looked forward to being an old man, quoting a story about General Boulanger (a favourite character of his), would-be dictator of France in the 1880s. Boulanger had been making a speech containing some Napoleonic reference, at which some member of the audience had shouted: 'Monsieur, à votre âge Bonaparte était mort.' Osbert Sitwell said: 'Nevertheless, all the things the old men told one when one was young turn out to be absolutely true.'

It may have been the same evening that Osbert Sitwell related a story about the Duke of Cambridge, Queen Victoria's first cousin, who, as Commander-in-Chief, had for many years opposed all change in the army; expressing the opinion (according to my father) that 'he saw no reason why one gentleman should not command a regiment as well as another'. News had come to the ears of the Duke that an outbreak of venereal disease had taken place at Sandhurst. He set off for the Royal Military College at once, *en civil*, carrying as ever a rolled umbrella, to deliver a rebuke. When the cadets were all assembled, the Duke of Cambridge waved the umbrella above his head. He thundered: 'I hear you boys have been putting your private parts where I wouldn't put this umbrella!'

If Dru was an unusual brother-officer, so too in quite another manner was Major E. C. Bradfield, lightly outlined as Dempster in *The Military Philosophers*. Bradfield, who some called Ted, some Charlie, was on the whole known to most of the Section as Bradders. He worked with the Norwegians, with whom he communicated in fluent Danish, the two languages being sufficiently similar to make no great matter. The Norwegian Government in exile did not dispose of many soldiers, but controlled an extensive merchant navy, of great importance in the war.

Now in his middle fifties, Bradfield had been awarded a Military Cross on the Western Front in the first war, a Bar to it in the War of Intervention against the Bolsheviks, 1918/19, when he had served in the neighbourhood of Archangel. Smallish, wiry, quite bald, Bradfield's features, anyway the upper part of his face, resembled that of the Emperor Vespasian, oddly enough a Roman head to be seen in Bradfield's adopted capital, Copenhagen. Bradfield was a man of notable good nature where his colleagues were concerned (if not handled carefully could be at first suspicious of officers from other Sections), and, highly strung not to say neurotic, would yell with wild laughter in which always lurked a sense of the deepest melancholy.

On one occasion, when the general in charge of the Intelligence Directorate (not the one who had enrolled Dru) arrived in the MIL room early one morning to make some enquiry, he found Bradfield (demonstrating that he could perform that gymnastic) standing on his head. As well as this exuberant side, Bradfield had an obsession with personal cleanliness, Dru alleging (something not denied by Bradfield's complexion) that he scrubbed himself all over every morning with a wire brush. He was a feverishly energetic worker, ever agitated by problems of 'security', especially in relation to how much more or less secret information might safely be released to the Allies.

An altogether phenomenal egotist when it came to talking about himself, Bradfield would treat his own past history as something with which everybody in the room should be thoroughly conversant. At the same time a few matters in that respect always remained obscure in a life story recited at the length, somewhat in the manner, of a Norse Saga. Dru and I used to reach a pitch of near hysteria, when, for the thousandth time, Bradfield would invoke some hero or heroine of his personal myth, phantoms indeed often strange enough. Bradfield accepted this helpless laughter as tribute to his own anecdote.

Bradfield's history was as out of the way as his personality. Ostensibly the son (youngest child by several years in a comparatively large family) of a Norfolk farmer and his wife, he seemed from his earliest days to have been under the wing of a Danish margarine tycoon named Horniman, who had formed the habit of making an annual visit to East Anglia for the fox-hunting season. Finally Mr Horniman (always referred to as 'my guardian') more or less adopted Bradfield as his son. Speculation was irresistible as to whether a blood relationship did not indeed exist between them, an ambiguity by no means diminished by Bradfield's own features. In fact Dru—familiar with clerical aspects of Danish life from Kierke-gaard studies, and producing book illustrations to prove his point—used to say: 'All Bradders needs to make him look a typical 19th century Danish pastor is a black gown and ruff round his neck.'

When Bradfield left home at sixteen or seventeen employment had been found for him (no doubt owing to the good offices of Mr Horniman) at the Danish Consulate in London. There his first duty had been to escort an intoxicated Danish sailor from the Consulate to the Docks en route for his ship. During their longish journey in a horse-cab the sailor had spent the whole time masturbating, an incident Bradfield could never banish from his mind, and would repeatedly iterate.

Later Bradfield was transferred to Copenhagen with a view to initiation into the operating of the margarine business his guardian controlled. Mr Horniman also presumably arranged the lodgings which his ward now occupied in Copenhagen. These were kept by the widow of Paul Gauguin, the French post-Impressionist. Gauguin, in his days on the Paris *bourse*, had picked up two Danish girls in a restaurant, and subsequently married one of them. She was called Metta Sophia Gadd, and came from a fairly prosperous family. After Gauguin abandoned the stockmarket for painting in Tahiti, his wife (without appreciation of her husband's pictures as works of art, but later not indifferent to their increasing financial value) returned to her own country, where, no doubt having to earn some sort of a living, she let rooms.

Madame Gauguin—Madame Gau*guing*, as Bradfield always called her

—was one of the major figures in the Bradfield Saga. She must have been in her sixties when he lodged with her, plainly a formidable lady, both from his own account and surviving photographs of the early 1900s. Bradfield's anecdotes were hard to piece together for preservation, as he laughed so much while telling them, but a recurrent one was how a fellow-lodger, a Danish young man, being one day too lazy to visit the lavatory, relieved himself into a piece of brown paper, made up a parcel tied with string, which he then threw out of the window. Unfortunately a caller *chez* Madame Gauguin was at that moment approaching the front-door. The package, bursting on impact, scored a direct hit. Understandably, there was a colossal row; a Scandinavian incident worthy of Strindberg at his grimmest.

Mr Horniman owned a castle in Jutland, Nørlund, which he left to Bradfield for life; would indeed have bequeathed the property absolutely, had Bradfield agreed to go into the margarine business. I am not sure what Bradfield himself wanted to do, possibly become a musician, since he was a pianist of sufficient accomplishment to give public recitals from time to time. Before the war he had farmed the Nørlund estate, an occupation he thoroughly enjoyed, living most of the time in a small house nearby the castle.

After the war farming and music absorbed Bradfield's life, Dru in a letter to me saying: 'Bradders . . . gives (a) a report on the storm damage to the Nørlund woods in cubic feet (b) a piano arrangement for the Londonderry Air . . . which would sound like three pianolas playing simultaneously.'

Though not badly disposed towards women, Bradfield always spoke disparagingly of his own powers in attracting them, and he never married. At the time of the German invasion of Denmark, April, 1940, he was lending a hand at the much overworked British Embassy in Copenhagen, since he was a passionately patriotic Briton in spite of domicile abroad. Having no diplomatic status he was held by the German authorities, the question of internment arising. No doubt partly owing to his age, he was told he would be less trouble, administratively speaking, if he proceeded to England, where German troops would in any case arrive within three weeks. Bradfield immediately rejoined the army on return to London, and was at once posted to MIL.

II

In the summer of 1949 Bradfield invited Violet and myself to Nørlund. The Castle (which had never belonged to one Danish family for more than at most a couple of generations), though much reconditioned, dated from the 12th century, the architecture characteristically Scandinavian. Crossing a bridge over the moat, which completely surrounded the inner buildings, a courtyard was entered through the archway of a kind of gatehouse or stable block. Here, dominated by an onion-domed tower, stood two wings at right-angles to each other, one used as an orphanage, the other inhabited by Bradfield only during the months of the year when he entertained guests. On the chimney of the orphans' wing storks appropriately nested.

At Nørlund, which was in the neighbourhood of Aarhus, notwith-standing six years of war and the German occupation, one had the impression of entering a world changed hardly at all from what provincial Denmark must have been in the 19th century. In the evening, lighted by the moon, we took long midnight drives in a carriage drawn by two horses, motor-tyre wheels designed to run smoothly over the sandy Jutland soil. On Sunday, at a long table in the dining-hall of the Castle, a crowd of neighbours, the pastor, the schoolmaster, local farmers, would sit down to *smørrebrød*, beer, aquavit, gossip, beasts, the crops.

If much seemed unchanged from an earlier epoch that was not because the record of the Danish Resistance had been less than a very fine one; something perhaps insufficiently appreciated in other countries. When Bradfield took us visiting in the neighbourhood one constantly heard of Danes who had sacrificed their lives in this cause.

The Castle itself had been used by the Germans as some sort of military school. When Bradfield returned to Nørlund to get his home into working order again, the moment came to light the stove in the Great Hall. The fuel was about to be put in, when an old retainer counselled the wisdom of making a thorough examination before that was done. A long iron bar was thrust into the deepest recesses of the stove. Right at the back of the fire-place floor, deliberately concealed, was found enough high-explosive to have blown up at least one wing of the Castle.

Among other Jutland neighbours we were taken to see was Bradfield's

Danish friend, Ole Benson, who had played a courageous part in the Resistance. Mr Benson's lifelong hobby was miniature railways. He had spent many years in perfecting a railway system in one of the rooms of his house (which we were shown), not only an impressive toy famous in the neighbourhood, but the superstructure under which the munitions of the Resistance fighters had been concealed.

During the German occupation Benson's underground activities had never been discovered by the German authorities, though there had been some bad moments. The worst of these had been when an officer of the Gestapo had called at the Benson house to say that the Chief of the Gestapo in Denmark wished to talk to Herr Benson himself. The officer had come to arrange an appointment. Benson thought that now all was up. There was no alternative but to name a day.

The Chief of the Gestapo arrived in due course and was shown in. At first he only made conversation. Benson became increasingly uneasy. The German seemed in some way embarrassed about getting to the point. At last with an effort he brought out what he had come to say. All was revealed. The Chief of the Gestapo was a railway fanatic. He had made the visit in person in order to ask whether Herr Benson would be kind enough to allow him to come round one afternoon a week to play with Herr Benson's model railway. Benson agreed, but only on condition that the Chief of the Gastapo wore plain clothes. This he did, while he sent the miniature engines rattling over a cache of Danish Resistance arms.

VIII

Departmental Exchanges

In wartime London, owing to the blitz, houses and flats were easily found, large scale sharing of these a commonplace of the times. Dru had belonged to such a commune in a relatively large and luxurious flat in Arlington Street, Piccadilly, but by the time I first met him, his co-tenants had sunk to one, a Treasury official seconded to the Cabinet Office. This Arlington Street accommodation becoming expensive even in war-time for only two persons, they moved, remaining together as a matter of convenience, to one of the blocks surrounding the Roman Catholic cathedral in Westminster, a flat Dru eventually took over when he married.

One of the earlier temporary inhabitants of the Arlington Street flat had been a former Cambridge undergraduate acquaintance of Dru's, a barrister in civil life, then a major (perhaps already lieutenant-colonel) on the military staff of the Cabinet Office. Dru (combining play on this friend's double-barrelled name, creed, demeanour, personal appearance) used to speak of him as The Papal Bun, regarding him as a never failing source of laughter, even if a useful contact in the lofty governmental sphere in which The Bun now operated.

Apart from that last practical potential of The Bun, I myself never quite saw his point, while at the same time wholly accepting that, from Dru's field of view, special rules might apply. Where early contemporaries are in question, school, university, anywhere else before the age of twenty, the essences and memories of adolescence, with all their intensity, are largely untransmittable in primitive meaning to those who have never shared them.

'Believe it or not,' Dru used to say, with much laughter. 'When The Bun went down from Cambridge people used actually to *worry* that he would not be able to earn a living.'

That certainly seemed a misplaced valuation of someone evidently proving himself unequivocally successful in wartime, but I could not see precisely why Dru thought that so funny. On the two or three occasions when we met (always with Dru) The Bun had been—to use a favourite Edwardian expression—perfectly civil, no more. I did not find his personality particularly sympathetic; indeed rather the reverse. In such circumstances I was not much less than staggered when one day The Bun announced that he required an assistant for his Cabinet Office job, and would like me to fill the appointment. I can't remember throughout life anything of a similar kind having come my way as quite such a surprise.

This proposed change of employment signified something a little different from a move within the War Office, say gaining promotion by transfer to one of the 'country' Sections (which specialized in information about given geographical areas), or being posted as Intelligence Officer or Liaison Officer to a formation. Military Assistant Secretaries at the Ministry of Defence and Cabinet Office, ranging in rank from major to full colonel (possibly higher), were, Assistant Secretary being a civil service grade, in theory equal with each other in their work. The Cabinet Office—often loosely referred to as the Cabinet Offices—represented not only the focus of government of the country, but also fount of war strategy, expressed in the persons of the Chiefs of Staff of the three Services, the War Cabinet, the Prime Minister himself.

I very much liked working with Dru, the whole Section was agreeable, Polish liaison rewarding. Nevertheless these duties had continued for some fifteen months. Unless the officer establishment of MIL was increased (at that moment no prospect) little likelihood existed of what used to be called in old-fashioned army parlance a 'step'. Not long before his death I had run across Hubert Duggan in White's (the London clubs allowed membership in common when one of their number was bombed), a fellow captain, who had remarked: 'Of course you don't get into the Big Money until you're a major.'

Apart from what would be a very acceptable rise in pay (majors in the Cabinet Office usually not long before becoming lieutenant-colonels), the prospect of viewing the war from this dizzy altitude (in actual practice, from the bowels of the earth) seemed a chance not to be missed.

Carlisle was by no means pleased when informed of this proposal, though he could not very well stand in the way of one of his officers' promotion. He played a delaying tactic, brought abruptly to an end by the arrival of a signal from the Ministry of Defence stating that, unless I reported forthwith to the Cabinet Office, Great George Street, the order would come over at Adjutant-General's level. This awful threat, particularly fearsome to Carlisle, seemed to underline the importance attached to my setting about this job as soon as possible. That was in February, 1943.

To forestall the least suggestion of appearing to make excuses for myself, let me emphasize at once that, to put it mildly, I was not at all a success at my new employment. At the same time—so it seemed to me —I was confronted with a set of circumstances which have cropped up more than once in my life (Balston at Duckworth's providing a slightly similar example), that is to say someone going out of their way to involve me in undertakings of their own, then, that accomplished, showing an extraordinary unwillingness to concede a minimum of initiatory instruction in what was required; indeed almost displaying satisfaction in consequent shortcomings. Perhaps in this, and other instances, I am being unjust. As remarked earlier, probably no job is done well unless done instinctively.

The Joint-Intelligence Staff (Navy, Army, Air Force, Foreign Office, Economic Warfare) included a group of committees, hierarchical in ascent, reaching their apex in the Chiefs of Staff, the last reporting to the War Cabinet and Prime Minister. These committees produced a continuous flow of 'papers' devoted to every conceivable aspect of how the war was, or might be, waged: what would be the result if Portugal joined the Allies; if the Axis invaded Sweden; if the Soviet Union declared war on Japan; every other potential eventuality, usually of a more or less urgent nature.

The main duty assigned to me was to act as secretary (usually two in number, of whom the other was The Bun) summarizing the findings of one of these committees. Arrival at the office was soon after nine, the meeting began at eleven, its sessions as a rule running on to at least half-past seven or eight in the evening. Two or three hours later than that was far from uncommon, though only occasionally did discussion close with midnight. When talk was ended its substance was boiled down by the secretaries (such as myself), a typed copy of the summary being made for each member of the committee to go over first thing the following morning, before returning to register approval or disapproval (in the latter case revision required) at Great George Street. The process would then begin all over again on a new subject.

In short, a fourteen-hour day was quite normal, occasionally an extension of that, protracted effort being expected of the higher echelons in wartime. Such working stretches required considerable physical as well as mental resilience, particularly if the blitz had extinguished sleep the previous night. No doubt the principle of utmost effort was good, though it was possible to wonder whether the best results were always achieved by weary men poring over complicated documents night after night into the small hours.

The duties of a secretary recording minutes of a meeting need a certain flair even at a quite humble level, if they are to be discharged with skill. Where the often conflicting view of the three Services and two government departments were in question, agreement was not always easily arrived at. Much argument could arise over the difference between what had been said, what set down in the 'paper'. The Bun was preternaturally gifted in bringing about acquiescence.

I lasted about nine weeks, relinquishing the appointment without regret, though not without a sense of having fallen abysmally short in failing to give satisfaction in the job. This inadequacy was rubbed in on receiving my *congé*. All ranks of an emergency-commission were temporary, but, if a rank were held down for three months, the rank below became 'substantive'. Thus a major for three months could not go below the rank (and pay) of a captain. A request that I should be allowed to hang on for the tail end of my three months, a fortnight or so to go, was refused. Another appointment as major would certainly have been sought for me by the War Office branch concerned, no doubt found, but, anyway in theory during the interim of unemployment, I should sink from major to lieutenant.

It happened just at this moment that Carlisle required a replacement in MIL. Hearing I was *en disponibilité* he at once applied for me by name. Acceptance would mean a return to the rank of captain, a demotion in principle not well looked on by the appointments branch; nevertheless, as I myself was willing to descend, no serious difficulties were raised. An immediate posting to duties already carried out satisfactorily seemed a great deal preferable to a potential period of unemployment, followed by something out of the lucky dip, which might well prove even more thankless than my recent assignment.

Kenneth Bell, my Balliol tutor (probably recalling his own less than happy publishing experiences before returning to Oxford as a don), used to say: 'Only after a series of ghastly humiliations does one begin to learn the extent of one's own capabilities.' There is much truth in that opinion. The interlude in the sub-basement of Great George Street, however ill-omened, made for clarity in that particular sphere. It brought other advantages too in glimpses of how government worked, what the individuals were like who controlled the machine, much else in the way of previously unfamiliar elements calculated to stir the imagination.

2

While at the Cabinet Office I was impressed on the whole by the relative unimportance of those 'secrets' which play so large a part in novels, and journalism, dealing with official life. One knew, several months before its launching, about the projected invasion of Sicily; a few other operational matters that were *en train*. No doubt certainty on such matters would have been useful to the enemy. Nevertheless, what broadly speaking made up the picture were the varied statistics dealing with such subjects as man-power, munitions, vehicles, oil, above all accurate information as to Axis morale. These things were always changing, needing perpetual collation. They were what mattered.

As war service went, duties at Great George Street did not, on the face of it, constitute a notable hazard. A bomb might fall on military personnel off duty; two floors below street level they were likely to be as safe as anyone could reasonably expect to be in a frequently bombed city. All risks, however, are not from enemy action.

In 1945, not long after the surrender of Japan, the United Nations Charter was signed at San Francisco. Certain members of the Cabinet Office Secretariat were flown to California for duty at this conclave, among them the officer who had in the first instance suggested I should be his assistant. On the return journey to England the plane never reached London. All were lost. How that happened I have never heard, but I could not help reflecting that perhaps greater ability in performing the duties required of me might have led—perhaps as a special treat owing to the prestige attached—to being included in the San Francisco party.

On this subject of violent death during the second war, some reviewer (probably too young to have been alive at that period) complained that too many characters in my novel lost their lives in the Services, implying that casualties had been negligible. It would be mistaken for such a legend to grow up. Casualties in the armed forces were certainly less than in the first war, that did not mean they were non-existent; while in the case of bombed civilians they were much increased.

To catalogue individual instances from my own personal acquaintance is scarcely practicable, but, to quote a single example from the novel, the episode of a husband and wife, each out to dinner with another person, both killed by bombs on the same night, was paralleled by a case known to me. The (already quoted) 1150 dead on the Eton Roll of the first war contrasts with 750 in the second, but of the last over forty were at least familiar to me by sight, five of these members of the same house during the years I was at the school.

3

I returned to MIL duties with Czechoslovakia (henceforward referred to for brevity as Czech) forces, and the Belgian; liaison with these two Allies being handled by one officer. As well as their military attaché, the Belgians employed a major supervising affairs of the Congo (now Zaire), a colony possessing an army of its own (somewhat comparable with that of the former Honourable East India Company), the Congo's products being a valuable card in the Allied hand.

The Czech military attaché, Colonel Kalla, appears in *The Military Philosophers* more or less 'as himself' under the name of Colonel Hlava; the Belgian military attaché, Major Kronacker, also not much altered, as Major Kucherman; but the Belgian Colonial Officer, Major Offerman, is a composite picture in Major Clanwaert.

Naturally the exiled governments in Great Britain were not without all political troubles, some of these abutting on to military affairs. For instance, the Poles numbered a proportion of officers who had been adherents of Poland's former semi-dictator, Marshal Pilsudski, their loyalties to Sikorski accordingly suspect. The conduct of one Polish general in the early stages of the war had been regarded by his compatriots as so unsatisfactory that they had wanted to court-martial, probably shoot him. In the event, retribution was commuted to banishment to Northern Ireland, where he worked as an agricultural labourer, Dru and I from time to time receiving reports as to how he was getting on. The Poles in any case possessed a large surplus of officers in relation to other ranks in their army, several hundred of these unemployed Polish officers quartered at Rothesay in Scotland, one of our concerns (moderately well achieved) being to get these absorbed so far as possible into civilian life.

The Czechs, a much smaller force, suffered their occasional political disquiets too on a lesser scale. A Czech soldier once arrived at the War Office asking to see the officer concerned with Czech affairs. When I went downstairs to interview him he told me he was really a German (presumably Sudeten Deutsch) and wanted to be interned. He looked a typical Czech, though that was no doubt beside the point. There was nothing I could do about his case but note name and details, then report the matter to Colonel Kalla.

Of all the states bordering the Soviet Union in those days, Czechoslovakia (with the possible exception of Bulgaria, bound by special links related to Russia's liberation of the country from Turkish rule in the 19th century) was the only one to look on the USSR with favour, both officially and as a matter of popular feeling. The Czechs would literally sentimentalize about their 'Big Brother', and were genuinely taken by surprise at the treatment they received when the Red Army marched into Prague. Since that day Czechoslovakia has experienced only too much opportunity to appreciate the practical consequences of having the Soviet Union as neighbour.

Colonel (later Brigadier-General) Josef Kalla, whose career—like that of many Polish officers too—had begun in the Imperial and Royal Austro-Hungarian army, had transferred from the infantry to air arm during the first war, becoming a noted flying ace and test pilot. He had been military and air attaché at the Czechoslovak Legation (later Embassy) in London for several years when war broke out, and was now doyen of the Corps of Military Attachés. Kalla was a delightful man, quiet, musical (he looked rather like Liszt), with much firmness of purpose. In 1939 he had armed his office staff against a possible take-over by supporters of the German-orientated Government in Prague. I have a little to add of him that is not implied in *The Military Philosophers.*

Pleasant relations with Kalla and his staff were brought to a melancholy end, when, by now aware of the tragic turn political circumstances were taking in his country, he went back to Czechoslovakia. Kalla himself had been one of the most determined champions of the Soviet Union through-out the war. Now, seeing the way things were shaping at home, his last words to me were: 'We can only hope for the best.' Not long after his return, by then under house arrest (some of the Czech officers who had fought with the Allies were shot out of hand by the Communists), Kalla died of heart failure.

4

If the Slav Allies preferred, so far as possible, to keep their political differences to themselves, rather than ventilate them in public, that was far from the habit of the Belgians (or, indeed, the French), who possessed no such inhibitions. The Belgians (as they themselves were always assuring me) are a nation much given to internal quarrelling, saying what they think about each other in the plainest possible terms. Indeed, their military attaché, Major Kronacker, told me that, when woken in a wagon-lit by the sound of a fearsome row going on in the next compartment, he knew he was back in his beloved country. The Belgian approach, which required a little getting used to, has much to be said in favour of its forthrightness, a national characteristic which could often be very entertaining.

Belgian circumstances at that moment offered scope for rows. One delicate matter, rivalling perennial discords between Flemings and Walloons, was the Royal Question. When in May, 1940, after a brief but stiff resistance, the Belgian forces had been compelled to give way before the invading German army, King Leopold III—automatically Com-mander-in-Chief on outbreak of war—had been faced with an impossible choice. If he went into exile with the Belgian Government, headed by the Prime Minister, Hubert Pierlot, the King laid himself open to the charge of deserting his kingdom; if he remained in Belgium, there was no alternative to becoming prisoner of the Germans.

Leopold, who (albeit an Old Etonian) had tried to show himself Neutral, rather than pro-Ally, during the period leading up to the war, chose the latter course. He was imprisoned in his own palace. Some of his subjects thought their King had not guessed right; others insisting he had taken the preferable path. There was another source of contention. Leopold's Queen (killed some time before in a car accident with himself at the wheel) had been beautiful and popular. His second marriage to a commoner (also good-looking) was not at all well received by most Belgians, a race with strong feelings about social distinctions. Nevertheless, in spite of these discords, a portrait of King Leopold hung in all the official buildings in Eaton Square, the Belgian wartime Whitehall of government offices in exile.

Belgian determination not to appear over respectful to their own authorities was well illustrated when, on some official occasion, I had to attend the showing of a Belgian propaganda film. The main picture was preceded by a short British satirical documentary called *Yellow Caesar*, constructed from shots pasted up from old news programmes about Mussolini, done in such a manner as to guy the Duce's pretentious public appearances. Several Belgians were sitting immediately behind me. When the title *Yellow Caesar* was flashed on the screen, one of them said: 'César jaune—mais c'est qui? Pierlot?'

5

At the outset of my new liaison job the relationship of the War Office with the Belgian military attaché's office was a far from happy one. In *The Military Philosophers* the Belgian military attaché, Kucherman, projection to some extent of Kronacker, is represented as holding the appointment at the time the Narrator takes over Belgian liaison. In fact Kronacker did not occupy that post until about nine months later. A world should be said of the circumstances.

Major (later Baron) Paul Kronacker, a Reserve officer just old enough to have served in the first war as lieutenant of Horse Artillery, commanded a battery at the time of the German invasion of Belgium in 1940. After various campaigning ups and downs he had been taken prisoner, but, soon released, managed to escape to England in 1942. Since then things had not gone too smoothly with him.

Kronacker, scientist, businessman, politician, was a well-known figure in Belgian life. He had received high academic honours for chemical research, was an industrialist whose concerns, Belgian and foreign, included the presidency of the big Tirlemont sugar refinery, and, in becoming a Senator not long before the outbreak of war, followed his Belgian maternal grandfather. His German-Jewish father had begun life as a German subject, only later taking Belgian nationality.

Kronacker himself had retained certain German business interests even after the advent of Hitler. His second wife was British, but at this period he was still married to an Austrian *Gräfin*, by then living in America. These two aspects of Kronacker's background—German business associations, Austrian wife—provoked uneasiness, Belgian and British, at a time when an eye naturally had to be kept on the bonafides of everyone entering the United Kingdom.

The Belgians, at least those responsible for such matters, showed the national taste for polemics mentioned above by disregarding the caution counselled, not only by their own authorities but the British ones too, and almost immediately appointing Kronacker as their assistant military attaché. This particular example of one lot of officials not caring a straw for the view of another lot caused a great deal of agitation. In neglecting the normal usage of sending a formal letter giving the name of the officer designate to take over an appointment in the military attaché's office, courtesy must be admitted to have been less than conspicuous on the Belgian side, the sitting Belgian military and air attaché being taken by surprise as much as the Foreign Office and War Office. In fact Kronacker's entrance on the scene was perhaps not unnaturally taken to be a piece of political manoeuvring within Belgian governmental circles, and for some time all was not well.

Correspondence between MIL and the military attachés normally took the form of the DO (demi-official or 'Old Boy') letter, in which rank was dropped in favour of the simple surname or first name. ('Do I call him Emil?', 'Do I call him Bronislaw?', Carlisle would mutter as he headed and tailed letters brought for signature). The current incumbent being, as it happened, an airman, all purely army matters were left to his subordinate, Kronacker. Accordingly, at the time I took over Belgian liaison, Kronacker would write direct to me, but, Kronacker's appointment never having been referred to the British authorities, I had instructions always to send the answer back to his boss.

This was obviously not a state of affairs to promote good relations, and naturally Kronacker himself—who had done everything a man could to show his patriotism and enthusiasm for carrying on active Belgian antagonism towards the Germans—was furious at being so treated. He insisted that his case should be investigated to the fullest extent, the result of this enquiry being that he was totally vindicated by both Belgian and British authorities in every aspect of what had been a most unfortunate conjuncture. Kronacker's honour was agreed to be unassailable. This final clearing up was brought about not long before the moment when Kronacker's superior officer was promoted to another job, Kronacker himself becoming Belgian military attaché.

In person Kronacker was small, neat, somewhat severe in manner, obviously accustomed to getting his own way in whatever he took up. Two years of existence as assistant military attaché in a somewhat anomalous state had no doubt left a certain mark. In our earlier dealings Kronacker seemed a little inclined to treat army matters as if cornering a commodity on the stock market, but it was not long before he showed himself capable of grasping that not being too serious is at times the best way of dealing with relatively serious army matters.

In fact, notwithstanding this rather sticky start, when we met face to face, Kronacker and I got on together pretty well. He was not only extremely efficient where routine affairs were concerned, but quite uncircumscribed by a professionally military point of view, often unjustly disparaged in its own field, but at times an impediment to the complex problems of armies in exile. Of all the Allied officers with whom I came in contact during the war Paul Kronacker was certainly the outstanding figure.

Kronacker did not often speak of his pre-war life as a tycoon, but he once mentioned an incident that should not be lost to history. The doorman at his main office building in Belgium was a White Russian, former general or diplomat. In the lapel of the Russian commissionaire's uniform

Kronacker noticed the rosette of a high grade of the Légion d'Honneur. Every day, when the Russian opened the door of Kronacker's car on arrival at the office, Kronacker felt uncomfortable that a man of such distinction should perform so humble a diurnal service. Finally he could stand it no longer, and sent for whoever was in charge of the office staff. 'The Russian who opens the door of my car every morning—he is obviously a man of ability. Give him a better job in the firm. There are plenty of other things that could be found for him.'

For a day or two the White Russian remained, Kronacker supposing other employment was being sought for him. Days grew into weeks. The doorman continued to open the car door, Kronacker's inner discomfort increasing rather than diminishing. At last Kronacker sent for the personnel-manager again.

'The Russian commissionaire I spoke of—he is still doing the same job. I said he was to be promoted. Why has that not been done?'

'Excuse me, sir, the Russian has been offered half-a-dozen better jobs. Opening the door of your car is the only one he likes. He insists on no change being made.'

6

When I first took over Belgian liaison, the Belgian forces included an artillery battery made up of Luxembourgers, that is to say subjects of the Grand Duchy of Luxembourg, rather than the Belgian province also called by that name. A customs union existed between Belgium and Luxembourg, but Luxembourgers felt themselves quite separate, detesting the Germans, not specially drawn towards the French, the last being critical of a language in which, I think, it is possible to say, for instance, '*Ich glaube que c'est zehr gentil*'.

After invading the Grand Duchy of Luxembourg the Germans annexed that prosperous little state, declaring its citizens German nationals, therefore liable to be shot as traitors if found fighting on the side of the Allies. They sent many Luxembourgers to concentration camps, and pillaged the Grand Ducal palace. In short there was nothing funny about the way Luxembourg had been treated, nor the courageous resistance to the Germans that had been put up. Nevertheless something of Comic

16. AP with platoon at Gosford Castle, Co Armagh, 1940

17. AP with Col. Carlisle in Normandy, 1944

18. Bradfield (with cigarette) arrested by the Germans in front of the British Embassy, Copenhagen, 1940

19. Allied Military Attachés at Field-Marshal Montgomery's
Tactical Headquarters, 21 Army Group, near Roermond on
the Netherlands/German frontier, November, 1944:
(*left to right*) Lt.-Col. J. D. Carlisle (MIL), Lt.-Col.
Schoonenberg (Netherlands), Maj.-Gen. Strugstadt (Norway),
Brig.-Gen. Peabody (USA), Maj.-Gen. Regulski (Poland),
Gén. de Brig. Noiret (France), F-M Montgomery (C-in-C,
21 Army Group), Col. Kalla (Czechoslovakia), Col. T'ang (China),
Maj.-Gen. Skliaroff (USSR), Maj. Al Ansari (Iraq), Col.
Zobenitza (Jugoslavia), Maj. Comdt. Basnyat (Nepal),
Commandant Lechat (Belgium), Maj. A. D. Powell (MIL),
Col. de Almeida (Brazil)

20. Montgomery puts the Military Attachés in the picture:
Gen. Peabody (nose), Col. Schoonenberg (hand to face),
Gen. Regulski (just hidden), Col. de Almeida (spectacles),
F-M Montgomery, AP, Gen. Noiret, Col. Carlisle,
Comdt. Lechat (just hidden)

Opera inescapably attached itself to the affairs of the Grand Duchy, those in charge of them not at all discouraging a certain atmosphere of high spirits and gaiety of tone.

'After all,' as the Prince of Luxembourg once remarked to me, 'as the Austrian Netherlands, we are quite separate from the Spanish Netherlands like Holland and Belgium', a splendidly historical point of view. Prince Felix, the Prince of Luxembourg (a Bourbon-Parma, brother of the ex-Empress Zita of Austria), was consort of the sovereign, Grand Duchess Charlotte, a lady of great distinction of character and bearing. Prince Felix had fought with the Austrian army on the Eastern Front during the first war, when it had been understood that he must never serve against France.

The demeanour of Prince Felix, a genial figure (who once confided to Carlisle that 'being a consort is a rotten job'), by no means diminished the air of opera bouffe that brightened the Grand Duchy's Legation in Wilton Place, off Belgrave Square. If Prince Felix played a kind of *buffo bass*, whose humour with a touch of sentiment sometimes steals the show, the foil was André Clasen, Luxembourg Minister (later Ambassador), the man who did all the work, and lively, witty, with a taste for practical jokes, acted as *raisonneur* in the performance.

Clasen, who at the outbreak of war had been (like his father and grandfather) Luxembourg's Consul-General in London, handled all the Grand Duchy's military affairs, in the course of which he would sometimes become a trifle exasperated with Prince Felix's always well-meaning arrangements with the War Office, sometimes made over Clasen's head. The two of them might have sung a magnificent comic duet on the subject from opposite corners of the stage.

By the time I ended my liaison duties with the Grand Duchy, its forces had increased from a single battery to three battalions of infantry, and the Heir Apparent, Prince Jean, was serving with the Irish Guards.

One morning, leaving the Legation after talking with Clasen, I saw Prince Felix (who wore the uniform of a brigadier) coming from the direction of Belgrave Square. He was carrying a large paper bag.

'I've just bought some buns, Major Powell. Come back to the Legation. We'll go up to my room and eat them.'

Wartime food shortages made one very ready to accept such an offer.

The Allied landings in North Africa of 1942 greatly changed French political circumstances. The special mission with the Free French in the UK was now dissolved, MIL dealing directly with the French army authorities, the liberation of France in due course bringing about the return to St James's of a French Ambassador and military attaché. At one moment it seemed that General Giraud might displace General de Gaulle as leader of the French in arms against Germany, but de Gaulle turned out too astute for anything of the kind to take place.

This absorption of the French into MIL's work resulted in an increase of the Section's establishment. I was once more promoted major, and, with two captains to help, added France to an existing empire of Belgium, Czechoslovakia, Luxembourg. When Italy left the Axis and joined the Allies, two Italian liaison officers were sent to London to undertake military contacts there. Owing to the exceptional nature of their position —neither former Allies, nor former Neutrals—no one had been deputed to look after them. They were offered to me. I should greatly have liked to take them on, but existing pressures of work made that impossible, something I have always regretted.

I do not remember what finally happened to the Italians, but one of the problems was what they should wear—if anything—when they appeared in London. The terms of the capitulation laid down that Italian military personnel must not wear uniform out of Italy, while former enemy nationals, who had borne arms against the Allies, were forbidden to appear in civilian clothes in the United Kingdom. If not precisely that, the difficulty of dress was in those areas.

A somewhat similar question (apparently one for the Admiralty) was inexplicably brought to MIL, when Charles Morgan's play, *The Flashing Stream* (1938), was put on in Paris towards the end of the war. British naval uniforms (mess-kit, I think) were required for some of the scenes, but regulations forbade the export of all British uniforms in time of war. The problem must have been surmounted because the play was certainly performed in Paris.

During the interim period between the dissolution of the special mission and return of a French military attaché, liaison was held together not so much by various officers of more senior rank as by Captain Jean Kéraudren (Kérnevel in *The Military Philosophers*), a convivial Breton in his fifties, long chief-clerk in the pre-war French military attaché's office, who, on the Fall of France, had been one of the first to volunteer for the Free French Forces, at a time when many Frenchmen in official positions preferred to return to their own country. After the war he became one of the vice-consuls in London.

Kéraudren, whose doctrine was that by twelve years of age a child should be drinking half-and-half wine and water, was an admirable colleague, a mixture himself of French humour and French seriousness. When I spoke of Proust, he pointed out that Proust was a writer not taught in the schools, and, after dining with us at Chester Gate, wrote a letter of apology to Violet for having shown lack of knowledge '*sur les guerres de réligion*'; consequence of some historical discussion during which he kept repeating '*Nous avons perdu un Louis*'. He would say: 'I'm going to write you another letter this afternoon asking you to tell us how to construct a Bailey bridge, but I quite understood that your people will not allow you to give the information.'

Kéraudren was once lunching with me at the Junior United Services Club (now no more), where, at the top of a staircase leading to the dining-room, a massive bust of Napoleon Bonaparte stood on an equally massive pedestal. As we passed into the room Kéraudren remarked: 'When you lunch with me in Paris you won't find a statue of Wellington at the top of the stairs—those two Bonapartes did more harm to France than any other two men in the country's history.'

8

In November, 1944, the Allies having penetrated about two miles beyond Germany's frontiers, it was decided to take the military attachés on a Continental tour to see something of the progress of the campaign. This was to be accomplished in two waves: first the Neutrals, conducted by Bradfield; then the Allies, fourteen in number, shepherded by Carlisle and myself.

Kronacker (soon to join the new Belgian Government as Minister of Economics, a portfolio he was to hold for a long period of years) had been summoned to Brussels at about this time for consultations as to the country's future policies. His place was taken by his assistant, Captain Albert Lechat (in whose honour one of the most notable of our cats, a tabby, was later named Albert), who had made a dramatic exit from Belgium to join the forces in exile, including jumping across the last few feet of water into a ship already sailing for England.

In *The Military Philosophers* I have described this tour of duty fairly circumstantially. A few points may be confirmed. In Normandy a night was indeed spent at Cabourg, one model for Proust's Balbec, Carlisle and most of the party being billeted in the Grand Hotel, which had meant so much to Marcel, while, with four of the other military attachés, I was accommodated in the smaller Hôtel de Paris, a more modest affair. Although at the time I was struck by an indefinable charm the resort possessed even in wartime, I attributed that to the moving feelings that overwhelmed one on this return to France in such circumstances; not very discerningly, failing to grasp the Proustian significance of the town itself and the hotel. Only on return to England did the experience suddenly crystallize into appropriately Proustian shape in memory.

In the summer of 1955, with Violet and our sons Tristram and John, I revisited this strip of coast. The 'season', as ever rigorously observed by the French, was almost at an end, and we could do no more than stroll through the central hall of the Grand Hotel, observe the two lifts which the renowned Proustian lift-boys had operated. Now a small memorial to Proust stood in the municipal garden in front of the hotel facing the sea. The little railway that had once transported guests to the Verdurins no longer existed, nor, so far as could be seen, did the ostentatious brothel which had once caused offence to local residents. Nevertheless much remained unchanged, not least the high prices charged in the famed restaurant at Dives.

9

Main Headquarters, 21 Army Group (the designation given to the British invading force), gave the feeling of entering the precincts of a minor public school which had just defeated its chief rival on the foot-ball field. Everyone seemed young, aggressive, enormously pleased with himself, so much that normal army courtesies were sometimes forgotten.

From Main HQ the military attachés' party, inspecting various things on the way, proceeded to the Army Commander's Tactical HQ. In *The Military Philosophers* the Narrator passes through units of his former Division, no literary contrivance, actual personnel of The Welch Regiment being seen en route. It was also true—as I was able to remind Field-Marshal Montgomery, when he mistook my cap-badge for that of the Prince of Wales's Volunteers (a South Lancashire regiment)—that an officer of The Welch had recently been awarded a VC.

Having attempted in *The Military Philosophers* to convey something of Montgomery I have little to add here about the man himself. The atmosphere of his Tactical HQ was far less swaggering than Main HQ, though the two caravans (over which the military attachés were given a personally conducted tour), the brace of yapping dogs, the smiling sergeant suddenly materializing out of thin air with a camera, had all the marks of a set-piece.

Montgomery was then at the peak of a triumphant advance still just short of universally acknowledged victory. Already a stylized figure (which to some extent Montgomery had no doubt been throughout his career), he had not yet hardened into an exhibit, the immensely energetic mobile waxwork that his outward appearance seemed instantly to resemble after accomplishing the task appointed by history.

On arrival at 21 Army Group Tactical HQ the military attachés were drawn up in single rank (in order of their appointment, Kalla the senior), and presented one by one, as Carlisle accompanied Montgomery down the line. Lechat, the most junior, was next to me at the far end. On hearing Lechat was Belgian, Montgomery spoke the words recorded in the novel, to the effect that, if the Belgian Resistance groups gave trouble (as they were showing signs of doing), he would 'shoot 'em up'. Lechat, dissatisfied with much that he found on return to his own country, was not in the least disposed to disagree with this principle. Kronacker would certainly not have dissented either, but I should have liked to witness Kronacker's confrontation with Montgomery. The question of the Belgian Resistance groups was soon to arise again in London in an acute form.

I have always found a certain fascination in the style of individual generals, even at the rank's lower levels, far more so those destined to find a place in the annals of war. On this very superficial contact Montgomery seemed to me to inspire confidence rather than admiration or devotion, but (tactical skills apart) no doubt his own instinct for what was required in our age for the army he was to command, the war to be fought, was substantially a sound one.

There was something incongruous about the two badges in his béret, the battle-dress cut from smooth service-dress khaki cloth. Montgomery's personality was not well adapted to military chic. He looked better in an old pair of flannel trousers, pullover deliberately shown beneath battle-dress blouse, a fashion several of the military attachés had followed, then, seeing the mode had changed, hastily tucked up pullover ends. Yet the badges, the service-dress cloth, seemed to suggest in Montgomery a yearning for sartorial panache that some hiatus in taste precluded.

One used to hear of Montgomery's quirks when he had been a mere Corps Commander, but I do not remember him spoken of as inevitably marked out for great things. He was as far from being a rough diamond (displaying petty envy of officers close to him) as cutting a figure as *beau sabreur ;* in some ways a very 'typical' soldier, in others never fitting comfortably into the extensive range of military eccentricity. There were unexpected sides to him. Nancy Mitford told me that Montgomery had expressed a wish to meet her at dinner in Paris, when he had revealed a perfectly competent knowledge of her novels.

Montgomery, his own consummate ad-man, was as different in exterior from such few other Great Captains of the time I have had opportunity to observe superficially, as they from each other. I have recorded in *The Military Philosophers* how, as he burst through the hall of the War Office, the bare shout of 'Good-morning' on the part of Field-Marshal Sir Alan Brooke (later Lord Alanbrooke) released a galvanizing out-give of energy. There too is recorded the tongue-tiedness of Field-Marshal Sir William Slim when distributing decorations, broken only when Slim put his hand on Kéraudren's shoulder (whose citation was withheld as technically 'Intelligence', and had done no more than write me ten thousand letters), saying '*You* are the real heroes of this war.' Nevertheless, one could understand Slim's hold on his troops, probably not hindered by something of the ogre about his appearance.

A contrast to all of these was Marshal of the Royal Air Force Sir Charles Portal (Lord Portal by the time I came across him after the war), who some have supposed the outstanding leader of all. Portal, a member of The Travellers, used to lunch in the club every day during the war, where it was a recognized precept that even those who knew him well left the Chief of the Air Staff undisturbed during this brief respite from duty.

It was alleged that Portal was sitting in The Travellers reading one of the weeklies after luncheon, when a heavy descent beside him on the sofa gave warning of the arrival of another member of the club long deceased, Lord Cecil Manners, elderly, vast in size, by then with some reputation as a bore, who observed in his very resonant voice: 'I hear the Flying Corps are doing splendidly.'

If the story has any basis in fact, I have no doubt whatever that Portal replied with, at worst, mild discouragement, certainly delivering no snub. For some years after the war he was Chairman of The Travellers' General Committee, on which I myself for a time sat. Even if club committees are likely to be composed of those who know how best to get quickly through the work required, occasionally an individual will speak too long, fail to grasp an obvious point, ride some hobbyhorse of his own. With the immense prestige Portal had acquired in the war, he also possessed an infallible ability for summarizing the needs of the Club. At the same time I never saw him by the flicker of an eyelid show impatience, much less crush a speaker who was stupid or prosy.

The furthest I ever heard Portal go in implied rebuke, when someone complained that other clubs made larger profits from cardroom and bar, was to answer: 'I'm afraid we cannot force our members to drink and play cards.' His own inclinations were perhaps revealed for a second when, a candidate for election being described as collecting Impressionist pictures (in those days a possibility) and breeding shorthorn cattle, Portal said: 'We hardly need hear any more, do we, gentlemen? He sounds suitable.'

Portal was indeed a leader for whom one guessed it would have been easily possible to feel devotion, though I never knew him personally. The only conclusion seems to be that all sorts are required at the top if a war is to be won.

When Kronacker returned to London after his Brussels consultations he telephoned at once, asking me to come over to Eaton Square. When I arrived at his office he said immediate danger was threatened by the Belgian Resistance groups, some of which were getting daily more out of hand.

These groups were chiefly recruited from young men of exemplary patriotism, grown up under four and a half years of German occupation, now desperately needing some sort of active employment. Few had been in action against the invaders, and naturally a great deal of frustration was felt, even though members of the Resistance had by now been cadred into some sort of army. More sinister was the fact that some of these groups were dominated by Communist elements, whose aim was to spread confusion with a view to revolution. One form of doing that was by inciting antagonisms (at best a chronic Belgian problem) between Flemish-speakers and French-speakers. The King's abdication was demanded in some quarters. In short, obstruction to the sorting out in a peaceful manner of the many difficulties arising from the liberation, indeed actual threats to democratic government, were very serious indeed.

The Belgian Government's suggested solution to the Resistance Question was that about 30,000 of those who made up this irregular force —say two Divisions—should be sent to the United Kingdom for training. On the face of it that seemed an excellent idea. The point was how soon such a proposal could be first agreed, then implemented.

Clearly the importation of 30,000 Belgians into the UK would have to be a Cabinet decision. Speedy arrangement of the move was not so much menaced at this height, as by details which would have to be worked out lower down: the financial side; logistics applying to the troops themselves; above all the geographical areas of Great Britain throughout which formations and units would be distributed. Senior civil servants at the War Office were capable of acting without delay; at lower levels, on the other hand, a love of obstruction was in places deeply rooted on the civil side. This was just the kind of administrative undertaking—where an actual military 'operation' could not be pleaded—to get bogged down in a tangle of petty argument among the lesser bureaucrats.

Kronacker was clearly very worried. In any case it looked as if nothing could be done until Monday, because this was the end of the week; as it happened, the Friday before I went away for a fortnightly two days of leave. The normal process to set things in motion would be for a War Office File (a more portentous affair than a mere Branch File) to be opened. I should draft the minute (memorandum)—to be approved by Carlisle and one of the two Brigadiers of the MI Directorate—which would then be signed by the Director of Military Intelligence, and circulated at major-generals' level. Brussels might well be in flames, the Belgian Cabinet hanging from lamp-posts, while the Finance Branch of the War Office was still discussing the monetary minutiae of the proposal.

Then I remembered that, some months before this, Kronacker—who went about more in London than most of the military attachés—had mentioned as worthy of note that on some social occasion he had come across 'Major Morton'. At that we both smiled. Major (later Sir) Desmond Morton, Personal Assistant to the Prime Minister, was universally regarded as a powerful figure, not less so because a certain aura of mystery surrounded his activities. He was a former Gunner officer, who had moved over to duties with the Foreign Office. To what extent Morton did indeed command Mr Churchill's ear was uncertain, but he was generally looked on as an *eminence grise*, whose name was likely to crop up whenever byways of government were being discussed.

This seemed an excellent opportunity to test the authenticity of Morton's reputation, while at the same time seeking a manner of cutting a corner or two in resolving the problem of the Belgian Resistance groups. I reminded Kronacker that he had spoken of meeting Major Morton not long before. Kronacker agreed that they had been introduced.

'Ring up Morton and say you would like an interview with him as soon as he can possibly give you one. Tell him it's vital. He won't object. That what he's there for. Repeat to him exactly what you've just told me. Say the War Office has been informed through the usual channels, and your contacts there are at once putting forward the Belgian Government's suggestion. Ask Morton to consider setting the matter before the Prime Minister himself as soon as possible.'

'Shall I tell Colonel Carlisle?'

'No—certainly not.'

Carlisle would have been horrified by the notion of approaching Morton, not because in principle he himself objected in the least to backstairs intrigue, but on account of the enormous respect he felt for his superiors in rank. The Prime Minister loomed in Carlisle's mind as a godlike essence. The idea of getting a buccaneer like Morton—albeit the PM's private and personal buccaneer—to tell Mr Churchill how he should act would have seemed carrying intercession to the point of rank sacrilege; blasphemy liable to call down departmental nemesis of unthinkable horror.

Kronacker turned the matter over in his mind for a minute or two. 'Very well,' he said. 'I'll get in touch with Major Morton, if you really recommend that.'

I returned to the War Office, and reported to Carlisle (leaving out Morton) the situation Kronacker had outlined. Carlisle went at once to the appropriate Brigadier, the two of them then conferring with the DMI. The consequence was, as envisaged, that a War Office File was put into circulation on the subject. That night I went off to Dunstall for the weekend.

Soon after my arrival in the MIL room on Monday morning, Carlisle rang down to say I was to see him at once. I found him in a state of some excitement. A message had been transmitted direct from the Prime Minister (in itself calculated to make Carlisle assume what Dru called 'his religious face') to the effect that movement of the Belgian Resistance Force to Great Britain was to take place forthwith, and be treated as a matter of urgent priority. Accordingly, said Carlisle, a meeting presided over by the Director of Staff Duties (major-general of branch deciding, so to speak, which bit of the army does what) would take place in an hour's time. I was to be there.

'This is an extraordinary thing to have happened, Tony,' said Carlisle. 'I can't understand it. Somebody very high up must have spoken the right word.'

At the meeting the DSD announced that 30,000 Belgian troops were to be transported as soon as possible to Northern Ireland, quarters vacated not long before by the US Expeditionary Force. The various War Office branches concerned were briefed as to their duties in connexion with this move. It occurred to me that, in a country where feelings ran high between Roman Catholics and Protestants, their discord should at least not be forgotten. The DSD, himself an Ulsterman, smiled rather grimly. He said he thought differences in religion should not be allowed to stand in the way of the many advantages of that training area.

The Belgians were installed in Northern Ireland within a very creditably short space of time. They did not at all like their new surroundings, among other things complaining greatly about the inadequacy of British army rations, probably meagre enough in comparison with what had been available throughout the war on the mainland of Europe. They were much happier when in due course shifted to England, where they found better facilities for training. Belgians, as I have said, are the first to admit that they represent a nation of grumblers, something that may well help to bind their disparate strains together. Neither Kronacker nor I ever spoke of our initial collusion in the matter, which I used without much change of circumstances in my novel.

12

One of the dramas witnessed in slow motion by MIL—though not, I am glad to say, an affair in which I was compelled personally to be involved —was British disengagement from Allied support of General Mihailovich's Nationalist partisans in Jugoslavia, in favour of transferring all assistance to the Communist forces headed by Tito, later Marshal Tito.

This political decision, later to be looked on as of questionable wisdom, was largely founded on dubiously reliable advice sent in by some of the British elements in the structure at work on the spot. I have myself read reports circulated on the situation applauding the Jugoslav Communist irregulars in a tone more suitable to an adventure story in the *Boys' Own Paper* than a sober appreciation of what was happening; while it now turns out that, if indeed Mihailovich may, as alleged, have allowed for tactical purposes his forces to declare occasional truces with the Germans, so too did Tito for those partisans under his command.

Jugoslav liaison in MIL, as already noted, was in the charge of Ker, who was responsible for a laughable by-product of what was in itself an essentially tragic turn of events. I have given examples of circumventing bureaucracy. It is only fair to show how bureaucracy can have its uses. The matter fell out in consequence of some contact made by me, how I don't remember, with a certain Professor of Political Science and Fellow of All Souls, John Plamenatz.

John Plamenatz, rather unexpectedly for a Fellow of All Souls, was a Montenegrin. His family had emigrated from Montenegro at the end of the first war, whether or not on account of that small Balkan kingdom being absorbed (without the least by-your-leave) into the newly created state of Jugoslavia, I do not know. Whatever the reason, in due course Plamenatz himself grew up to be an academic of some distinction at Oxford.

When the second war broke out in 1939, Plamenatz, who must have been a British subject by this time, joined the Royal Artillery in the ranks, but when Jugoslavia came in on the side of the Allies, was transferred to the Free Jugoslav Forces, in which he became an officer. I confess that I am not quite clear how this could have happened. I should have supposed him to have been given a commission in the Intelligence Corps, and sent to the Jugoslavs as an attached liaison officer, but no doubt there were conveniences in such matters as pay, for example, to approve otherwise. Plamenatz was employed, so far as I remember, in the King's Office of the Jugoslav Government in exile.

When the unedifying transference of British patronage from Mihailovich to Tito took place—after which Mihailovich was judicially murdered by his Communist compatriots—Plamenatz, without giving the least thought as to what would happen to him in a changed military status, simply resigned from the Free Jugoslav army. This left him in his earlier condition of being a gunner in the British Royal Artillery.

By this stage of the war Plamenatz's original unit was in Burma. It is unlikely that he would have been posted back to them—though one can never tell in the army—more probably sent to some draft-supplying centre of the RA. He had behaved honourably in joining the army in the first instance (which as an academic, not to mention an academic of Montenegrin parentage, he could certainly have sidestepped), and it was not unreasonable, after serving as a gunner in the British army, followed by two years as an officer of the Kingdom of the Serbs, Croats and Slovenes, that he should feel less than disposed once more to revert to the ranks. For the moment he had been granted extended leave, but the prospect of being recalled to the British army hung over him. He asked me whether MIL could do anything to remedy his case.

I consulted Ker. Cupping his ear occasionally, Ker listened to the Plamenatz story. At its end his expression did not change. He nodded his head several times sagely. Ker's exploits on the field of battle had by no means inhibited a keen sense of legerdemain in handling bureaucratic intricacies.

'I'll go into the matter', he said.

Some days later Ker invited me over to the table where he sat between his two G 3s. He did not speak at first, merely shaking his head from side to side.

'I can't get your man out of the British army', he said at last. 'No. I can't do that. There's no machinery to do that. He's bound to be called up sooner or later, if no further action is taken about him. That's what we don't want. Don't want that, do we? I've thought about his position a lot, talked it over with several of the Sections concerned, or those who might be concerned. It's a difficult question. Seems no way out. Still we'll have to do our best. This is what I consider the most hopeful course to follow. I'll get a file circulating on him, setting out his position from both the British point of view and the Jugoslav point of view. I'll send that file off to all branches that might be interested—there are a good number of those in the case of a man like that—circulating it in such a way that the question can never, if you understand me, be disentangled. The file, with all the facts about him in it, from the manner in which I've worded my minute, can't avoid going backwards and forwards from Section to Section. Questions not at all possible to sort out. No action can really ever be taken. So long as nothing is decided, he can't be called up. If you agree, I'll go ahead. Would that suit him, do you think? Sorry I haven't been able to do better than that.'

I said that seemed an admirable solution. Ker nodded gravely, and returned to his many other files. I passed on the information to Plamenatz. He was delighted. Now he could earn a living by lecturing on Political Science, a vocation he followed undisturbed until peace came. The Plamenatz file is perhaps still circulating through the corridors of the Old War Office, a unique example of perpetual motion.

IX

Demob Outfits

While Violet was living at Dunstall she came to know a widow in her late fifties, Margaret Behrens, who was a very good friend to us at about this time. Just before the flying-bombs began Margaret Behrens invited Violet, with Tristram, to stay for a week or two's holiday in a cottage she had taken at Lee, a seaside village three or four miles from Ilfracombe. This was of some consequence in our lives, as we not only decided later to go to Lee for a month or so after I left the army, but often subsequently revisited its bay with the children.

During this stay in North Devon the flying bombs settled down to a regular twenty-four hour transit over Shoreham on the way to London, explosions often taking place prematurely, while efforts were also made to shoot them down before reaching built-up areas. Violet had already done her share of standing up to bombardment from the air, and it seemed wise to delay return to Kent until this infliction had at least lessened. Accordingly she led a nomadic life for some months, going back to Dunstall for a short time only after the Allied invasion of Europe. We then moved once more into Chester Gate, where the worst of the bomb damage had been more or less repaired. For a time we were joined there by Alick and Gabriel Dru.

Margaret Behrens, without exactly belonging to a literary world (though she had written several novels in the manner of E. F. Benson with Scotland as background), was used to writers, and it was through her during the later years of the war that we first met T. S. Eliot. Eliot was also an old friend of a great crony of Margaret Behrens, Hope Mirrlees, unmarried, with Bloomsbury associations in early life, though now settled down to a less exacting intellectual condition of comfortable upper-middlebrowdom.

Hope Mirrlees lived with her mother, a well-off widow, and a disgruntled spinster aunt. The aunt was for some reason supposed not to smoke. When Eliot called at the Mirrlees house, the aunt (like Harold Brookenham borrowing a sovereign from his parents' guests in *The Awkward Age*) would waylay the poet as he passed through the hall in an effort to scrounge cigarettes. Tom Eliot, a good-natured man, would bestow a few, but, being also strait-laced, assuaged his conscience by never releasing quite so many cigarettes as were demanded by the aunt.

On the night of VE-Day—festival of Allied victory in Europe, 8-9 May, 1945, a two-day holiday—as we listened to the singing in the pub across the way from our house in Chester Gate, Violet remarked that I was probably the only person in England at that moment lying in bed reading the *Cambridge History of English Literature*. We did, however, celebrate the occasion less soberly the following day by having Hope Mirrlees and Colonel Kalla, the Czech military attaché, to lunch. Quite why these two, admittedly an incongruous couple, were asked together I cannot remember. No doubt for some reason connected with the exigencies of entertaining at that moment, such as the day that the meat ration was drawn. Luncheon was marked by an unforgettable incident.

The scene took place when we were having drinks before going down to the dining-room. Suddenly Kalla, who must have been sitting ten or twelve feet away from Hope Mirrlees, rose from his chair, his eyes fixed glassily on her. He moved across the room in the slow motion of the old-fashioned silent film. Both Violet and I thought it was love at first sight. Madame Kalla had already returned to Prague. Would she ever see her husband again?

Hope Mirrlees, whose emotions so far as known were orientated towards her own sex, seemed to share our fears. A look of absolute terror came into her face. She straightened her somewhat dumpy figure in readiness for the final pounce.

Kalla's deliberate advance continued. Waiting for the climax imposed an agonizing nervous strain. When he stopped there was a rapid movement. His hand shot out towards the bare neck of Hope Mirrlees.

'Ladies are sometimes frightened of these.'

With a courtliness of gesture, recalling his own military beginnings as an officer of the long departed Dual Monarchy of clicking heels and Strauss waltzes, Kalla removed an earwig from her scarf.

2

By the time of the Thanksgiving Service for Victory at St Paul's (an occasion described fairly fully in *The Military Philosophers*), 19 August, 1945, Carlisle, Ker, Bradfield, Dru, the Old Guard of MIL, had returned to civil life. This erosion brought me, so far as seniority went, into the position of second-in-command of the Section, which had been taken over some months before by a mild Regular, who had spent most of the war as a prisoner. Iron Curtain military attachés now abounded, unfriendly men, who wrote crusty letters beginning 'Dear Sir'. Their dispossessed predecessors did the best they could to keep alive. I sometimes caroused with the French. Violet, expecting another baby, had returned to the comparatively quiet life of Lee, where I was to join her when free of the army.

Before that liberation was accomplished we had existed as a rather strange household at Chester Gate, which for a time included the Drus, occasionally Malcolm Muggeridge, who was living out his last days of army life in London. Muggeridge used to take the same crowded bus as Dru and myself every morning, the densely packed upper floor not discouraging him from an unremitting calling down of anathema on all mankind at the top of his voice. I remember Dru bursting into a terrible *fou rire* on one of these journeys, because, from the painful twitchings of the back of the man's neck, Dru recognized in the seat in front of us the same passenger who had listened to Muggeridge's similar stream of invective behind him on the previous day.

One evening at Chester Gate—regarded by Violet as an act of supreme cruelty—I read aloud to Dru after dinner Kipling's poem *Tomlinson*, but on the whole it was Dru who introduced me to unapprehended literary fields. He was not a great reader of novels, though he had some favourites, and was keen on the distinction drawn by Coleridge (*Biographia Literaria*) between Imagination and Fancy, attributing brilliant powers of the former to Evelyn Waugh, holding reservations as to his brother-in-law's gift as to the latter. I felt I might have benefited myself by being introduced to that discrimination earlier, though personal inquisitions can be overdone in writing a novel.

One of the novels Dru liked (a copy of which he gave me, and I found marked at some time by himself) was Étienne Pivert de Sénancour's *Obermann* (1804), written in the form of letters, which describe its hero's melancholy and frustration from an unhappy love affair and other troubles. Obermann finds release through religion. The Kierkegaardian parallels are clear enough, but Sénancour (1770–1846), who influenced many French writers including Balzac, is interesting for his early emphasis on childhood. No doubt he owed something to Rousseau, but also anticipated later 'psychological' writing for instance (marked by Dru):

'Plus je rétrograde dans ma jeunesse, plus je trouve les impressions profondes . . . si, dis-je, je cherche ce que j'éprouvais à sept ans, à six ans, à cinq ans, je trouve des impressions aussi ineffaçables, plus confiantes, plus douces, et formées par ces illusions entières dont aucun autre âge n'a possédé le bonheur.'

Matthew Arnold, another Switzerland addict and thwarted lover, wrote two long poems (not his best) about Obermann, when he visited—and revisited—Sénancour's Swiss haunts. Arnold also names Obermann in the poem (remembered for the pageant of Byron's bleeding heart) on the Grande Chartreuse:

> Or are we easier to have read,
> O Obermann! the sad, stern page,
> Which tells us how thou hidd'st thy head
> From the fierce tempest of thine age
> In the lone brakes of Fontainebleau
> Or chalets near the Alpine snow?

The chances are that most English readers would find the reference obscure, but it is an instance˙of Arnold's closeness to a later period than his own.

Another favourite novel of Dru's was *Volupté* (1834) by Charles-Augustin Sainte-Beuve. No one should be misled by the title. *Volupté* is not light reading. Sainte-Beuve was a very different kettle of fish from Sénancour (for that matter from Kierkegaard), but again the theme is the torments of love sublimated by religion. The narrator of the novel is a priest; Sainte-Beuve's own passion, on which the story is modelled, being for Adèle Hugo, wife of Victor Hugo.

Dru also gave me a set of Sainte-Beuve's *Causeries du lundi* in translation, collected critical pieces comparable with *Times Literary Supplement* 'fronts' of the old days, though Sainte-Beuve wrote at decidedly greater length each week; a heavy stint for any literary journalist. Dru, interested in Sainte-Beuve, was far from an uncritical admirer. He wrote to me (4 February, 1947): 'After reading a number of the *Causeries* I am still in the dark: why is he considered a critic? He was really a voluminous Austin Dobson, diabolically malicious, with the unctuous style of a Second Empire monsignore.' Proust, severe not only on Sainte-Beuve's bad guesses about contemporary writers, but also his whole critical method, would not have disagreed.

I was also introduced by Dru to Benjamin Constant, who, though immeasurably more entertaining, has some affiliations with Sénancour's psychological reconnoitrings. *Adolphe* (1816) is one of the best short novels ever written about a love affair; the *Cahier rouge*, Constant's posthumously published account of his own first twenty years, also very enjoyable in a somewhat Stendhalian manner. Although he developed into a political bore in later life, the young Benjamin Constant remains a figure to hold the attention.

Another of Dru's letters (21 February, 1947) says: 'For years I have owned most of Péguy's work, and am running through it with the greatest possible interest. The titles bear no relation to the subject which is annoying enough, but the style is a nightmare of heavy repetition. But he is the only man I have ever read who makes sense of French history, and (most flatteringly) confirms all my suspicions about the nineteenth century. Orwell (superficially) has some links. Indeed, I have wondered several times whether he has not read him. You know my weakness for Taine and Renan, so you can imagine my pleasure at finding those two heavenly twins the subject of Péguy's longest *Cahier*. With the usual mysterious foreknowledge, I have just finished Boulanger and Dreyfus, and came perfectly prepared for Péguy. Need I add that he is an existentialist.'

During my War Office association with Dru I had brought him and Orwell together, but the meeting of the three of us at lunch was not a great success. That was not, so far as might be guessed, because either Dru or Orwell took a dislike to the other, but, each possessing an intermittent tendency to withdraw into his own shell, this happened almost the whole time throughout luncheon. There was no apparent antipathy; equally no communication.

Dru's suggestion that Orwell had read Charles Péguy (1873—1914), French essayist and poet, whose earlier socialist convictions turned to patriotic enthusiasm and mystical Catholicism, is interesting in the light of a letter (10 July, 1948, *Orwell Letters IV*) from Orwell to Julian Symons, sent about eighteen months later than Dru's remarks to me on the subject. Orwell (at that time in a Lanarkshire hospital) wrote: 'He [Léon Bloy] irritates me rather, and Péguy, whom I also tried recently, made me feel unwell.' This seems to indicate that Orwell's reading of Péguy must have been subsequent in time to Dru's finding some resemblance between the two of them; suspicion of some such similarity perhaps additionally fretting Orwell.

The references to Boulanger and Dreyfus are no doubt in connexion with books Dru had been reading, either with a view to writing something about the Third Republic, or just reviewing. The period was one he knew a good deal about, and General Boulanger, as mentioned earlier, a figure he liked discussing. Nevertheless, religious mysticism was always closer to Dru than history, and later the same year (8 July, 1947) he wrote: 'Yesterday I began reading Swedenborg, who seemed to me very sensible, all things considered, but I daresay one's standards are dropping.'

This familiarity with Continental writers not much known in Great Britain might have been used to great advantage by someone of more ambitious temperament, especially if Dru had managed to retain the lightness of touch of these letters, which never quite managed to survive in articles he wrote. Dru's preference for rambling about in a world of ideas, rather than putting what he knew to some more or less utilitarian purpose, gave him much of his unique character and charm. He would have been a less remarkable person had he been a more systematic worker.

As it was, Dru produced a fair amount in a leisurely manner after the war. Together with what he contributed about Kierkegaard from time to time, he edited a selection from the Letters of Jacob Burckhardt (author of *The Civilization of the Renaissance in Italy*), and wrote a book about religious controversies in France under the Bourbon Restoration; the last, rather eclectically, published only in German translation. On the whole Dru's post-war energies were devoted to farming, though he would always have been the first to point out that on the farm Gabriel Dru did most of the work. He himself would chat of cows and crops with the same imaginative wit that he brought to religion and philosophy.

3

One of the works Dru caused me to read was Amiel's *Diary*, celebrated on the Continent, inexplicably little known in this country, even among professional intellectuals. Indeed Cyril Connolly's lively squib—in a sense Connolly's swan-song—about Logan Pearsall Smith, in *The Evening Colonnade* (1973) invokes Amiel (with Joubert, Vauvenargues, and Logan Pearsall Smith himself) as typification of literary oblivion. So far as the UK is in question, the US probably no less, this is no unjust estimate, though it might be fair to add that very few Frenchmen or Germans have ever heard of the Revd Francis Kilvert's *Diary*, Kilvert being more or less contemporary with Amiel, no intellectual competitor, but perhaps Amiel's superior in poetic observation.

The interest that Dru aroused in me for the *Journal intime* of Henri-Frédérique Amiel (1821—1881) had a small public repercussion after the war, which may be recorded out of chronological order. It also made me reflect on Amiel's possible influence on Joseph Conrad, something which, so far as I know, has never been investigated.

Amiel, a professor of philosophy at Geneva, fits into Dru's canon of 'psychological' writers who seem to anticipate Proust and Freud in observations about human character, in Amiel's case notably his own. A somewhat ineffective heterosexual, Amiel was perfectly conscious of a lack of enterprise with women, treating with deprecatory humour the fact that he was verging on forty before acquiring a mistress. *Fragments d'un journal intime* appeared posthumously, Mrs Humphry Ward undertaking a translation in 1885, and further selections in English were published from time to time.

Conrad visited Geneva more than once. In 1891, after the Congo experiences embodied in *Heart of Darkness* (1902), he recuperated at a sanatorium in that neighbourhood, where he wrote some of *Almayer's*

Folly (1895), his first published novel. *Almayer's Folly* has for epigraph a sentence from Amiel's *Journal intime*: '*Qui de nous n'a eu sa terre promise, son jour d'extase et sa fin en exil.*'

This strikingly Conradian rhetorical question (no mark of interrogation in my copy) makes me wonder if Conrad had already come across the *Journal*, perhaps in translation, before these Swiss visits, or was introduced to Amiel from staying at Geneva. At all events he places most of the action of *Under Western Eyes* in Geneva, the pervasive atmosphere of that city somehow keenly suggested with few if any passages of descriptive writing, in a novel about Russian political exiles.

Under Western Eyes again shows Conrad's familiarity with Amiel's *Journal*. The narrative revolves round a group of Russian refugees in Switzerland, one of whom, Peter Ivanovitch (presumably the two names of a Russian patronymic, rather than surname), has made an incredible escape across Asia from imprisonment in Siberia. Peter Ivanovitch's adventures, somewhat satirically recalled by Conrad, seem based on Amiel's reference to memoirs the diarist had been reading, written by a Polish political prisoner, who had made a similar flight from a Russian prison.

Conrad may well have seen his own compatriot's book, but the tone in which he writes—making fun of Peter Ivanovitch's pretentiousness, while not denying the genuineness of the experience—suggests that he borrowed Amiel's recorded amazement as a reader in order to strengthen the picture of the character in *Under Western Eyes*. Indeed Amiel's reference could have started Conrad's train of thought in using the whole Genevan connexion.

Amiel, without Conrad's painful knowledge, as a Pole, of Russian political attitudes, was himself free of illusion on that subject. He goes out of his way to define at some length just how he saw Russia of his own day. The *Journal intime* (1 July, 1856) comments: 'What terrible masters the Russians would be if ever they should spread the might of their rule over the countries of the South! They would bring us a Polar despotism—tyranny such as the world has never known, silent as darkness, rigid as ice, insensible as bronze, decked with an outer amiability and glittering with the cold brilliance of snow, slavery without compensation or relief; this is what they would bring us.'

Towards the close of my army service, while on leave, I wrote a couple of pieces about Amiel. These appeared in print (*The Cornhill*, December, 1945; April, 1946) after return to civilian life. Among other passages quoted from the *Journal intime*, some illustrating Amiel's views on the characteristics of different nations included this estimate of the Russian political character.

The article appeared at a moment when the Soviet Union's policies were hardening into unconcealed antagonism towards the West, in short the beginnings of what was to be called the Cold War. Great Britain, saturated with sentimental wartime propaganda about Russia as an ally, taught to think of Stalin as a genial uncle, was on the whole not at all aware of Soviet aggressions that were taking place. Mr Attlee, the Prime Minister, was confronted with the task, by no means an easy one, of creating throughout the country a more realistic appreciation of foreign affairs relating to Central and Eastern Europe.

In one of Attlee's speeches aimed at that clearer understanding, the Prime Minister, attributing the words to a 'wise old Swiss philosopher', quoted Amiel's reflections on Russian political characteristics quoted above. They seem likely to have been brought to his notice by what was in *The Cornhill;* something that might have surprised Amiel, but in which he would have found quiet satisfaction as a diary-entry.

4

My three months leave, routine period preceding final demobilization, began in September, 1945. Chester Gate had been let to General Regulski and his wife (our Polish allies in London now in a grievous state owing to recognition by the British Government of the Communist administration set up in Poland by the USSR), and, the Regulskis by no means the only Poles who came to live in the house, my last week at home was spent among entirely Slav surroundings, which included moving all the furniture and pictures to different positions. I handed in returnable military equipment, obtained a demob outfit from the governmental store at Olympia, and travelled down to North Devon, where at Lee we hoped to restore ourselves, after nearly six years of war, with a month or two's holiday paid for by my army gratuity.

At one time or another Violet had put up at various houses in Lee. She was now established at Chapel Cottage, belonging to Miss Maud Armstrong, where I joined her. Circumstances caused us to remain there only a week or two before moving to a furnished bungalow standing on one of the high cliffs enclosing the bay, but in subsequent years we often returned to Chapel Cottage (said to have foundations on remains of a small religious edifice of the Celto-Roman period), and Maud Armstrong became a friend.

Lee's little bay and white houses were not much changed from 19th century pictures. The former manor, now an hotel, was set some way back from the shore, a few modern bungalows scattered here and there on the slopes above. The long sea-wall stood above a rocky beach, over which tides of the Bristol Channel periodically strewed mauve seaweed. Among the stones and shingle would occasionally appear green glass spheres about the size of a croquet ball, used for weighting the fishermen's nets. In summer, tourist infiltration from Ilfracombe withdrew in late afternoon; in winter, shore, cliffs, the inland valley where fuschsias flourished, were all unpeopled, an emptiness greatly to be valued after wartime's unremitting contiguities.

Leaving the army, sudden liberation from a cluster of responsibilities varying in dimension, brought its own sort of fatigue. Out for a walk, I would suddenly feel scarcely able to reach the summit of a hill, if at all steep, though the anaesthetic Devonshire air may have had something to do with that. On waking in the morning the prospect of death seemed curiously inviting. These glooms were likely to dissipate themselves as the day advanced.

I began to sort out the fairly extensive collection of notes on John Aubrey which had by now accumulated. Even if the war had left a kind of jet-lag there could be no doubt one had been on the whole advantageously shaken up as a writer. From now on, although certainly bad days might occur when nothing much could be produced, I never again suffered quite the same succession of bad days on end, when all writing seemed out of the question.

5

Maud Armstrong, owner of Chapel Cottage, was a preponderant figure in Lee's social hierarchy. She was indeed generally recognized as its summit. Then in her early seventies (she lived to ninety or thereabouts) an attractively gnomelike appearance made her seem, in the best and most complimentary sense, a witch. Her life had known romantic aspects. She was a doctor's daughter without much in the way of prospects. Then the young and beautiful widow of a well-to-do parson had unexpectedly bequeathed to her a small but comfortable sufficiency. The story would have made a good frame for a novel, one of I. Compton-Burnett's perhaps, or, in another manner, Iris Murdoch, but open to all kinds of treatment. Maud Armstrong, who possessed a keen humour, could provide at a moment's notice a Proustian analysis at any and every social level, of Lee's complex society.

Soon after our own arrival at Lee, T. S. Eliot turned up there. He lodged at a farm, but spent most of the time with the Mirrlees family, mother and daughter, who had also taken rooms in the neighbourhood. Eliot was known to us then only from one or two meetings in London, and a dinner at Chester Gate. Now we saw a certain amount of him, usually in the company of Margaret Behrens and Hope Mirrlees.

When I had first set eyes on Eliot in 1927 or 1928, dining by himself at a Charlotte Street restaurant, I remember feeling a sense of excitement at the sight of a figure whom the Sitwells, Bloomsbury, even Wyndham Lewis, treated with respect. He seemed a remote unapproachable person to most of my own generation. The scene was The Étoile, Eliot (no doubt on his way to a party) wearing a dinner-jacket. Someone remarked: 'They say Eliot is always drunk these days.' I found that fascinating too, though he seemed perfectly sober when, walking rather quickly, he made his way out into the street.

When one came to know him better Tom Eliot was inscrutable only in his mild amiability. The undemanding chit-chat of tea-time and cream cakes (if procurable) seemed the stimulants he needed, giving a rest from poetry, high thinking, very genuine 'good works'. He was the incarnation of his own pronouncement (made in the context of writing rather than behaviour) that 'no artist produces great art by a deliberate attempt to express his own personality'. Eliot, encountered in the Mirrlees household, drinking a pint or two of cider in the pub, dropping in at our bungalow on the cliffs at the end of one of his long solitary walks (wearing a cap and carrying a stick), always kept conversation to light topics, making fun of *The New Statesman* about as far as seriousness was allowed to stray.

"sketch for a gigantic mural to be placed
coffee-room at White's by public subscription
being the theme "Connolly at Canossa"

21. *Connolly at Canossa*—drawing in ink and sepia by Osbert
Lancaster, 1950: Evelyn Waugh, Cyril Connolly, Pope Pius XII,
Fr D'Arcy, Vatican official, Swiss Guard (perhaps the artist)

22. Leslie Hartley and AP
at The Chantry, 1959

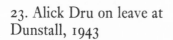

23. Alick Dru on leave at
Dunstall, 1943

24. Gerry Wellington at
The Chantry, 1961

25. Harry d'Avigdor-Goldsmid
at Somerhill, 1969

Osbert Lancaster
The Chantry, 1956

27. AP and Malcolm
Muggeridge,
Kitty Muggeridge (in
between heads) passing
National Gallery about 1946
(street photographer)

28. Powell family at Cabourg, 1955:
Tristram, AP, Violet, John (street photographer)

Eliot must, I think, have been rather different as a young man: the violent enthusiasms; the boxing; the attempt (precluded by ill health) to join the navy in the first war. No doubt forces from which such elements had taken shape were still active enough within, but they were now concealed. I used to wonder what impression would have survived after an encounter with him during which for some reason Eliot's name and identity had remained unrevealed. Would one, for instance, have guessed American origins? His faint accent was not exactly English, at the same time not recognizably American, anyway to an English ear used to the general run of Americans who come to England.

Friendly, easy, picking up instantaneously the most lightly suggested nuance in conversation, Eliot had also just a touch of the headmaster, laying aside his dignity for a talk with the more intelligent boys, boys from whom he was quite prepared to pick up something for his own use; indeed a headmaster who had learnt deep humility from shattering experiences. None the less the façade of buttered scones and toasted crumpets—both representing a perfectly genuine taste in Eliot—was by this time all but impenetrable.

> I smile, of course,
> And go on drinking tea.

This amalgam of tea-party cosiness with a cold intellectuality, the more menacing because strictly implicit rather than explicit, gave Tom Eliot's personality that very peculiar flavour, which even the most high-powered of his contemporaries seem at times to have found, if not exactly intimidating, at least restraining.

Eliot could be entertaining about embarrassments suffered by himself as a famous poet. Discussing with Violet the restorative effects of massage, he described how his own masseuse, at a moment when he could not escape from her clutches, said: 'Mr Eliot, I dreamt last night that I saw a child drawing with a reed on the water. I knew this child must be the spirit of William Blake. Do you know why Blake revealed himself to me, Mr Eliot? It was so that I should tell you to write more poetry than you have been doing lately.'

'Although I look at everything from an English point of view now', Eliot said, 'at times my Americanness returns like a flash. That's when I hear someone over here assume as a matter of course that, if an American is described as a gentleman, he must of necessity come from the South.'

Eliot liking ghost stories, I told about the haunted bungalow (*Infants of the Spring*) in which I had lived as a child. He responded with a story I record with diffidence, being neither my own, nor anything to do with me, but seeming to deserve preservation in giving support to the existence of hauntings lacking what vintners call bottle-age. Eliot had not known personally the member of the Faber family concerned, but had been told the story by the publisher of that name, in whose firm Eliot himself worked.

In the 1930s Mr Faber, hero of the anecdote, had been one of a fishing syndicate renting a house in Scotland for the season. He travelled north to take over this house, a comparatively modern one, before the others arrived. A severe attack of toothache developing in the train, he had a painful night at the house, but managed to find a dentist the following day, who sufficiently put things right for a satisfactory fishing holiday to follow.

Some years later this Mr Faber (or possibly another member of the syndicate) was talking to a fellow fisherman in a club or on a train; one of those classic encounters which provide the dénouement of so many ghost stories. The stranger turned out not only familiar with the sport as practised in that corner of Scotland, but revealed himself as having been member of a fishing syndicate renting that very same house.

'Did you catch a lot of fish?'

'The fishing was all right. Very good. There was one drawback, rather an unusual one. The house was haunted. Did none of your party notice that when you stayed there? Several of ours saw the ghost. It was a man walking up and down in one of the rooms, holding his face, as if he had terrible toothache.'

6

In about 1952, just before we moved to the country, the *Times Literary Supplement* (then edited by Alan Pryce-Jones) gave a party for its contributors in the 'private house' at Old Printing House Square. (At one of these *TLS* parties, the traditions of the paper being less than prodigal in payment of its contributors, Harry d'Avigdor-Goldsmid, who as an MP and City magnate used to review an occasional political or financial biography, said: 'How nice to meet you both at a gathering of the worst paid workers in England'). On this particular occasion I don't think Harry Goldsmid was present, but Tom Eliot was there, and John Hayward in his wheelchair.

About halfway through the party Hayward beckoned me.

'The Bard's accountant has been complaining that he doesn't get sufficient documentary evidence for the Inland Revenue that the Bard spends money entertaining other writers and publishers, so Tom's asking a few friends to dinner at the Savoy Grill tonight, and hopes you'll both join us.'

Hayward's passion for parties caused him almost always to remain until what was often no empty phrase in being termed the bitter end. As someone had to wheel out the chair before his own withdrawal was possible Hayward was in an exceptionally strong position with all but the most ruthless.

At the close of the *TLS* assemblage there might have been two or three guests over and above the half-dozen or so making up Eliot's dinner-party (Violet the only woman), these remnants unlikely to hold out on their own, if supporting elements represented by Eliot, Hayward, the auxiliaries, retired in a body. Meanwhile the host and proprietor of *The Times*, Colonel John Jacob Astor (later Lord Astor of Hever), had no means of knowing that the retreat of the Eliot/Hayward forces would terminate the jollification. Colonel Astor's face, drawn with anxiety at the prospect of apparent unending festivity, suddenly brightened and beamed into a happy smile, as Eliot turned and firmly took hold of the back of Hayward's wheelchair.

7

Return to London from North Devon shortly before Christmas, 1945, opened up a régime of working on Aubrey at Oxford during the middle of the week, spending only long weekends at Chester Gate. I lived austerely in Balliol, sitting all day in the Bodleian, where, in Duke Humphrey's Library, a portrait of Aubrey himself hung appropriately on the wall.

Duke Humphrey's Library was one of the most agreeable refuges for that sort of research, which consisted chiefly in going through certain of Aubrey's own manuscripts, together with many letters from Anthony Wood and other Aubrey contemporaries.

In the second week of January I found a telephone message at Balliol (accepted, it seems, rather unwillingly at the porter's lodge, where it was assumed I was in hiding at the College), instructing me to return to London. When I rang up the nursing-home the following morning (11 January) I was told Violet had given birth to our second son, John.

I worked hard on Aubrey, glad to have made provision for this immediate post-war period of writing, which would otherwise have been not at all easy to handle, as I was not yet feeling at all like sitting down to work on another novel. The job itself was enjoyable. Aubrey's personal history is comparatively unbedevilled by the wars and politics of his epoch, which history lessons at school imposed. Set free from Tonnage and Poundage, or the Three-fold Advance on London, I became captivated with 17th century life in England.

A long-standing interest in genealogical investigation had made me fairly familiar with consulting documents like wills, lawsuits, ratebooks, records of that kind. People who have never undertaken this sort of first-hand research perhaps miss something in life, a peculiar magic which makes time-travelling practicable. As one becomes increasingly steeped in a period like Aubrey's, one acquires for the moment a strangely intimate acquaintance with a crowd of deceased persons. After such burrowings into the past come to an end, so equally does the sense of existing in another century; the names of Aubrey's friends hard to remember like those of some wartime colleagues.

An example of odd insights attainable was given when going through a section of Aubrey's private library, which has found its way to Worcester College, Oxford. Not every volume held in this particular group of books is known for certain to have belonged to Aubrey, who sometimes, though by no means always, wrote his name on the fly-leaf of books he speaks of owning. I discovered that his signature was often followed by a little spatter of blots from probably a quill pen. These blots, I found, appeared in some of the volumes without Aubrey's signature. There was, therefore, a reasonable presumption that they too belonged to him.

Very little of this sort of enquiry had previously been devoted to

Aubrey. I was struck by a derivative common to both genealogical potterings and Aubreian research, that is to say their common service-ableness in refuelling the novel-writing engine within. In early days I had felt a certain guilt in spending an afternoon at the Record Office to inspect Subsidy Rolls or Early Chancery Proceedings, in which my own family might occur, until I found such activities were often followed by a release from what had recently been a stagnant writing interlude.

The whole business of a novelist's incubatory periods, what can produce or prolong them, is naturally of great professional consequence. Although at times it is certainly necessary to force oneself to write, as one might exert any other form of self-control, while at others a holiday from writing is obviously needed, the process of occupying the mind with some different mental activity, pleasant but relatively onerous in itself, seems to have a stimulating effect in getting the necessary machinery going.

X

Upper Grub Street

London life had been drastically changed by the war. Before things settled down to a new pattern a pause between the Acts took place, an interval of time which seems now to have possessed a pungency of its own. The bomb-defaced weary squalid town, still suffering shortages of every sort, had to endure the gruelling winter of 1946/7, the worst months of which began in January of the New Year, snow still falling in mid-March on the solid hillocks of sooty ice over which the buses skidded and bumped.

This was a grisly period, in some respects—fortitudes now relaxed—harder to put up with than the war. In Chester Gate the house next door, with which we shared a water-main, had been gutted in the blitz, so that every time its roofless frozen pipes were systematically unfrozen during the day, they froze again at night. For three weeks baths depended on the charity of friends whose taps still ran hot water.

Apart from work on Aubrey, I was reviewing for *The Daily Telegraph*, *The Spectator*, anywhere else available. *The Spectator*'s literary editor, W. J. Turner, poet ('Chimborazo, Cotopaxi, took me by the hand') and music critic, was an Australian. Turner (whose accent Bloomsbury found 'distressing') had known D. H. Lawrence and kindred writers and painters of the pre-1914 world. He and his wife had been staying at Garsington on one of my visits there in undergraduate days, but naturally enough no contacts had been made. Turner must already have been brooding on his Peacockian dialogue, *The Aesthetes* (1927), where guests gathered in a country house discourse on art and letters, in which Lady

Ottoline Morrell is herself caricatured. *The Aesthetes* gave great offence at Garsington, a bad situation being made worse by W. B. Yeats, one of Lady Ottoline's most prized lions, writing in praise of the book.

Walter Turner, sallow, slight in build, his movements quick and nervous, gave the impression of being eternally fed up with the human race. He had a name for antagonizing people, especially in the musical sphere, but I found him not at all unsympathetic when I collected books for review at *The Spectator's* offices in Gower Street. I should have liked to hear something of his early days in London, but that was prevented by Turner suddenly dying in his late fifties. He was followed on the paper by a much younger literary editor, barely thirty, one of only two or three persons I have known to be murdered, though that was many years later.

Murder, as it happened, was twice in evidence in our own neighbourhood at this period, when we also ran some risk from a nocturnal fire that broke out during the cold spell (we were existing on buckets of water obtained from the pub opposite) in Cambridge Terrace, at right angles to Chester Gate, where, paint stored in a long row of empty houses surrounded by scaffolding, the night-watchman had decided to go home. We were aroused, and with the children spent an hour or so with a neighbour. If the wind had brought the huge blaze in another direction things would have been very awkward indeed. As it was only our side wall was singed.

One of these local murders was that of a youngish woman in Regent's Park. She turned out to be a virgin, and the motives were never traced. I am not at all fascinated by crime (in the army the occasional near-criminal in the ranks always seemed, as an individual, among the least interesting, standing out only through egotism and stupidity, not at all one of the charming sinners often represented by intellectuals), but when some workmen, arriving early in our house, said the body was still there, curiosity overcame me. I walked a few hundred yards up the park to find a police cordon, the corpse removed a minute or two later in a parti-coloured blanket, a macabre scene.

The other murder did not take place in our immediate neighbourhood, but we knew the victim by sight, indeed Violet had exchanged an occasional 'Good morning'. He was an Iraqi secondhand-car salesman, who did his business in Fitzroy Square, but parked his own vehicle in front of the house next door to us. He was called Setty, and his murderer afterwards dismembered the body and dropped it piecemeal from an aircraft on to the Essex Marshes. Violet happened to be in hospital soon after this, and was told by one of the nurses that Setty had been a fellow-patient not long before. He had gone into hospital to have his nose altered, as he judged that feature unbecoming, as it was, under the peaked cap of a yachting club of which he had recently become a member.

2

Within about a year of returning to civil life, Malcolm Muggeridge, with all his family, moved into a flat just round the corner from us in Cambridge Gate, a continuation of the terrace in which the great blaze had taken place, but itself a grey stone block in Renaissance style, barbarously inserted by John Galsworthy's father, a speculating builder, among the neo-classical architecture of Regent's Park.

Muggeridge was then leader-writing for *The Daily Telegraph*, of which newspaper he was later to become Washington Correspondent and Deputy Editor. Seeing a good deal of him led as a matter of course to meeting again Hugh Kingsmill, Muggeridge's lifelong friend, whom I had come across years before (*Messengers of Day*), when Duckworth's published some of his books, though never known well.

Kingsmill was now literary editor of the *New English Review*, to the book pages of which I became a contributor. This magazine, which had its eccentric side, was edited by Douglas Jerrold, whose more substantial position was as chairman of Eyre & Spottiswoode, the publishing firm of which Graham Greene, soon after the end of the war, had become managing director.

The Eyre & Spottiswoode/*New English Review* axis largely revolved on the Authors Club, an odd little backwater housed in Whitehall Court, the massive block of flats standing between the Old War Office building and the River. The Club, its interior dominated by Edwardian literary memories and a gargantuan black cat, had most of its policies settled by Jerrold, the most prominent member of its committee and in general guardian angel.

Kingsmill, Muggeridge, Greene, myself for a short period, were all members of The Authors, from the smoking-room of which Kingsmill virtually edited the book pages of the *New English Review*. If consultation about some book was necessary—or talk about literature, love, marriage, the meaning of life, anything but politics—Kingsmill was always to be found asleep every afternoon in one of the upright chairs; a coma from which he would emerge for tea at about four o'clock.

Greene, like Muggeridge, had spent the latter years of the war in the Secret Service. A man of very considerable practical ability (unlike many writers), his nervous energy, organizing faculty, taste for conflict, sudden bursts of rage, would have made him successful in most professions; indeed I can think of few in which he might not have made a mark. He soon set humming the veteran engine of Eyre & Spottiswoode, by no means so broken down an equipage as Duckworth's (when shaken to pieces by Balston's mild efforts at cranking up the machine), nevertheless a chassis set rattling ominously under the force of the new dynamo.

As an actor on this stage-set, Douglas Jerrold seemed in certain respects to have strayed in from another play. He belonged to Kingsmill's generation, was a Roman Catholic convert like Greene, took a vehement interest in politics as did Muggeridge, but at the same time could hardly be said to belong to the accustomed world of any of those three. The *New English Review* reflected Jerrold's own particular brand of Conservatism, which did not necessarily at all coincide with that of the rest of the Tory Party; indeed Jerrold was forever breathing out dire threats to withdraw his own support from Winston Churchill.

If Kingsmill's demeanour always suggested a touch of Victorian moral complacency, a far more pervasive whiff of another form of Victorianism was habitually borne in the wake of Jerrold, the Victorian Englishman's determination to stand up for his rights. Indeed, Jerrold always seemed to me a genuine survival from an epoch when, for a man to be less than aggressive, was thought effeminate; days when a coffee-room would echo with the words: 'Are you aware, sir, that you have been monopolizing *The Times* throughout the whole of breakfast?'

Jerrold's life was a perpetual round of making paper mountains out of political molehills, and breaking literary butterflies on the wheels of publishing. Muggeridge used to call him Mr Forcible Feeble. Large, sombrely dressed, immensely gloomy (sounding on the telephone as if already in Purgatory) Jerrold had been employed as a young man in the

Treasury. One cannot help wondering sometimes about those recruited for the Treasury. Does it explain otherwise incomprehensible aspects of how we are governed? Jerrold, for instance, could bring instantaneous and inextricable confusion to the simplest transaction.

Nevertheless, if Jerrold's capacity for making heavy weather was, in its own field, unsurpassed, he was also exceedingly long suffering in putting up with Kingsmill's occasional vagaries as literary editor of a magazine which was Jerrold's pride and joy. In most respects Kingsmill did the job (his principal means of support) extremely well, but from time to time Jerrold would be dissatisfied and issue an enormously verbose screed in his best Treasury style.

'Douglas gets as much pleasure from writing me a pompous letter,' Kingsmill once cried aloud in his exasperation, 'as other people do from having a good fuck.'

3

When *John Aubrey and His Friends* was finished, having a vague idea that the book might benefit from the semi-academic affiliations of the Oxford University Press, I let the OUP see the manuscript. The suggested advance being unexciting, I took Muggeridge's advice, and gave the biography to Graham Greene to read. Eyre & Spottiswoode offering better terms, a contract was signed in May, 1946, undertaking that the book would appear within nine months from that date.

After the second war, owing to shortage of paper and many other causes, book production slowed up lamentably; an ill from which publishers have never wholly recovered, having invented other reasons for delaying publication. In the good old days, when I had been employed in Duckworth's, an author might be thought exigent if, delivering a manuscript in August, he expected the printed book to be in the bookshops by October, but, in practice, such optimism was rarely disappointed.

By this post-war period things had become very different. The publication of *John Aubrey and His Friends* was continually postponed, until at last, two and a half years after the delivery of the manuscript, the biography was scheduled to appear in the late autumn of 1948.

Not very long before this projected publication date, Greene, Muggeridge and I, all three lunched at The Authors. In the course of the meal Greene revealed that Eyre & Spottiswoode's had decided once more to delay publication of *John Aubrey and His Friends*, this time until some unstated moment in the New Year. I had raised no difficulties at all about previous deferments, knowing something of current publishing difficulties involved, but 1946 to 1949 was too much. I made a fairly vigorous demur. There was a brisk exchange, in the course of which Greene said: 'It's a bloody boring book anyway.'

Having myself worked in a publisher's office, I know how tiresome authors can be, especially when—showing complete disregard for a publisher's carefully worked out programme—they merely fuss about the precise date on which their own (indeed often bloody boring) book is due to appear. At the same time, even in post-war conditions, nearly three years might be looked on as approaching a near Olympic record in making an author wait.

In addition to that, Greene's comment, perfectly acceptable as the bluff judgment of some friend not much conversant with the 17th century, or salutary criticism of a fellow novelist dissatisfied with the technical arrangement of biographical material, was, to say the least, discouraging from the managing director of the firm responsible for marketing the book in question. This scene now strikes me as hilarious. At the time I was ruffled.

I said it was to be presumed that Greene's words implied release from a contract that offered further books of mine to Eyre & Spottiswoode. Greene agreed that consequence was implicit in the view he had expressed. The rest of the luncheon passed without incident.

A disharmony of this kind was one calculated to motivate an absolute torrent of verbiage in Jerrold. Letters poured from him. One of these included the piquant image: 'Graham has no more power to release you from your contract with this firm than I have to sell the company's furniture.'

I was, however, unaware of the Second Act of the drama, the First Act of which had been played in the Authors Club dining-room. Greene's brusqueness with me on account of the dissatisfaction I had expressed about his firm had been followed apparently at the office by a row about the firm's treatment of myself. That at least is the impression given by his own subsequent letters. The antithetical gestures would not be out of character. No doubt there were many other reasons why Greene no longer wished to remain a publisher; my own case, at least to some extent, seems to have provided a *casus belli* for resignation from the Eyre & Spottiswoode board.

4

In the end all terminated comparatively happily, because *John Aubrey and His Friends* (a very respectable piece of book production in the light of the difficulties of that moment) was after all published late in 1948. The biography sold well for a study of that sort, going into a second printing, and leading to a good deal of correspondence with scholars concerned with that period. A revised edition, in which a certain amount in the way of correction and new information was incorporated, was issued by Heinemann in 1963.

By this time I felt ready to set about another novel, the method and content of which I had been pondering a good deal, but (as in the game of Snakes and Ladders when a path is closed) another impediment to novel-writing was put in the way.

John Hayward had by now become literary adviser to The Cresset Press, a publishing firm (rather than strictly speaking a press) belonging to Dennis Cohen, a friend who—although somewhat older and decidedly richer than most of those to be found there—had to some extent moved in the bohemian party-world of the Twenties. Cohen, a kind, quiet, rather melancholy man, had taken a series of emotional knocks in that party milieu, but, as a married publisher, now seemed to be existing more happily. Under Hayward's direction The Cresset was launching a series of 'classics' (including some foreign translations), chiefly books now hard to obtain. For editing these they offered no royalty, but paid a small lump sum down.

Hayward asked for a volume from me to be called something like *Brief Lives; and Other Selected Writings by John Aubrey*, the title which was eventually used. This was to present Aubrey in a form more congenial to the 'general reader' than any then available. Although I was greatly looking forward to saying goodbye to Aubrey, at least for the moment—as one might to a close friend with whom one had been confined for several years on a desert island—it seemed advisable not to turn down this proposition, even though the financial reward was modest, the work considerable, and I wanted to get down to a novel. By this time I knew a fair amount about the subject, had developed a great affection for Aubrey, and, not least, was no doubt influenced by Hayward's accustomed determination to get his own way.

Aubrey's manuscripts and letters are beyond words chaotic. Most of the *Lives* were recorded for the use of his friend, Anthony Wood, who was compiling the *Athenae Oxonienses*, a biographical dictionary of all writers and bishops educated at Oxford, Aubrey's notes being not designed for publication until they had been stringently revised. They were mostly jotted down in a haphazard manner for his own information, to be worked over later. Much of the censure visited on Aubrey for disseminating unreliable gossip stems from that fact not being properly understood. Aubrey collected what information he could from every source to be found, wrote down what he was told, intending that in due course its accuracy should be sifted, where that was not possible simply recording what people had said.

History has thereby benefited, but, on account of Aubrey's illegible handwriting, muddled arrangement of paragraphs, difficulties of interpretation often arise. For example, seeking traditions about Shakespeare, Aubrey questioned William Beeston, an old actor, whose father had been master of one of the Elizabethan playhouses. Aubrey notes: 'would not be debauched; and if invited to court was in pain'. Some writers have assumed this refers to Shakespeare. It may, but that is by no means clear. The point at which the words are inserted on the page might just as well be applicable to Beeston himself.

In 1898 Andrew Clark edited a two-volume *Aubrey's Brief Lives* (previously published only in a scrappy ramshackle manner), a name which has stuck. Clark, augmenting the *Lives* from Aubrey's letters and other writings, performed on the whole a useful and scholarly job, but, prudish even by the standards of his time, omitted racier passages, such as (to name only three): 'they [apparently including Ben Jonson] did take also of my Ladye's Shee Blackamore'; Mary Countess of Pembroke's taste for watching stallions coupling, before having sexual relations herself; the 2nd Duke of Buckingham, bored with geometry taught by the philosopher, Thomas Hobbes, quietly masturbating.

Clark, apart from his primness, coped in a scholarly manner with the complexities of editing Aubrey's material, but his two volumes are not easy to follow unless the reader takes some trouble. Entries such as the following, with regard to the philosopher and chemist Robert Boyle (1627—1691), are not untypical:

Mr Robert Boyle—vide Oliver Hill's . . . , where he is accused of grosse plagiarisme. Dr Wood went to school with him at Eaton Colledge.

Mr R. Boyle, when a boy at Eaton verie sickly and pale—from Dr Woode, who was his school-fellow.

The honourable Robert Boyle esq, son of Richard Boyle, the first earle of Corke, was born at Lismor in the county of Corke, the . . . day of . . . anno.

Hayward's aim was an Aubrey selection which a reasonably literate person might, say, read in bed. How then were the examples given above —with much else in the same manner—to be summarized? Should the dates Aubrey omits (to be ascertained by himself later) be inserted? Either the various passages must be synthesized and consolidated, or whatever was produced would be as unwieldy as Clark. But could a version renovated in this manner be looked on as Aubrey's own work? These and many other questions had to be settled.

In due course I assembled my selection from the *Lives*, and elsewhere, to the length of the volume agreed with the publishers. I was then told that owing to printing and publishing exigencies of the moment, the book must be cut by thirty thousand words (say, seventy-five pages), a chilling demand which had to be obeyed, but made hay of my choices, especially those taken from Aubrey sources additional to the *Brief Lives*.

What eventually appeared in my edition of *Brief Lives: and Other Selected Writings by John Aubrey* (1949) was in a handy and readable form, but would have been that equally without the severe excisions. The problem of presenting Aubrey's *Lives*, much less his whole works, in an edition at once scholarly and unencumbered, is one scarcely to be overcome. Indeed, even a scholarly and complete edition of the *Lives* has not yet been achieved.

The publication of my own Aubrey selection was followed by a tedious incident, which to this day I find hard to understand. Soon after *John Aubrey and His Friends* appeared (perhaps while I was still writing the biography) a London publisher told me that a young man of his acquaintance had the ambition to edit Aubrey's *Lives* in a manner to replace Clark, and asked, as this edition would be published by his firm, if I would make myself available for help and advice.

So far as I was personally concerned there was no professional objection to a proposal likely to promote the Aubrey market. I told the publisher I would do anything I could to assist, mentioning that my own selection was due to appear soon. There the matter rested. I was never approached by the publisher again on that subject, nor by the young man.

This other edition of the *Lives* appeared a short time after my own selection. It contained more material—in some degree to be accounted for by what had been removed at the last moment by The Cresset Press—but, apart from inclusion of supposedly obscene passages, was in no scholarly competition with Clark, merely another volume for the 'general reader'.

At the end of this edition occurred a bibliography in which very disparaging comments were made, not only about my own Aubrey selection, but also on the subject of *John Aubrey and His Friends* (to some of the first-hand documentation of which the other editor had helped himself in his Introduction); a touch of farce being added to these strictures by his high praise of an anonymous article I had, in fact, written about Aubrey, which he supposed by another hand.

What was said in the bibliography went well beyond normal comment. I should myself have been inclined to ignore what seemed mere spite as not worth bothering about (especially as schoolboy howlers in the Introduction included, by careless reading of a printed source, the attribution to Aubrey of an autobiographical passage by another writer), but Dennis Cohen, very angry at imputations levelled at one of his firm's books, had the defamatory passages removed, and caused a public apology to appear in the main papers.

I have always been at a loss to comprehend this affair. I did not set eyes on the young man (who committed suicide some years later), either then or subsequently, so there was no question of mutual antipathy. I was supposedly on good terms with the publisher, with whom I had never had business dealings. I had offered to do anything I could to help. In the event, it was true, a selection more like my own was produced, though longer and with illustrations. Having been first in the field with Aubrey, it might seem that I, if anyone, might have felt put out by rivalry. The severe detraction of *John Aubrey and His Friends* was not the view expressed by a respectable assemblage of historians and critics.

Aubrey himself would certainly have ascribed this tiresome episode to the malign influence of astral bodies. The evil stars which plagued his own life were particularly obnoxious in bringing lawsuits. Perhaps the afflictions of the Zodiac were calculated to cause litigation even to those perpetuating his memory three centuries later, because, in a field other than Aubrey's and The Cresset Press, I had found myself a short time earlier than this in the midst of another literary libel action.

5

I have mentioned (*Infants of the Spring*) that I first became aware of Alan Pryce-Jones at school, when, at the age of about thirteen, competing for a declamation prize, he was reading the Bible aloud for the judgment of Edmund Gosse. Since then he had written several travel books, occasional critical pieces. During the war he worked in the Section of the War Office scrutinizing the organization of the German army. We used to exchange a word in those corridors, but I did not know him at all well. He had always seemed to take the life of a man of letters in a fairly leisurely manner, so that I was surprised when, meeting in the London Library soon after my own return from Lee to London, Pryce-Jones remarked: 'Of course what one wants to do is to edit the *Times Literary Supplement*.'

The fact that Pryce-Jones was established in the editorial chair of the *TLS* probably less than two years later suggests certain powers of the will. In the autumn of 1947, when he was working there just before taking over, he suggested I should come in two or three days a week to supervise novel-reviewing. I accepted the offer, remaining for several years, during which I reviewed a novel myself most weeks, sometimes other books, and from time to time wrote (features now abolished) 'fronts' and 'middles', the second of these running to an awkward length of 2600 words, too long for one sort of article, too short for another; the former, probably three to five thousand.

In one sense, at least outwardly, Pryce-Jones continued to pursue a professional path that appeared the reverse of strenuous. When parties began slowly to come into being again there were truancies from the office, but at the same time *TLS* reviewers seemed to become a shade less stodgy overnight, a faint but perceptible odour of chic sometimes drifting through the dusty caverns of Printing House Square.

Pryce-Jones's own literary equipment, an all-purpose one, moved across a broad spectrum, few if any books outside his reviewing sphere. He possessed that useful editorial characteristic of keeping the reader guessing, while giving him a good run of his money, together with a social acquaintance that was legion, and next to no prejudices.

This was a period long anterior to signed reviews in the *TLS*. It is commonly supposed that reviewers take advantage of the cowl of anonymity to be more vindictive than if the critic's name were made public. I'm not sure that is true. No doubt in certain specialized fields, where only a handful of experts are qualified to give a useful opinion on their own subject, bitter rivals sometimes pay off old scores without revealing 'an interest'. More generally, to be forced to speak as the voice of the paper, rather than express one's own opinion, seems to me to inhibit both praise and blame. Personally I feel less hampered in both if signing my name.

The reviewing of novels presents insoluble difficulties, if only on account of their dreadful abundance. On the one hand critics, quite gifted in other areas, can go through life without the smallest inkling of how or why a novel is written; while, on the other, every professional novelist is likely to feel that he (or she) would have composed almost every given novel in a manner slightly different from that of its author.

In a sense novelists, 'good' or 'bad', have more in common with each other in the mental images they manipulate than with any critic, but they can be just as inept at reviewing novels as non-novelists. Reviewing (of novels or anything else) may be a humble craft, but it is a craft. No amount of wit, scholarship, technical knowledge, political acumen, can take the place of the down-to-earth abilities required in a competent reviewer.

The method of classifying the torrent of novels arriving in a literary editor's office is no easier than finding suitable persons to review them. In the 1920s and 1930s the *TLS* used to pick out at most three or four novels a week to treat seriously, the rest (where I commonly found myself) dismissed in a couple of hundred words of small print at the back of the paper. Such arbitrary division seemed so far as possible to be avoided. I tried to cover the ground by having—at worst—two novels reviewed together.

This two-at-a-time system was not always satisfactory, as sometimes the pair turned out not to 'go' together, or I guessed wrong about an appropriate reviewer (all reviewers having their own particular bugbears), but the method seemed preferable to a savage separation of recognized sheep from conjectural goats; or (as sometimes advocated) reducing the goats to a herd of 'recommended titles'. Within the bounds of allowing freedom for severe criticism—certainly never to be averted if needed—there is much to be said for Rilke's opinion that all works of art should be approached in a spirit of sympathy. For those so disposed, nothing is easier than making knockabout fun of, say, *Hamlet* or the Sistine Chapel, and little is gained by giving reviewers books they are bound to dislike on sight.

6

Early in 1947, while still working for *The Daily Telegraph*, I had reviewed a batch of novels that included *The Age of Reason* (*L'Age de Raison*), first volume of Jean-Paul Sartre's trilogy, *The Roads to Freedom* (*Les Chemins de la Liberté*), the second volume of which, *The Reprieve* (*Le Sursis*), arrived at the *TLS* towards the end of the same year.

When, long after this, Sartre's account of his own childhood, *Les Mots*, appeared in English as *Words* (1964), I reviewed that too, and was impressed with the sardonic humour with which the author examined his early years; the approach—as Connolly himself noticed—having something in common with the autobiographical passages of *Enemies of Promise;* the theme of juvenile intelligence, recognized too early, bringing disadvantages to the hero.

I found much less to like in *The Roads to Freedom*, a 'committed' sequence, Communist in flavour, forgoing the humour of which Sartre later showed himself capable, though not, as things turned out, without all touch of impishness. The style, again in contrast with the pungent French clarity of *Les Mots*, was influenced by the experimental schools of twenty or thirty years before, whose language was usually English. In

Sartre's trilogy nothing was found to be so extreme in method as Joyce or Stein, but, when recording events taking place at different levels of the narrative, sentences and paragraphs were sometimes dovetailed together by a colon, in a manner to disregard time and space in the course of events there described.

The translation by Eric Sutton (met years before as a congenial older friend of John Heygate's) was well done. Notwithstanding, so it seemed to me, Sartre's trilogy never came to life.

In spite of having cavilled earlier at *The Age of Reason*, I took on (somewhat contravening Rilke's principle of sympathy) *The Reprieve* for the *TLS*. That was partly because I had read the first volume, a qualification that might not have been easy to find elsewhere, partly because my job was to tackle novelists who might be regarded as of consequence.

The action of *The Reprieve* takes place in late summer 1938, the week of Neville Chamberlain's negotiations with Adolf Hitler at Munich. The *dramatis personae* of the book include the major political figures of the meeting, certain members of their entourage, together with characters of the author's invention. Some of the last, for example, Mathieu Delarue, more or less hero of the trilogy, and Ivich Serguine, a White Russian girl living in Paris (whose virginity Delarue takes without much enthusiasm), had already appeared in *The Age of Reason*.

In order to illustrate the intricate nature of the style employed by Sartre I quoted towards the end of my review of *The Reprieve* in the *TLS* :

Messrs. Hubert Masaryk and Mastay, members of the Czechoslovak delegation, were waiting in Sir Horace Wilson's room in the company of Mr Ashton-Gwatkin. Mastay was pale and perspiring, with dark circles under his eyes. Hubert Masaryk paced up and down. Mr Ashton-Gwatkin sat on the bed: Ivich had slipped away to her own side of the bed, she wasn't touching him, but she could feel his warmth and hear his breathing: she couldn't sleep, and she knew he wasn't asleep either.

This paragraph of the novel terminated with these further sentences, which I did not quote:

Electric discharges sped through her legs and thighs, she longed to turn over on her back, but if she moved he would touch her: so long as he thought her asleep he would leave her alone. Mastay turned to Ashton-Gwatkin and said: 'It's lasting a long time.'

I closed my review with the comment: 'But what purpose is served by suggesting to the reader's mind that Ivich was taking this silent share in the negotiations?'

7

Surnames rarely if ever seem droll to those who themselves bear them. In the case of the double-barrelled name of Ashton-Gwatkin, the hyphenation had been a matter of deliberate choice on the part of its owner. No one before him had been so styled. To a writer's ear there could be no doubt about the whimsicality of the linked syllables. Not only that, a writer's instinct in Sartre—I like to think in myself also—immediately recognized something invisible on the surface; that the man named, if he really existed, had some additional characteristic, which added savour to the merely documentary interest of invoking him as an official.

F. T. A. Ashton-Gwatkin, CB CMG, was in fact Counsellor in the Diplomatic Service and Head of the Economic Relations Department of the Foreign Office, from which he had that very year retired. He did not take Sartre's mention of himself in at all good part. In fact a lawyer's letter imputing libel speedily arrived at the offices of *The Times* and to Sartre's London publisher. So far as I know, Ashton-Gwatkin did not seek to pursue the matter further with the French publisher of *Le Sursis*, which had first appeared in Paris at least two years before.

Under threat of legal action both publisher and newspaper capitulated at once. Ashton-Gwatkin received an apology and 'sum which recognized the force of his complaint and emphasized the sincerity of their regret' for what was defined as 'the unconventional literary style adopted by the author'. The trouble was the colon. If there had been a full-stop, had all the sentences in the book—even in the paragraph—terminated with a colon, things might have been different. The mixture of the two forms of punctuation, especially within the narrative's terms of reference, was seen as inadmissible. In any case, I fear, a line of least resistance would probably have been adopted. That was a pity, because, as suggested above, there was more in the case than met the eye.

Ashton-Gwatkin, a clergyman's son, had been at Eton (by odd coincidence at the same house as my own years before), proceeding to Balliol, where he had won that laurel, sometimes fairly lightly proffered, the Newdigate Prize Poem: the subject that year (1909) being *Michelangelo*. From Oxford he had entered the Far East Consular Service, later exchanging into the Diplomatic.

As the Newdigate suggests, Ashton-Gwatkin himself aspired to literary ambitions, which he did not abandon in later life. He wrote several novels under the pseudonym John Paris, also producing a volume of verse with the title *A Japanese Don Juan*. Ashton-Gwatkin's thinness of skin regarding Ivich may have had something to do with his own books, of which I have read only *Kimono* (1921), a work put into paperback only a few months before publication of *The Reprieve* in England.

In *Kimono* a good deal of expertise as to Japanese life is displayed. The story opens in 1913, with the fashionable marriage of Captain the Honourable Geoffrey Barrington (a peer by the end of the book) at St George's, Hanover Square, to a Japanese girl, beautiful, rich, orphaned. The photograph of the author on the cover makes one suspect that Barrington, a huge bearlike simple-hearted Englishman, is a self-portrait. During an extended honeymoon the Barringtons visit Japan, a country unknown to the bride, though she had many relations there.

Barrington (apparently even after marriage) 'had never gazed on a naked woman except idealized in marble or on canvas', but in Tokyo licentious friends take him to brothels, where 'against the yellow skin the violet nipples glowed like poisonous berries'. Barrington, profoundly disturbed, becomes preoccupied with the evils of prostitution in Japan.

Although his wife's income is £20,000 a year neither Barrington nor she have ever bothered to explore the sources of this money. At a moment when other matrimonial tribulations beset them, her riches turn out to be derived from a chain of Japanese brothels. This unhappy news threatens the marriage, some sort of a Japanese divorce is arranged, but, on the outbreak of war in 1914, all is patched up, quite how is left rather vague.

Violet-coloured nipples like poisonous berries are by no means the only gaudy images of sex, conjured up with a good deal of relish, in *Kimono*. If, as it was rumoured he planned, Sartre had come to London to defend his novel in court, a great legal comedy—not to say farce—was missed.

When Aubrey was finally out of the way, much to my relief even, if in some respects the most enjoyable work I have ever attempted, the question of writing another novel could be at last seriously set about.

Sickert used to insist that every picture tells a story. Equally perverse reasoning might urge that every novel has a plot. What individual artists (in the general sense) make of either principle is another matter, but the abyss between abstract and realist in painting is scarcely wider and deeper than in writing. In practice the term 'novel', after every kind of variation has been tried out, has come to be thought of as comprising a work with some sort of a beginning, middle, end, taking up a length of about 80,000 words. Although well disposed in the arts towards discipline in structure (a phrase again to beg all sorts of questions), I have never felt particularly at ease in the eighty-thousand framework as an end in itself.

On reading—and rereading—the works of even the greatest novelists, one is apt sooner or later to become aware of what seems in effect, the same character reappearing under a different name, the same situation cropping up in another setting. Certain specific types and happenings haunt every individual novelist's imagination. There has lately been some rebellion, literary and philosophic, against novelists seeing life through those 'Balzacian' spectacles at all. So be it. Other approaches have their own built-in limitations and handicaps too. *Si monumentum requiris circumspice*. The menace of repetition is common to all, particularly for runners in the eighty-thousand-word stakes.

For a time, therefore, I had been turning over in my mind the possibility of writing a novel composed of a fairly large number of volumes, just how many could not be decided at the outset. A long sequence seemed to offer all sorts of advantages, among them release from the re-engagement every year or so of the same actors and extras hanging about for employment at the stage door of one's creative fantasy. Instead of sacking the lot at the end of a brief run—with the moral certainty that at least one or two of the more tenacious will be back again seeking a job, if not this year or next, then in a decade's time—the production itself might be extended, the actors made to work longer and harder for much the same creative remuneration spread over an extended period; instead of being butchered at regular intervals to make a publisher's holiday.

At the same time there were many objections to setting out on such a hazardous road, chiefly the possibility of collapse, imaginatively speaking; or, like Robert Musil (a novelist of immense gifts, though I don't care for the mass-murderer theme in *The Man Without Qualities*, *Der Mann ohne Eigenschaften*), simply dying (something bound to happen sooner or later) before completing the book.

The eighty-thousand-word fetters would not be entirely struck off, if normal processes of commercial publication were accepted (some novelists have chosen their own special form at their own expense), but such disciplining of the writing might have advantages in checking too diffuse a pattern, by imposing a series of shorter sections each more or less complete in itself.

Certain technical matters had to be settled at once for early establishment of a sufficiently broad base at the start from which a complex narrative might arise; fan out; be sustained over a period of years. This meant that undeveloped characters, potential situations, must be introduced, whose purpose might be unresolved throughout several volumes of the sequence. Perhaps understandably, only very few critics of the opening volumes showed themselves capable of appreciating that, in reality, quite simple principle.

An essential point to decide, from the opening sentence, was whether to use a first-person or third-person narrative. A third-person narrative (though not necessarily so) is apt to include a character more or less representative of the author's point of view (from which, in fact, all novels must ultimately be written), some such comparatively explicit unification particularly needed to maintain a novel of exceptional length.

This 'telling of the story' can be seen at a popular level in the use of, say, an improbably reflective or articulate cowboy, while even relatively accomplished novelists will contrive dramatic contrasts by changing, or even falsifying, the values by which different characters are judged by the author. Such aspects of novel-writing are easier to recognize than to avoid.

I concluded that the first-person narrative was preferable in dodging the artificiality of the invented 'hero', who speaks for the author. For example, when in my own early novels Atwater (*Afternoon Men*) is described as having 'failed for the Foreign Office', or Lushington (*Venusberg*) as possessing 'Anglo-Catholic leanings' when younger, these labels, not applicable to myself but giving body to a character, would merely false-card the reader as attached to the narrator's point of view throughout a dozen volumes.

But, if the narrator is not to have invented characteristics, to what extent must they be the author's? Are we back with Eliot's distaste for an artist 'deliberately expressing his own personality'? In any case, the moment the 'I' of the novel is embroiled with 'invented' characters, the 'I' ceases to be the author, who is henceforward having experiences not before known.

Besides, if too literally 'himself', the surrounding characters risk being put out of focus. Proust's Marcel, though much described in one sense, lives in the novel chiefly through the persons with whom he comes into touch. The same is true of Musil's Ulrich, though Ulrich is a more self-satisfied projection. The very occasional introduction of 'I' throughout *The Devils* (*The Possessed*), though in an odd way the reader has some sense of knowing him, is given no physical substance by Dostoevski at all.

9

At a fairly early stage in tackling this matter, I found myself in the Wallace Collection, standing in front of Nicolas Poussin's picture there given the title *A Dance to the Music of Time*. An almost hypnotic spell seems cast by this masterpiece on the beholder. I knew all at once that Poussin had expressed at least one important aspect of what the novel must be.

The precise allegory which Poussin's composition adumbrates is disputed. I have accepted the view that the dancing figures (three female, one male) are the Seasons, though some suppose they represent the Destiny of Man, as conditioned by Pleasure and Riches, Poverty and Work, an explanation perhaps now more fashionable. The young man, lightly clad, wears a crown of laurel, so he may be Fame. Wealth (if she is Wealth), in a yellow petticoat, does no more than touch the wrist of her sister, Poverty (if she is Poverty), whose head is crowned with a turban. Phoebus drives his horses across the heavens; Time plucks the strings of his lyre.

There is no doubt a case for asserting that the dancers are not easily identifiable as Spring, Summer, Autumn, Winter. They seem no less ambiguous as Pleasure, Riches, Poverty, Work, or perhaps Fame. In relation to my own mood, the latter interpretations would be equally applicable. The picture was painted (probably between 1637 and 1639) for Clement IX, and its subject may have been based on personal fantasies chosen by that Rospigliosi pope. The one thing certain is that the four main figures depicted are dancing to Time's tune.

10

When *A Question of Upbringing*, the first volume of the sequence, was finished—and I was free to find another publisher—Malcolm Muggeridge, at that moment literary adviser to Heinemann's, persuaded me to go there, where I have remained for close on thirty years. In those early days I used to deal with A. S. Frere, whose choleric humours I found sympathetic, and some good laughs were shared between us. At Heinemann's I first met Roland Gant, then recently emerged from a notable war career (which had included digging his own grave, at the end of which the Germans thought better of shooting him), who had a period of infidelity to Heinemann's with another publishing firm, but, reconciliation taking place, returned there to look after me and my books.

A small bibliographical point may be recorded regarding the 'prelims' of *A Question of Upbringing* (1951). It was my intention that an additional half-title, indicating the name of the whole sequence, *The Music of Time* (followed by asterisks denoting the number of the volume), should appear on the page preceding that opening the narrative. After I had passed proofs some overenthusiastic supervisor altered this subheading to *A Question of Upbringing*, already used on the first page as half-title. This was soon put right, so that a 'first state' exists in the first edition.

In 1961, when I was applying for a US passport visa, a breezy young woman at the counter of consular officials in Grosvenor Square asked me for documentary proof of the authenticity of my purpose in visiting Dartmouth, Amherst, and Cornell. I showed her a letter from John Meck, then Vice-President of Dartmouth, which referred in flattering terms to *The Music of Time*.

'Is it a book about music?' she asked.

I tried to explain. She still seemed puzzled, but endorsed my passport with the words: 'Informal lectures to Ivy League colleges'. This mis-understanding caused me thenceforward to use the full title of Poussin's picture, *A Dance to the Music of Time;* though no doubt the inference might then be drawn that the books were about dancing.

II

Two friends dating from this period of the late 1940s were Osbert Lancaster and Harry d'Avigdor-Goldsmid, who both belonged to the Oxford generation following my own, a less fruity undergraduate vintage perhaps than its antecedent, but one with plenty of bouquet.

Osbert Lancaster's first marriage was to Karen Harris, daughter of Sir Austin and Lady Harris, who had a house in Catherine Place, West-minster, where parties took place from time to time. Although Violet had met him before our own marriage, I scarcely knew Lancaster himself before the war, though familiar with his work. I had also come across his sister-in-law, Honey Harris, a sculptress, at a party of Dorothy (Warren) Trotter's, and (because both of them came to see us at Great Ormond Street) it was no doubt through Honey Harris that I met her mother, a fan of my early novels.

Sir Austin Harris was a banker and picture collector, his wife Cara a remarkable personality, who retained her good looks and wayward charm well into her sixties, together with the high spirits of days when, with the Edwardian 'younger set', she had been accustomed to play Hare-and-Hounds through the departments of Harrods. Lady Harris and her family made a film at their house in the Isle of Wight, in which she doubled two parts, the climax being the moment when she was bitten by a Black Widow spider (convincing mechanical models then procurable), and performed the Dance of Death, an unforgettable piece of choreography.

One of Lady Harris's skills was in massage, and she once massaged Violet for pains in the back. In the bedroom at Catherine Place, hanging from the bedpost, Violet noticed a rosary and a motor-horn; and wondered of what mysterious rites those were the emblems. Eccentricity is never easy to convey, but enough has been suggested to show that Cara Harris was well adapted to be mother-in-law of a cartoonist.

At this period Osbert and Karen Lancaster, who later moved to Henley-on-Thames, were still living in Addison Crescent, West Kensington, a district dear to Lancaster from childhood memories of having been brought up in those parts, no less as former habitat of Victorian Academicians and sages. Leicester House, Henley, Georgian with Victorian embellishments, was on the outskirts of the town, with a large garden. We often used to stay at this delightful spot, until Karen Lancaster, whose health was never good, died in 1964. Efforts were made to prevent Leicester House from being demolished after sale, but such things can be safeguarded only up to a point; sadly, a housing estate now standing on the spot.

Henley, especially at the season of the Regatta, gave the impression of being largely peopled by figures from Lancaster's own cartoons: beefy young oarsmen in shorts and pink Leander socks; white moustached ancients wearing sere and yellow flannel trousers under blazers and college-crested caps, who grasped megaphones; over all an aura of cider-cup, cold salmon, strawberries-and-cream.

Lancaster, having severely stylized his own personal appearance, produces subtlely in his subject matter by manipulation of an extreme stylization of type. At first sight this principle might seem to threaten the reverse of subtlety, even a certain crudeness, but, like an extended Commedia dell' Arte, the assembly of easily recognizable puppets can be used to express and relay, in all sorts of unexpected ways, their creator's wit.

Lancaster enjoys the comparatively rare advantage (instanced in the case of Constant Lambert) of being at home not only in the graphic arts he practises, but also in writing and music. His early training as an architect, imposing an academic preoccupation with the Orders of Architecture, has left its mark in a similarly firm adherence to the Orders of Human Society (inescapable whatever the political régime); in the delineation of which Lancaster is one of the few cartoonists who can handle military uniform at once satirically and correctly.

Although best known for his cartoons and stage-sets, Lancaster's watercolours and lithographs—particularly of the Ægean—have an atmosphere very much their own, Greece (he was besieged in the Athens Embassy during the Communist attempt to take over the country) exercising a strong hold on him pictorially. Nevertheless, Lancaster's most resolute expeditions have been among the swamps and jungles of

London's parties and clubs, a safari in which he has excelled himself in capture of fauna to be transmogrified into terms of satire.

Not long before the *Annus Sanctus* of 1949/1950 was inaugurated by the Pope—naturally an occasion for pilgrimage to Rome—Cyril Connolly (according to himself) saw Evelyn Waugh in White's Club, of which both were by that time fellow-members. Waugh said: 'I am thinking of going to Rome for the Holy Year. I shall be staying in an *hôtel*. I wondered whether you would care to join me? If there were likely to be money difficulties, I could arrange.'

Had Connolly ever flirted with the Roman Church—of which sounder proof than any known to me would be required to speak affirmatively—that flirtation had remained in every sense Platonic. Connolly declined Waugh's offer to 'stand' him a visit to The Eternal City during the Holy Year, but did not hesitate to dine out on the story.

The news of the Waugh/Connolly interchange had scarcely reached me, when the Lancaster drawing (plate 21) arrived by post. It is captioned: *Rough sketch for a gigantic mural to be placed in the coffee-room at White's by public subscription celebrating the theme 'Connolly at Canossa'.*

The biretta-capped ecclesiastic standing behind Pius XII (easily recognizable) seems a generalized Vatican functionary, but the bare-headed cleric of lean and hungry look is undoubtedly Fr Martin D'Arcy SJ, celebrated for his conversions in the *beau monde*. The helmeted Swiss Guard, grasping a halberd, has every air of being a self-portrait by the artist.

When Waugh was once in our house I showed him Lancaster's picture, by then framed on the wall. He gazed for a long time, finally saying: 'Not in the least like.' Connolly was never given the chance of expressing an opinion. Opportunities arose, but courage failed me.

12

When in 1948 we took Evelyn Gardner's cottage in Kent for a few weeks' holiday with the children, Somerhill, the d'Avigdor-Goldsmids' house near Tonbridge, was not far away. Violet had known Rosie Goldsmid (*née* Rosemary Nicholl) since deb days. We dined at Somerhill, the beginning of a long series of visits.

The Goldsmids had married soon after the outbreak of the second war, only a few months before Harry Goldsmid's father died, when he inherited the baronetcy and Elizabethan house. In a remarkably short while after peace came Rosie Goldsmid put Somerhill into working order, and, by the time we went over from Evelyn Gardner's cottage, hospitality was already on an heroic scale. After six years of wartime austerity one could feel very grateful for a bucket or two of champagne.

Harry Goldsmid (whose family had owned the house for about a century, and traditionally derived from the 2nd century BC Maccabees) had served with great dash in the local Territorials, being profusely decorated. He returned from the war to be a banker and bullion broker in London; in the country performing many public duties, and later becoming an MP (Con) for a North Midland constituency.

Goldsmid's knowledge of the City, the complexities of financial dealings, expecially on their comic side, was of incalculable value to me where such matters played a part in my novel. He would give advice, read proofs before publication, make suggestions that were not only well informed about the City, but showed grasp of the literary exigencies that govern writing a novel. In this last respect he was a rare friend, somehow seeming himself to share the life of the novel's characters, without at the same time imposing too much exterior influence in what he recommended.

Harry d'Avigdor-Goldsmid had, in short, brilliant gifts: courage, physical and moral; generosity; a keen and independent intelligence in both intellectual matters and business affairs; an individual wit; and— something that can perhaps at times prove an inconvenience to certain temperaments—a great deal of money. He was also (as Isaiah Berlin observed at the West London Synagogue Memorial Service in 1976) the most easily bored man he, Berlin, had ever met. No one who knew Harry Goldsmid is likely to dissent from that assessment. Almost in the middle of a sentence in which he had been laughing about something (quite likely sparked off by his own wit), boredom would strike him down, melancholy descend like an unwanted guest impossible to exclude from the table. Gloom might easily take over for the rest of the evening.

Latterly, there was reason enough for the Goldsmids to be sad. They had two daughters, beautiful, intelligent, well-behaved, whom they adored. In 1963, the Fates enacting one of their dreadful rôles, tragedy came. The elder girl was lost in a sailing accident. Harry Goldsmid's life was utterly, irretrievably, laid waste.

There had been talk of his writing a book about Disraeli. From reading short pieces achieved by him on this subject I am confident that, had Goldsmid been able to summon up the staying power, he would have produced an acute and unusual study. He would have appreciated the minutiae of the exotic beginnings as much as the world of high politics ending with the Beaconsfield earldom. Unfortunately Goldsmid, involved with a thousand other activities, could work at Disraeli only in short bursts, and was in any case unsuited to the drudgery of writing even the shortest book.

Goldsmid entered the House of Commons with plenty of enthusiasm and ambition. He was Parliamentary Private Secretary to a Minister, chaired many important committees on financial matters, took a keen interest (uncommon among MPs) in promoting art and letters, including grants for indigent writers. Nevertheless, in the political dog-fight, Goldsmid's critical intelligence, his impatience with bores, humbugs, knaves, was a fatal impediment. He once showed me a letter he had written, rapping the knuckles of a Minister in his own Party for answering a question with a jumble of half-baked pompous clichés. Such an attitude is refreshing in an MP, but unlikely to appease ministerial stupidity.

In short, Goldsmid's years in Parliament were useful and honourable, but a disappointment to himself. He characteristically expressed his own feelings by quoting a story taken, I imagine, from Sir Richard Burton's translation of *The Arabian Nights*. The tale concerns a man who is brought by some magical means to a magnificent house, the door of which is guarded by a gigantic Nubian. He is admitted. Within, among luxurious surroundings, gorgeous women are playing chess. The man is invited to play with them. It is explained that, if he wins the game, he will enjoy the favours of his beautiful opponent—but, if he loses, he will be buggered by the Nubian.

'That's the House of Commons,' said Goldsmid. 'I lost. I'm being buggered by the Nubian.'

13

If this was a decade when new friends were made, its close was saddened by the loss of two old ones; George Orwell (*Infants of the Spring*) and

Constant Lambert (*Messengers of Day*). They belonged to very different areas of my life, and never, I think, came across each other.

Orwell had been seriously ill for months before the end came in January, 1950. He had expressed a wish to be buried in the rites of the Church of England (constituting, in the view of Frazer of *The Golden Bough*, adherence, anthropologically speaking, to a given religion), and the Revd W. V. C. Rose, kindly vicar of Christ Church, Albany Street, took on Orwell's funeral service at short notice.

It fell to me to choose the hymns: *All people that on earth do dwell* (I felt Orwell would have liked the Old Hundredth, if only for the name); *Guide me, O thou great Redeemer* (chiefly for my own wartime associations, though *Jehovah* is more authentic); *Ten thousand times ten thousand* (Why, I can't remember, perhaps Orwell himself had talked of the hymn, or because he was in his way a sort of saint, even if not one in sparkling raiment bright). The Lesson was from Ecclesiastes, the grinders in the streets, the grasshopper a burden, the silver cord loosed, the wheel broken at the cistern. For some reason George Orwell's funeral service was one of the most harrowing I have ever attended.

14

Constant Lambert's first marriage had gone wrong a short time before the outbreak of war in 1939. He was in The Hague the following year, on tour with the Sadler's Wells Ballet Company, when the Germans launched their attack on Holland. Bombs and parachutists descended wholesale from the sky, the city was in flames, but the Company managed to get back to England without casualty. During the war years Lambert had a fairly gruelling time keeping the Sadler's Wells dancers going, something for which, it has often been said, he never received as much credit as he deserved.

In 1947 Lambert married again, this time to the painter and stage-designer, Isobel Nicholas, who had herself been model for many well-known painters and sculptors. She executed the sets of Lambert's last ballet, *Tiresias*.

After their marriage Constant and Isobel Lambert took part of a house, 197 Albany Street, only a short way up the road from Chester Gate. I had come across Lambert only a few times during the war, but now began to see him again more regularly. By this period he was in rather a shaky condition. In general his drinking had not diminished, but he would have interludes when he hardly drank at all—that happened once when the Lamberts came to dinner, again when they themselves gave a party— but during such abstinences he would be in an odd state, sometimes silent, sometimes convulsed with laughter.

Our chief exchanges, anyway most coherent ones, began to settle into a pattern of Lambert making long telephone calls to me relatively late at night. He would ring up between half-past eleven and midnight, discussing at great length things which had amused him during the day. This would happen especially on Sunday evenings, when Lambert liked to go through what had appeared on the book pages of the Sunday papers.

Sacheverell Sitwell (an old friend of both of us) was then contributing an unsigned column to one of the Sunday papers, in which he wrote of anything that had caught his attention, no intellectual or aesthetic holds barred, resulting in a panorama of esoteric items altogether unfamiliar to most newspaper readers. A wide field was usually covered by Lambert's telephone conversations too, but these were likely to begin with the words: 'I say, *have* you read Sachie this Sunday?'

Lambert was making these calls two or three times a week, when, at the beginning of August, 1951, Violet and I went with the children to Lee; returning a fortnight later. My mother rang up Chester Gate the same evening, 21 August, asking if we had seen in the paper that Constant Lambert had died. We had no knowledge of that, nor that he had been in a bad way for some days, then seemed to recover, followed by a terrible relapse that killed him.

The next night an old Oxford friend, Matthew Ponsonby, with his wife, Bess, turned out to be in London, and came at short notice to dinner at Chester Gate. I mention their presence there as witness of what happened. At about a quarter to twelve the telephone-bell rang.

'It's Constant,' said Violet.

I went downstairs and picked up the receiver.

'Hullo?'

There was no sound for an appreciable moment, then a click, followed by the dialling tone.

Index

Illustrations in italics

223

Index